A PHOEN

By the same author:

Making Out

A PHOENIX RISING
Impressions of Vietnam

Zoë Schramm-Evans

An Imprint of HarperCollins*Publishers*

Pandora
An Imprint of HarperCollins*Publishers*
77–85 Fulham Palace Road
Hammersmith, London W6 8JB
1160 Battery Street
San Francisco, California 94111–1213

Published by Pandora 1996
10 9 8 7 6 5 4 3 2 1

A catalogue record for this book
is available from the British Library

ISBN 0 04 440965 6 (Paperback)
ISBN 0 04 440976 1 (US Edition)

Printed in Great Britain by
Caledonian International Book Manufacturer

For David McIlfatrick

CONTENTS

Acknowledgements

I would like to thank the following:
Helen Brazier, Phan Thanh Hao, Phan Thi Phuong Hoang,
Dwayne Jackson, Alan Micklethwaite, Debbi Murtagh, Tim Page,
Greg Pearce, David Pearson, Dr Adrian Richardson, Carol
Shergold, Louise Williams and the late 'Dunnett'.

Introduction

In 1950 writer Norman Lewis arrived in Saigon, then capital of a French colony called Cochin-China. In his acclaimed book *A Dragon Apparent*[1], Lewis explained his reasons for travelling to what is now Vietnam:

> Now that China had passed into the transforming fire, it seemed that the experience of Far-Eastern travel could no longer be safely postponed. What then remained? Which would be the next country to undergo this process of change that was spreading so rapidly across Asia, and would have to be seen now, or never again in its present form? I thought that Indo-China was the answer...

Most travellers have the desire to see a place before it changes forever. Almost half a century after Lewis visited the country, I left London for Vietnam, sharing with my fellow Welshman a desire to see Vietnam 'now, or never again in its present form'.

In 1950, the Vietnamese Communists led by Ho Chi Minh already controlled much of the country, while the French authorities were fighting a desperate rearguard action to keep their colony. Lewis was well aware that change was inevitable and wrote with steady conviction of the anti-colonial feeling within the country and with belief in the inevitability of a 'coming renascence' for the 'free nations of Indo-China'. Four years after his visit, the French were crushed by the Vietnamese Communists and freedom to follow their own five-pointed star did at last seem within the grasp of the people of Vietnam. What came after, even Lewis, for all his perspicacity, could not have foreseen.

1   Jonathan Cape, 1951

In 1966, at the age of nine, I first heard of a place called Vietnam, which was far away and full of people getting blown up for reasons I, a young girl growing up on the Welsh–English border, didn't understand. I subsequently absorbed the fact that the Vietnamese were 'baddies' and that the Americans, who wore helmets and ran in and out of helicopters on television, were the 'goodies'. I knew this for certain because the BBC, and my elder brother who was in the British military, told me so. My family connections also meant that I was as well informed on camouflage and automatic weaponry as any nine-year-old should be, which perhaps goes some way towards explaining my fascination with a country whose name was, and to some still is, synonymous with war. In 1966, both America and Vietnam seemed equally remote and equally exotic and I often daydreamed through classes at my convent school after late nights spent listening, on a small red radio pressed to my ear under the bedclothes, to the reporting of the war by the BBC World Service.

At the age of eleven, I became a pupil at a pleasant semi-rural establishment in what was then England and is now Wales. I discovered that the family of one of my new classmates actually lived in Vietnam, which immediately gave the country a more realistic dimension. Her father, though British, was a military attaché with the French embassy in Saigon and I was profoundly envious of the nonchalance with which she described mortars pounding the city where she spent the school holidays. Despite persistent interrogation, however, she never seemed able to answer my innumerable questions about the country, the war or Saigon itself.

By the time official American involvement in Vietnam ended in 1973, I had discovered flared jeans, afghan coats and boys. Vietnam was relegated to a remoter outpost of my brain. However, the media-fed memories of war never entirely faded; only years later did I realize the extent of their impact, as a desire to go to the place so vividly remembered from childhood grew rather than lessened with time. As an adult I understood that of all the sights and sounds witnessed through the unprecedented media coverage of that war, the only ones to remain with me were of Americans, in an American conflict. Somehow, in the telling, the land and people of Vietnam had been lost in an oversight of history. Within 25 years of Lewis' journey through Cochin-China and Annam, more than 10 million Vietnamese from all parts of the country and all walks of life would be dead or wounded, poisoned or deformed by toxic chemicals, homeless, bereaved, insane. Vietnam's victories over France, the United States and more recently China were expensive ones, and the degree of its success, which left Vietnam unified and independent for almost the first time in its very long history, is reflected in the scale of its sacrifices and tragedies.

The phoenix, or *phuong*, of the title is of course Vietnam, which Vietnamese literature refers to as the 'Land of the Phoenix'. I realized as I began to write this book and relive my experiences in Vietnam that in a very different way the phoenix was also myself. Most travel writers of recent decades have, with a few notable exceptions, been healthy, fit and male. I was and am none of those things. Two years prior to leaving England for Vietnam I had been diagnosed with cancer – merely the most recent in an over-long line of disabilities which had beset me for more than a decade. Planning my journey to Vietnam, the time spent there and the process of writing about it subsequently assumed a highly personal significance for me. I came to feel that in some odd way going to Vietnam would also be a journey into myself, a test of some kind from which, like the phoenix, I could emerge strengthened. For a person without full health, travelling in a country still described by the guidebooks as 'challenging' would in itself be an experience beyond the ordinary. So it was for a number of reasons that Vietnam beckoned me in the winter of 1994.

When I compare my experiences travelling in other parts of the world to those in Vietnam I am struck by the enormous differences in the depth and quality of my feelings. I often wondered, both while in the country and subsequently, how much of the extraordinarily powerful emotions Vietnam engendered in me was a result of my own susceptibility or due simply to the place itself. Of course, as with most such things, it was both. On occasions I found the clash of cultures deeply disturbing as my burden of 'Western guilt' came up against the everyday life and recent history of Vietnam in many guises, from the casualties of mine explosions to undersized and malnourished teenagers offering sex with a glance or a hand on the thigh. In order to move on, both literally and metaphorically, I had to learn to put that imaginary burden down and try at least to see the modern Vietnam as it is – a country whose people have the same everyday hopes, fears, difficulties and desires as anywhere else in the world; a country which has done more than most to leave its problems behind it and rise from literal ashes. Only by attempting to see Vietnam as it sees itself and not through childhood media memories, Hollywood films, or my own needs or wishes could I hope to come to terms with an incredible land. Only by such an attempt could I hope to change my own view of the world and of myself.

It was never easy, in any sense, to be in Vietnam, but then I didn't go for ease. I went perhaps with the words of a teacher at the 'pleasant semi-rural establishment' still echoing in my ears.

'What,' she once asked a half-attentive sixth-form studying *Hamlet*, 'is the most important thing one can have in life?'

To which question an unhesitating reply flew from the lips of one of the class's less deep thinkers: 'Happiness!'

The teacher – a 'Miss' whom I greatly admired for bringing literature to life, but also for smelling powerfully of gin at two in the afternoon and driving a sports car – gave the thoughtless respondent a truly withering glance before correcting her.

'The most important thing one can have in life, I assure you, my child, is experience.'

So this book is about a very personal experience of travelling: the humour and excitement, the discomforts and difficulties, the moments of magic and surreality and the tension between aloneness and companionship. Despite previous far-flung travels, only in Vietnam did I learn, not always readily, to appreciate the pleasures and benefits of solitude, and realize that, for me at least, any adventure worth the name happens as much inside as out and can only be experienced alone.

I remember Vietnam for many reasons, but perhaps mostly for being a place that was challenging in every sense, a place that obliged me to think and feel even when I didn't want to. At the time I fought all that. But I was just another sort of invader rejecting Vietnam's realities, wanting things my way – and failing, just as empires and nations had done before me.

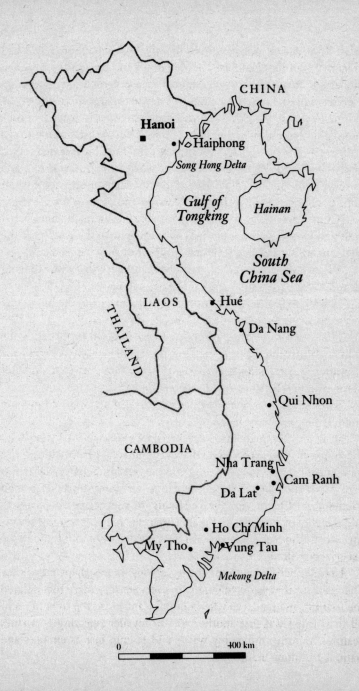

CHINA

Hanoi ■ ● ◁ Haiphong

Song Hong Delta

Gulf of Tongking

Hainan

South China Sea

LAOS ● Hué

● Da Nang

THAILAND

● Qui Nhon

CAMBODIA

Nha Trang ●

● Da Lat ● Cam Ranh

● Ho Chi Minh

My Tho ● ● Vung Tau

Mekong Delta

0   400 km

chapter one
GETTING THERE

In the autumn of 1994, having just handed in the manuscript of my first book, I decided to take a journey long promised in my imagination, a journey to Vietnam. Because my final decision to head east was sudden and near to Christmas, all direct flights into Vietnam from London were full at the time I wanted to leave. Having telephoned dozens of travel agents, I finally acknowledged that my only option was to fly to Hong Kong, with a connecting flight back to Ho Chi Minh City four days later. This news was bad enough, but I then learnt that the only carrier with seats available was Aeroflot which, empirical evidence suggested, would invariably mean several fuel stops, a great deal of chicken and no film between London and the soon-to-be-Chinese colony. It did suggest a new itinerary, however, and I began to plan my return journey from Vietnam, travelling north and east through China and back to Hong Kong by land. So, my book and visa purchases included not only Vietnam but China too.

Attempting to counter some of my own assumptions about Vietnam, I read what I could in the time between deciding to leave and departure. Although hundreds of books have been written on Vietnam since 1965, very few have been about the country or the people. The focus of such books is war – from an almost exclusively US perspective. However, reading Michael Herr's *Dispatches*[1] (the book which reputedly inspired the seminal Vietnam war film *Apocalypse Now*), followed immediately by Bau Nin's novel *The Sorrow of War*[2],

1   Picador, 1991
2   Mandarin, 1994

was profoundly enlightening. Herr's book is a spectacular, journalistic *tour-de-force* which I could barely put down. Place names remembered from my childhood, like Da Nang and Khe San, echoed as I read into the early hours of the morning. Herr had been there, he'd seen it. His words and those of men like him had made the news I heard as a child. My reading was enhanced by the fact that I had recently met a character in Herr's book, photographer Tim Page, who had brought names like 'I Corps' and 'DMZ' (Demilitarized Zone) vividly to life for me at his home in Kent and had given me what were to be useful contacts in Vietnam.

Dispatches fascinated me, but it was only as I read *The Sorrow of War* that I wept. Nin is a veteran of the Ha Noi side, the winning side, but his expression of loss and failure is intense and sensitive in its continual questioning of the purpose of war and the ephemeral nature of victory. Nin was *really* there, unable to fly in and out of the war as Western journalists did, and that 'thereness' is in every line of his novel. I found *The Sorrow of War* unremittingly depressing, but it moved me in a way Herr's brilliant, controlled writing could not. I was shocked to discover how deep my own prejudices had been, how I had unconsciously retained those stories of 'goodies' and 'baddies' where inscrutable 'gooks', 'dinks' and 'slopes' were always bad, and tall, square-jawed and invariably white college boys good. The experiences of Nin's hero Kien in the 'Jungle of Screaming Souls' taught me what I should already have known, that there is no occidental monopoly on emotion, on romanticism, on sentimentality, or on the expression of those things, though we in the West have occasionally tried to convince ourselves that there is. Kien's 'sorrow' became more real to me than the entire Vietnam *oeuvre* of Hollywood. It also made me more nervous.

Shortly before leaving London I read Anthony Grey's novel *Saigon*[3], which was different in every way from both Herr and Nin, but was a romping read and gave me some background to twentieth-century Vietnamese history in an easily digested form. Only days before my departure, my neighbour Al Micklethwaite, source of many good books over the years, asked me if I had read Norman Lewis' *A Dragon*

Apparent and was shocked when I said I'd never heard of it.

'Well,' he said, 'it's in hardback, but you'll just have to take it with you, it's brilliant.' Seeing me hesitate at the thought of the extra weight, he looked at me with a mixture of envy and generosity. 'You can't go to Vietnam without reading Norman Lewis, you know. I'll dig it out for you.'

A week or so later I thought of Al with gratitude as I smiled through the first pages of *A Dragon Apparent* sitting outside a Saigon street café. Unlike V.S. Pritchett, who carried Lawrence Sterne on his march through Spain despite acknowledging he had no interest in a 'beloved classic' while on the road, I was delighted to have Lewis as my 'classic' companion. I had learnt during days spent on Indian trains that reading about a country while in it can perform two useful functions: it can add to one's knowledge of a place while simultaneously blocking it out when required.

I had been right about Aeroflot chicken and a lack of in-flight pleasures. Entertainment between Moscow and Hong Kong was confined to watching the antics of one's fellow passengers. Bored with several hours of arguments, screaming children and vomit, I turned my attention to the tiny and almost opaque window through which I could just make out the dawn and sunset spectacle of black cloud meeting red sky, which recalled the fairytale pictures of Ivan Bilibin once glimpsed in a Delhi bookshop. I couldn't know, as I headed for Hong Kong, how very grateful I would be to Aeroflot before too long.

Hong Kong in December is cool and damp; the combined effect clammy as influenza. The whirr of the de-humidifier was a constant in the apartment where I stayed with an American friend Greg, a designer of the railway terminal for the new Hong Kong airport soon to spring up in the middle of the bay.

'It's all there,' he told me confidently as I peered down from the balcony onto a blank expanse of water. 'One day it'll just appear!'

After I'd turned the noisy de-humidifier off several times, Greg explained, with engineering precision, that the machine was necessary to prevent the place smelling like a mildewed hayloft and being overrun by a ubiquitous and indefatigable mould which could destroy the flat and its contents in a week. So the whirr continued and I slept in earplugs. But the view from the twenty-ninth floor of one of the tallest tower blocks on Hong Kong Island was stunning and just about compensated.

Greg's partner, Dwayne, had worked with Vietnamese refugees in Hong Kong for several years and although he was already in Australia preparing for an Oz Christmas when I arrived, I found the detailed, thoughtful letter he had left for me, pinned to the kitchen noticeboard. It read:

> Enjoy Hong Kong – it looks better from afar... I've written some notes based on my experiences in Vietnam. There are also a few addresses of people you might like to meet... If you don't catch me before you return to London, leave a message on the machine; tell me how you found Vietnam and whether you met any of my friends there.
>
> Good luck. Good luck. Good luck. You'll have a great time.
>
> Dwayne

This was followed by two hand-written pages of information, contacts and advice which I was to find most useful in the weeks ahead.

The apartment balcony, when I braved the chill wind, gave a brilliant view down over Hong Kong Island and beyond to Kowloon, where it lies, already China, on the other side of the curving bay. In the violet-grey distance are the rather un-Chinese mountains of the New Territories: Beacon Hill, Tates Cairn and Sugarloaf Peak. They draw an observer's eye and mind towards the vast country lying north and east, lying, Hong Kong appears to feel, in wait.

I learnt quickly that 'British' and 'popular' were diametrically opposed concepts in the soon-to-be-former colony. I discovered that it is better, if you can, to look out rather than down in Hong Kong – and not merely to avoid vertigo.

'Below' is invariably less attractive than 'beyond'. Beneath the soaring balconies small streets cluster among the roots of skyscrapers in a jumble of rusted corrugate, telephone wires and TV aerials. There was something slightly feudal and European about this urban scenery which recalled history-book pictures of peasant dwellings skirting castle walls. Only when looking out and away from the geographical and social fastness of Hong Kong's 'Peak' district did the panorama – smog permitting – become all the things I had imagined from book and magazine pictures. At night, Hong Kong comes into a tawdry but genuine beauty, as the shanty aspects of this decaying outpost of Empire are obscured by brilliant multi-coloured neon lights which hang in the thick dark air, vibrant as costume jewellery on some moth-eaten and outmoded black velvet frock.

Shortly after arriving at the Conduit Road apartment, I had a call from Peter, a young Englishman whom I had met on the flight out. Somewhere over Russia, Peter explained to me that one morning he'd woken up and decided to go to China, alone. Having made the mistake of telling friends this whim, he felt he had no choice but to go through with it. In subsequent conversation I elicited the startling information that he had never been in a non-English speaking country and had never spent more than half a day alone in his life. Despite the fact that he was armed with eight guidebooks, which he proudly displayed, I felt some slight maternal concern, having little faith in the efficacy of the guidebook as talisman.

Peter was almost in tears on the phone, having checked in – against advice – to the Chungking Mansions in Kowloon, a notorious backpackers' hostel described by the *Lonely Planet* guide as 'a coffin-shaped sweat box'.

'It's so awful here,' he said desperately. 'I can't stand it. There's no hot water, my room has no windows and I've just seen a beggar with gangrene; he had a big piece missing from his leg and I was eating a McDonald's at the time.'[4]

A feeling of grim smugness crept over me at the idiocy of the very young.

'So?' I replied rather unkindly. 'You really shouldn't eat McDonald's. It doesn't look like you're going to do very well in China, does it? Now, when I was 19...'

---

4   Back in the UK, I described this incident to a friend who told me that he had seen the same gangrenous beggar in exactly the same spot on Nathan Road and consequently never ate burgers in Kowloon.

The smugness faded somewhat as I recalled, silently, that at the age of 19 I hadn't been further than Scotland and China had been a closed country. More sniffling ensued and I decided it might be more helpful to engage with him on a compassionate level – he was, after all, a rather attractive young man – and as I invited him to Conduit Road for tea and a shower, any vestige of maternal concern I might have felt began slipping away.

Several hours later and still keen to avoid Chungking Mansions, Peter asked me to eat with him. Sadly, the choice of place and food were unfortunate and did nothing to fill Peter's youthful bosom with enthusiasm for the East. A large cockroach spread itself like a stain on the wall beside our table, its antennae waving with what seemed like suppressed excitement. The food, a dumpling soup with bits of green vegetables, resembled hard-boiled testicles floating in a stagnant pond. Trying to avoid looking at the small insects crawling in and out of the cracks in the table's faded formica, Peter did his best to swallow then gave up. Hungry after my efforts to inspirit him, I ate my own soup and then his while he looked on disconsolately.

Towards the end of my second bowl, Peter said, 'Um…I know someone here in Hong Kong – from school. I think I'll call him tomorrow.' Without looking at me he continued, 'His family live here, you know, perhaps they'll let me stay with them until I…um…until I go home.'

My attempts at solace and encouragement had failed; Chungking Mansions and the prospect of China had overcome, as I had already guessed they must.

Standing too long on the apartment balcony comparing the magnificence of the distant view with close-quarter shabbiness nearly finished me off before I ever reached Vietnam. Tiredness and Aeroflot air-conditioning had weakened my occasionally asthmatic lungs and this, combined with the damp, pollution-laden air which rose up and up to the eyrie of Conduit Road, made me sick with 'flu within 24 hours of arriving in Hong Kong. I had only three days in which to recover before my flight on to Ho Chi Minh City, I hadn't slept for nights from anticipation and body-clock confusion and I was feeling very ill and rather desperate at the thought that having come thus far I might not make it to Vietnam after all.

I was also alone on the twenty-ninth floor, as Greg had left to join Dwayne in Sydney the day after my arrival. Guessing I had some viral thing conventional medicine couldn't assist, I spent the next three days shuttling back and forth on the stainless steel subway trains to Nathan Road – haunt of 'The Gangrenous Beggar of Kowloon' – to visit the excellent Dr C. K. Lo, whose name I had chosen randomly from the phone directory, for acupuncture with free electrocution. I was very lucky with my choice.

On the first day of treatment I had staggered to his office, barely able to see, hear or breathe for the fluid simultaneously blocking and leaking from every facial orifice. However, as Dr Lo's card proclaimed, he was no mere needle-sticker but President of the International Acupuncture Society, President of the International Acupuncture Institute, President of the Institute of Oriental Medicine and an Honorary Consultant to the Medical Acupuncture Societies of the USA, New Zealand, Holland, India and Italy. I felt suitably reassured. Having only ever been treated by Western acupuncturists, I was frankly terrified of the 'real thing', a prejudice the gentle and highly skilled Dr Lo cured me of. I don't really know what he did, but daily treatments with needles in my face, throat and scalp cured me. The needles were wired up to a machine which sent out an electrical pulse every second or so. As I lay behind a curtain on the narrow bed of the treatment room, watching the needles jerk rhythmically just below my eyes and feeling utterly miserable, I wondered, for the first, but not the last time, 'Why *am* I here?'

The acupuncture treatment was enormously successful. However, Dr Lo belonged to that school of medicine which believes in trying every possible treatment on the grounds that one is sure to work. So after an initial lung X-ray, the daily needling was supplemented with a generous injection of something-or-other in the buttock, oral antibiotics, the most marvellously effective blue sleeping pills (which I subsequently discovered were not sleeping tablets at all but an oral anaesthetic), anti-cold tablets, a scarlet cough medicine which screamed 'E' numbers and seven tiny phials of traditional Chinese herbal pills, each type resembling the droppings of a differently sized rabbit. Every visit concluded with 15 minutes' hard pounding up and down my back with the 'medicinal roller', 'to bring up the lung damp', as the nurse smilingly assured me. The roller was pale blue plastic and looked like a giant baby's rattle with wheels. I found myself looking forward to that final quarter of an hour with the nurse as light relief after the electrics.

Thanks to Dr Lo, on the fifth day after my arrival in the East, I was able to breathe, able to stand and on my way to Ho Chi Minh City.

The two-hour flight with Vietnam Airlines from Hong Kong to Ho Chi Minh City was pleasant and uneventful and the in-flight service excellent. When *Lonely Planet* published its 1993 guide to Vietnam, the reputation of the country's national airline was not good, either for on-board comfort or the statistical chances of arriving with one's person intact. In December 1994, I was more than satisfied as the wine flowed freely and the aircraft soared over the South China Sea, invisible below the clouds we rose through.

I felt jollier than I had for some time as the trials of Hong Kong drifted away; I even began to consider how Vietnam Airlines could teach European carriers a thing or two about service and eventually found myself staring in slightly intoxicated fascination at the first 'real' Vietnamese people I had ever seen. The gorgeous and diminutive stewardesses had an ethereal perfection; their tiny waists and shoulders seeming even smaller under their skintight *ao dai*s. I had read about but never seen an *ao dai* (pronounced 'ow-yai'), a knee-length tunic with long sleeves and high collar. The tunic, split both sides from just above the waist, hangs loosely open to the knee, but is figure-hugging everywhere else, and trousers of the same or a contrasting fabric are worn under it. Detailed descriptions by various male writers of this elegant Vietnamese dress had not prepared me for baby pink crimplene with badly turned edges. The elegance, which was undoubted, lay not in the costume but in its wearers, whose grace was only matched by the perfection of their *maquillage*. The stewards, in their maroon nylon jackets, suffered a similar sartorial misfortune to their female colleagues, which they overcame with the same grace and impeccable courtesy.

I found myself wondering who these young men and women were. Were they perhaps the privileged children of some well-to-do party cadres? Maybe they were returned refugees? Were they from the north of Vietnam or the south? All inevitably remained a mystery to me. More prosaically I wondered, as I do on every flight, how much they knew about emergency procedures. Did they know, for example, where the descent chute was stored and were they hefty enough to move it? But I reminded myself that these were the people who had overcome the might of nations – or at least their progenitors had – though probably not wearing an *ao dai* or the precariously heeled shoes that went with it.

My fellow passengers were mostly South East Asian; many I guessed to be Hong Kong or Taiwanese businessmen from their dapper suits and expensive shoes. There were a few travellers like myself, but the airplane was only half full and the seats near me empty, so I relaxed and thought about a report I'd heard some weeks earlier on the *Seven Seas* programme broadcast by the BBC World Service about piracy in the South China Sea. I wandered into a minor fantasy in which, 30,000 feet below me, picturesque wooden junks with red sails and cargoes of oily, pungent opium were guarded by pirates dressed like Errol Flynn, but brandishing machetes instead of rapiers. Of course, modern pirates drive fast, big-engined boats and carry everything from AK47s to grenade launchers (and even the occasional machete), though I much preferred the idea of junks. But my fantasy wasn't so very far from the truth and I have since come across the words 'Piracy is common in the Gulf of Thailand and the South China Sea' more than once.

It was dark when we neared the Vietnamese coastline, so with nothing to peer at, I thought instead of Dr C. K. Lo and his presidencies and was grateful to be able to withstand the descent towards Tan Son Nhut airport free of unrelieved pressure in my Eustachian tubes. Walking down the steps of the plane towards the waiting bus I felt good for the first time since leaving England. The air was humid but the breeze was warm and soft and I breathed in deeply. Not yet able to see Vietnam except as shades of black starred with the blue, white and yellow lights of the airport, I could already feel it all around me.

On the bus from the aircraft to the terminal I met yet another young Englishman and as we were headed for the same hotel we agreed to share a taxi into the city. Any concerns I'd had about entering Vietnam, engendered by *Lonely Planet*, proved unnecessary. Our flight arrival was processed through passport control quickly and efficiently and baggage collected without mishap; all clearly the result of much practice. A few weeks later at Ha Noi's Noi Ba airport an Italian doctor, Damasso Maria Rosario, became the millionth tourist to visit Vietnam in 1994.

Hiring a cab to take us into the city centre proved equally easy, though the exchange was accompanied by a controlled version of the sort of experience I'd had many times in other Asian countries, where it seems every cab driver in the world is trying to tempt the unwary newcomer into his vehicle – and all at the best possible price. The chaos was controlled by men I presumed, from their ID badges, to be government officials and who seemed to have the task of allotting customers to drivers. 'What power!' I thought as an 'ID official' led us to a waiting car in front of the terminal building, assuring us of quality all the way. The ID man paused to talk to the driver of a very new-looking four-door Honda and I was surprised and impressed by the standard of Vietnamese transport. I soon realized, as we were marched on, that I had been impressed for the wrong reasons. The ID man had the power to turn a 1990s Honda into a 1960s American leftover and there was very little anyone could do about it. This was a lesson that, with hindsight, I should have stored in the very forefront of my mind for future reference, but some mistakes evidently need to be made repeatedly. So we set off on the four-mile ride in an ancient vehicle of questionable origin, towards the Hoang Vu Hotel and Pham Ngu Lao Street, Saigon.

The name 'Saigon' was causing all sorts of buried memories to cast their shrouds, images not only of the US war of the 1960s and '70s, but of French colonialism, of its officials and their ladies in the latest Paris fashions, strolling along the rue Catenat. I thought also of the work of Marguérite Duras and a steamy, exotic mysteriousness not, in my experience at least, to be found in former British colonies, its lack due no doubt to the differences between the Anglo-Saxon and Gallic temperaments.

I noticed, even before leaving Tan Son Nhut, that the names 'Ho Chi Minh City' and 'Saigon' were being used interchangeably by taxi touts and would-be guides, which was confusing at first. It took a little time to grasp the political and geographical complexities of place and name. 'Saigon' seems to have two distinct but overlapping usages. Many southerners still prefer to call their city by its former name of Saigon for ideological reasons. Others may refer to the central district, District 1, the heart of Ho Chi Minh City, as Saigon. Neither use of the name is politically acceptable, but Saigon is so much shorter and easier to say, particularly if you're a foreigner.

Ho Chi Minh City, which was created after the reunification of North and South Vietnam following the collapse of Southern resistance on 30 April 1975, is not, as I had thought, simply the old city of Saigon renamed; it isn't even a 'city' at all in the usual sense of that word. Over 90 per cent of its area is rural, a vast landscape of rice-based agriculture dependent on the waters of the Mekong River, with the occasional clump of palms, or village, breaking the horizon. This 'city' is divided into urban and rural districts and although they cover the smallest land area, the urban districts of Ho Chi Minh City are more numerous than their rural counterparts and form the most densely populated region of Vietnam, with over four million official inhabitants. The sprawling conglomerate stretches from the South China Sea in the east across the north-west delta region to almost touch the Cambodian border.

After Hong Kong, what little I could see of Vietnam seemed human. Driving south-east through the dark towards a glowing skyline that gave away the position of the central districts, I found the flatness and scale of the suburban buildings reassuring. The driver was silent as we rattled along at about 40 mph, the seating shaking badly due to defunct springs. My companion, a large, blondly hirsute young man, was pleasant enough; on closer acquaintance his manner and general appearance (excluding the rugby shirt) made me think of English travellers of the mid-Victorian era. We talked as the taxi trundled on through the brightening night and I felt increasingly certain that wherever life's aeroplane set him down, my compatriot would use the same peculiarly English combination of polite insouciance and lumbering *équivoque* to maintain personal dignity and the necessary status quo.

The air blew in through the wide open windows, any air-conditioning the car had once possessed now as defunct as the seat springs; the smells of dust and earlier sunshine on soil rushed at us

and mingled with the much fainter scent of cracked leather uphol-
stery. I was sorry not to be able to see more of what we were passing
– the street lights were not numerous and in the outer suburbs the
few people still about seemed faint and rather ghostly under the
yellowish electrics. The large moths which I glimpsed occasionally as
they flapped past the windscreen also seemed pale and insubstantial.
But despite being unable to see all I might wish, there was something
appropriately mysterious and in keeping with the spirit of the place
about this night-time approach to Saigon, as the pale darkness hid its
secrets from me a little while longer.

We entered District 1 at around 9 p.m. There were more people
and traffic now and the driver slowed and beeped his way through
thin streams of cyclists. As we drew to a stop outside the Hoang Vu
Hotel, it looked as though a riot must be going on. But pushing my
way through the crowd it was soon apparent that the seeming chaos
was simply end-of-day street socializing as food vendors, water sellers, children and beggars intermingled loudly on the broken but
clean pavement that was the hotel entrance. Odours characteristic of
heat and humanity seeped into my nostrils and I realized I'd missed
these smells and all the people and things associated with them.

Almost every aspect of the Hoang Vu Hotel was beige and
brown. The largish lobby was beige tiled and everything in it seemed
to be of brown wood or painted to look like brown wood. In one area
a few caramel-coloured sofas were arranged for the benefit of guests,
but all were empty except for a small, thin man in what looked like
dark brown pyjama bottoms with a beige shirt. The four women
sitting behind the hotel desk wore a variety of colours but still
seemed at one with their surroundings by managing everything as a
unit; smiles, the search for my booking, handing change to street
vendors, all seemed to happen directed by a homogeneous impulse.
As there were no single rooms, I took a double at $8 per night; the
Vietnamese dong and US dollar are currently as interchangeable as
the names 'Ho Chi Minh City' and 'Saigon' and the exchange rate
between them as flexible as the imagination of the buying and selling
parties will allow.

I had made several copies of my passport before leaving the UK
and having deposited one of these at reception was handed my keys

and, accompanied by the silent, brown-clad man, led to a very small, very brown lift which took us to the third floor.

Opening the door to room number 18 I felt a surprising sense of peace and relaxation which I didn't pause to investigate, as my English companion, now installed in number 19, had earlier suggested we head directly for a cocktail on the roof terrace at the Rex Hotel and, arrival excitement overcoming tiredness, I'd agreed. So, dumping my bag – I was proud to have only one small piece of luggage – we rendezvoused in the monotint lobby under the flickering, yellow-brown strip lights and went in search of a cyclo or two.

Vietnamese pedicabs, or trishaws, are the reverse of most Asian types, having the passenger in the front and the cycling driver higher and behind. This immediately struck me as being a decidedly pro-worker arrangement, designed as it is to ensure that in most cases of collision, the passenger would be the first to be involved. It was now between 9.30 and 10 p.m. and the streets of District 1 were beginning to take on the deserted appearance of the suburbs. Vietnam, even Saigon, closes down early and though life goes on behind doors and shutters, the streets can seem deserted by 11 p.m. I was surprised at our speed, given that in both cases the drivers were pushing body weights well above their own, and despite the Hong Kong hangover of tiredness, I felt a tremendous sense of exhilaration at our almost silent movement through the dark streets, though this was mixed with a slight awkwardness at being transported by the physical efforts of another.

A statue of monumental size held centre stage at one of the roundabouts we circled. Its scale I had come to expect in the urban statuary of Communist countries, the historic subject matter was more surprising: a warrior looking rather like a character from a Kurosawa film seemed to shake his sword as we passed, but whether in defiance or greeting I was already too tired to tell. As we moved eastward to the Rex through wide streets now almost entirely free of any kind of traffic, I looked to my right and in the distance, at the bottom of a long straight road, glimpsed what I thought was the Saigon River. Later I discovered that what I had seen was only the Ben Nghe Channel, a small waterway which separates District 1 from District 4 before joining the majestic Saigon.

Our drivers stopped in the empty boulevard named after the early fifteenth-century Vietnamese emperor-hero Le Loi and pointing to the corner said, 'Rex Hotel.' We understood that for some reason they weren't allowed to drive down certain roads or drop passengers outside some hotels. We paid, politely refusing their offer to wait for us, and headed across the elegantly wide road reminiscent of Paris, past what on first glance I thought to be children dressed up in camouflage gear. Noting that the 'children' carried sub-machine guns, I realized with some unidentifiable sensation that I was looking at Vietnamese soldiers. Their backs towards me, I was free to stare as I liked at these doll-like young men who in their close-fitting fatigues looked more like scaled-up Action Man models than part of the army which had overcome the might of the West and the menace from the north. These were the only soldiers I was to see on my journey and later I learnt about the extent of malnutrition in Vietnam and the consequent undersize of much of the younger population which so surprised me that first night.

The oft-written about Rex Hotel had precisely the faded, colonial grandeur I'd imagined. It was more faded than grand, however, with an absence of staff and a plethora of brass. We wandered around for some time before being grudgingly shown the lift that would take us up to the roof; clearly our dress was considered inappropriate for the magnificence of the place.

In the close proximity of the lift I began to feel a slight awkwardness at the Englishman's presence which I hadn't felt in the taxi with the windows open or racing along the roads in two cyclos. We were here together only because of the 'stranger in a strange land' cliché and because there is comfort in familiarity; yet in some ways he seemed to me more remote than the barefoot cyclo drivers I had just met. Imagining we'd have almost nothing to say to each other over the planned cocktail, I stepped onto the hotel roof with minor apprehension.

I needn't have worried. The roof terrace bar of the Rex Hotel was bizarre enough to sustain our conversation through most of his beers and my bright blue 'Saigon Dream', which was indescribably flavoured and had no alcohol in it that I could taste. I was glad to be seeing the place at night, softly lit, the holes in the strange animal topiary less evident and our elderly waiter less noticeably crusty. He looked as though he would have felt happier on a bicycle in Brittany wearing onions and a beret. He certainly looked disgusted at my companion's ignorance of the French language and my own feeble attempts at it.

Behind what looked like a heap of deserted building material, rows of caged birds twittered sadly as they fluttered around and around on their meagre perches. Searching for the toilet, I passed the waiter's Doppelgänger, a particularly depressed-looking mynah bird which scrutinized me closely. We eyeballed each other for some moments and I was about to make some suitably encouraging remark about life, when it threw a large soggy fruit rind at me through the bars of its cage. 'Go ahead,' I said to it, looking at the pulpy mess which landed on the floor, having missed my shirt by millimetres, 'get it out of your system, you'll feel better. A bit more to the right next time though.' I'm certain the bird sneered at me.

Inevitably the Englishman and I talked of home, the immediate scenery having given up its secrets and there being no view over the city. Rugby, unsurprisingly, was the main matter of my companion's life history and eventually I heard myself saying, part accusation, part statement, 'I suppose that means you're a jock,' to which the unhesitating reply was 'Of course!' accompanied by a look of pitying surprise that so simple a concept had taken me so long to work out. The word 'jock', which among my friends and acquaintances would be considered a sentence of social death, was evidently *de rigeur* in Tunbridge Wells.

Shortly after that we left and found our drivers still waiting on the permitted side of the road, feet up and chatting. I was grateful for them being there as it was now midnight and there were no other cyclos in sight, indeed no traffic at all. Already half asleep, I headed for the Hoang Vu; my companion, in need of some real excitement after a few hours with me, decided he wanted to 'do' the bars of Saigon and disappeared into the night. Our drivers laughed and called to each other through the silence as they cycled in opposite directions until I was alone with Nin, pedalling away behind me, who asked, a gentle smirk in his voice, 'You have argument?' Facing away from him, I nodded and smiled at the semi-dark street ahead.

Despite the tiredness I enjoyed pottering round my room, deciding which bed to sleep on and how to put up my mosquito net. After the freshness of my cyclo ride, the room had felt stifling, but the choice was between hot silence and noisy cool. The ceiling fan ground on and on like a football rattle but it did give the air some motion. I pondered about the net for some time as there was no hook in the wall over the bed. I supposed that the Saigonese didn't use nets, implying a comforting absence of malarial mosquitoes; but with paranoid visions of large, hairy and foully poisonous insects crawling over my face, I was absolutely certain that sleep without a net in a room with an unglazed window was an impossibility. Having chosen the bed the nearest the window as being the least rock-like, I finally improvised on the net-hanging situation by squeezing a tall metal coat-stand behind the headboard and hanging the net precariously from that, tucking the edges in carefully under the mattress as insurance against extra-intrepid spiders. The ultra-hard bed was matched by a single pillow, obviously one of a pair with the stone upon which Jacob dreamt of his ladder. The undersheet was white and spotless and I hunted for the oversheet until I realized it was the small piece of fabric similar in pattern and feel to my great aunt's parlour curtains folded carefully at the foot of the bed.

I laid my books, notebooks and maps on the desk in front of the grille-covered window, then checked under the desk with a torch for lurking creatures. Satisfied, I turned the inconstant strip light off and sat in the semi-darkness, elbows on the desk, looking out over the alleyways and flattish roofs immediately under my window. Temporary lights were strung across and along the alley; a few lights were still on in the houses only yards away and faint sounds of domestic activity wandered up to me. In the distance I heard the occasional motorbike whining by on its way to I couldn't even guess where. In the space of a few hours I had arrived in Vietnam, paid with US dollars and spoken in French. I was very tired but content to be sitting doing nothing for the first time in weeks and months, wanting to be nowhere else.

Eventually I made for the bathroom, wearing the loudly squeaking rubber shower shoes provided for guests. I wondered who had worn them before me but decided not to think about that and put them on anyway. There was only one tap on the basin but the water was a perfect temperature, neither hot nor cold; the light switch hung out of the wall on its wires and small black insects darted away from the glare of the naked bulb, but all of it seemed wonderful to me as I cleaned my teeth with bottled water and grinned at the rusting mirror. I hadn't quite got used to the Gatling-gun sound of the fan, but deciding against heat and humidity, the compromise of fan and earplugs was reached. To make absolutely certain of a good night's sleep I swallowed one of Dr Lo's little blue pills just in case the pillow proved too hard and, armed with torch, earplugs, bottle of water and *A Dragon Apparent*, got swiftly under the mosquito net and tucked it around me. I read only two pages, describing Lewis' arrival in Vietnam, before the pill did a tango with the remnants of my 'Saigon Dream' and I passed into a restful oblivion.

chapter two

PHAM NGU LAO

The scene the following day could not have been more different from the almost silent darkness of the previous night. When I emerged from the hotel it was into a confusion of people and bicycles moving through a haze of dusty heat. I walked up Pham Ngu Lao Street cautiously, the thought of crossing the road a terror best not contemplated, and sat at a table outside a friendly-looking café where there were already a few other Westerners. I ordered my first Vietnamese coffee and some of the French bread I had seen on stalls along the road.

Sitting drinking the intensely sweet strong coffee, I noticed that several of the street cafés along Pham Ngu Lao were raised to a level about 18 inches to 2 feet above the road; I supposed this was to lessen the risk of flooding during the monsoon. It was also helpful for the onlooker, as the small advantage of height gave a rather better view of the street. From the little I had yet seen of the city I had no sense of Saigon being anything like the 'French town in a hot country' described by Norman Lewis in 1950; too much of what he saw then would have disappeared during and after the war with the US for his image of Saigon to have remained for me to see 45 years later. Instead I saw a jumble of old and new buildings – 'old' meaning perhaps 1960s – some with flat roofs, others with an almost Alpine style, their balconies rickety and the corrugated gables now red with rust. The width of the streets, the open fronts and large signs hanging over every shop and café put me in mind of Tombstone, Arizona, rather than Montpellier or Bourges.

My first impression was of cleanliness; the streets were spotless and joss sticks burned in the swept gutters. Unlike India – one of my main aural memories of which is the sound of the ubiquitous but totally ineffectual broom on stone – I was not aware of anyone sweeping or cleaning in Saigon. Even the beggars seemed clean. A small girl, her hair shining and beautiful, came to my table selling postcards which I declined, smiling. She smiled back, even though I bought nothing. As the child moved on to more profitable exchanges, I was startled by the vision of a woman in short-sleeved, baby-pink 'pyjamas', long blueish gloves and a maroon velvet hat, driving a scooter. Before I could fully grasp what I'd seen she was gone, disappearing into the crush of cycles in the middle of Pham Nu Lao. I noticed afterwards that many women, while cycling or riding a motorbike, wore long gloves that reached over the elbow and up to the edge of their blouse, and guessed this was in order to keep their arms white. Although I never saw a single crash-helmet being worn, female cyclists and scooter drivers wore all sorts of head gear as protection against the browning effects of the sun. Flowered straw hats that would have looked *de rigeur* on the King's Road London in 1966 abounded, as did large floppy velveteen creations which made me feel overheated just looking at them. The hats and gloves rarely matched, which I found surprising in a culture that I had already observed to have much aesthetic judgement in other sartorial matters. Perhaps the most ingenious if unflattering sun-screen I saw while drinking that first coffee was a large plastic washing-up bowl held over head and face with one hand, while the rider steered a perilous path on her scooter with her other.

The women I saw, as I ate the rather good French bread, looked much like the air stewardesses of the previous evening, but with more naked faces. They seemed so small, almost fragile, though I guessed in a rice-winnowing or water buffalo-harnessing competition the likes of me wouldn't stand a chance. I noted the body shapes of the local women and those of the Westerners; most of us looked oversized and positively hefty in comparison with the small-boned and high-breasted Vietnamese women. Western men – particularly Scandinavians, many of whom seemed massive even to me – looked bizarrely hulking as they strode along the pavements, topping the cyclo drivers and local passers-by by up to 2 feet in height.

From among all the movement and colour passing me on legs and wheels, I noticed a big-bodied, short-legged dog step cautiously off the pavement opposite my table and wait, watching the oncoming cycle traffic with a practised eye and decidedly human cautiousness. Having made up his mind that there was a lull in the action, he trotted sedately across the road, looking neither left nor right, head and tail up. That dog, I later realized, epitomized the attitude of the Vietnamese towards road traffic, which, if verbalized, would probably be something like: 'Look cautiously before moving. Once moving, don't look at all, you'll only panic, and anyway, vehicles should avoid pedestrians, not the other way round.'

I found this attitude refreshing after witnessing the demise of road courtesy in Britain, but when there are almost as many cars as there are people in Vietnam, doubtless pedestrians will cease to stroll casually there too.

I began to consider what I should do with the rest of my morning and thought that attempting to organize further travel would be the best use of time. I needed to find out what local travel was available at short notice as before leaving London I'd arranged to meet a photographer friend and her partner in Saigon. They wouldn't be arriving for three or four days, which meant my remaining in the Ho Chi Minh region for at least that long.

Walking further along the street I noticed the very many Western-style cafés and bars, most of which seemed to offer travel arrangements, including organizing visa extensions and vehicle hire. One of the advantages of staying on Pham Nu Lao Street, or 'backpacker's alley' as I heard it referred to, was that a great many useful things were squashed into a conveniently small space. The disadvantage of such a place is that it's entirely artificial, constructed for the benefit of tourists and about as Vietnamese as a restaurant in Manchester or Milwaukee. However, it met some of my travel needs and I discovered ways of getting around Vietnam not recorded in my increasingly outdated edition of *Lonely Planet*. Vietnam is one of the most rapidly developing countries in the world and the *Lonely Planet* guide, normally a boon to any right-thinking traveller, was already proving a sad let-down in late 1994.

Towards the western end of Pham Ngu Lao I found the Sinh Café which, from the outside, looked pretty much like any of the many busy open-fronted cafés and restaurants catering specifically to financially restricted foreigners. Pham Ngu Lao, because it has the largest concentration of Western tourists and travellers in Ho Chi Minh City, attracts a special kind of street-life. That morning, as I sat down for a glass of mineral water (moving from café to café is quite standard behaviour for a person in a hot place with no definite schedule), most of Vietnam's 36 million under-25s appeared to be thrusting poor quality postcards and copies of Graham Greene's *The Quiet American* into my hand, whilst telling me – almost winking – that their mother would beat them if they didn't go home with the requisite number of dong. This was generally done with good humour and considerable wit. One very strange-looking young boy in particular I envisaged on TV with a comedy show of his own. None of the children who approached me looked hungry or dirty and certainly none seemed visibly beaten.

Two Vietnamese women in exceedingly short skirts and very tall heels half-hauled an overweight and ageing hippy into a seat near mine and set about ordering alcohol for him and tea for themselves. He looked like he'd already had more than he could hold, certainly more than he could perform with any dignity on, but perhaps that was the point. These women were the only prostitutes I saw in Vietnam whom I knew without any doubt to be members of that profession. Prostitution in Vietnam is increasing rapidly, but at present it remains largely hidden and still discreet. Many tea houses and coffee shops across the country are merely polite-sounding brothels, and restaurants are often staffed with 'hostesses' who service customers in side-rooms and cubicles between courses. As in most Asian countries, virginity, or rather the ending of that state, is highly prized and it is not uncommon for madames and women pimps to 're-create' child virgins in order to demand higher fees from customers. At present most men using the services of women and men in the Vietnamese sex industry are Vietnamese, but as more and more businessmen from the Far East visit Vietnam that is changing. Western men too see the beauty and apparent fragility of Vietnamese women and children and want it. Perhaps the most sinister aspect of this is the rising number of young girls and women who are kidnapped each year and smuggled over the borders through places like Lang Son into China where they are sold as wives or servants, or both.

Dragging my eyes away from the spectacle at the next table, I looked around again at the indigent of Pham Ngu Lao. Beggars over 35 I guessed to be mostly former ARVN (Army of the Republic of Vietnam) soldiers or their families or any other South Vietnamese foolish enough to have been on the losing side and impoverished enough to have been unable to flee the country in April 1975. Of all the tragic outcomes of the American–Vietnam war perhaps the most unfortunate are those soldiers and their families of the South who fought to keep a non-Communist Vietnam. They have no memorials, no honour and after 25 years, no real peace. Today the luckier men clean shoes and drive cyclos. The unlucky ones, those with no arms or legs or eyes, beg.

Sitting outside the Sinh Café on that first visit, I watched a man, terminated at the hips, use his elbows to pull himself along on a square 'skateboard' through the gutter where a drab yellow dog was pissing only inches from his face. As he looked up and caught my eye, I looked away. The blankness of his gaze was perhaps the result of heroin, the dirt ingrained in his face maybe a prop rubbed there to increase the effect of degradation. I later described this incident to a British NGO worker who told me that this man was almost certainly a professional beggar, probably part of an organized gang. At that moment, however, had the man been as grand a ham as Sir Laurence Olivier, what I saw in his face I knew to be absolutely real and my own feelings of shame, embarrassment, guilt, pity and more were only heightened by the money I bent down to hand him and for which he squeezed my foot. As in other developing countries where poverty and desperation are commonplace, beggars in Saigon reputedly barter and even mutilate their own children to attract more attention and sympathy from people like me. There are also real beggars, but apparently it's hard to tell the difference between the real article and the professional; I certainly wasn't able to.

I was subsequently told by aid workers the reason for the relatively small number of beggars and the apparent cleanliness and health of many of the street people I saw. The long-term indigent prostitute, HIV sufferer[1] or drug user – and these criteria often over-lap – is not visible to the average foreigner because she or he has been 'removed' to a 'social camp'. One official explanation for these camps is that Western tourists and businesspeople don't like to see 'problems' on the streets and so junkies, whores and beggars are 'tidied away' for the convenience of foreigners. I was also told, how-ever, that such camps – formerly called 're-education camps' and now given the less loaded name 'social' – have existed since the mid-'70s, when no tourism or Western business of any note existed in Vietnam. Camp inmates are seemingly not only from the Saigonese underclass but may be whole families of former ARVN soldiers, intellectuals or former Western sympathizers who do not possess a *ho khau*, which literally translated means 'family mouth' but refers to an ID card representing a social and political 'file' or 'history' acces-sible by the state. If a man or woman has no *ho khau* or a bad one, he or she and his or her entire family will almost certainly be tainted by this. No *ho khau* means no work except the lowest; it means having no legitimate existence.

There are reportedly up to a dozen social camps in the remotest rural areas of the south, holding many thousands of people. I was told that camp gates are surmounted by Ho Chi Minh's words, bor-rowed from the American Declaration of Independence, 'Nothing is more precious than freedom', which recalled that other maxim, 'Arbeit macht frei.' Foreign aid workers who have spent years with street people, working in camps and outside, believe that at least 40–45 per cent of the population of Ho Chi Minh City live without a *ho khau* and that this is explained away by creating an official pop-ulation figure far lower than the actual one. In 1950, Lewis noted Saigon's 'ten thousand sampans, harbouring an uncounted native population'; almost half a century later the population is still uncounted and vastly greater than that contained in Lewis' sampans.

This invisible aspect of Vietnam is just that, not seen by the aver-age visitor, though I was always conscious of the innate discretion of the Vietnamese, which I assumed informed all their activities, not

---

1 Vietnam currently has one of the more active HIV prevention campaigns in South East Asia.

merely the social or cultural. Discovering that things were not quite as they appeared saddened, but didn't surprise me. Post-war Vietnam is little different from its neighbours China and Cambodia in the way it has treated its former opponents and dissidents. I became aware in a matter of days of the North/South divide that still exists and the dislike some Southerners feel towards their Northern 'overlords'. I often overheard older men talking to tourists and telling them that they had been with the Americans during the war – which I understood to mean, among other things, 'I wasn't one of them – from the North.' Of course the feeling is not one-sided – many Northerners apparently view their Southern neighbours as lazy, greedy and superficial.

One of the South's enduring complaints against the Northern-based Communist government is the way in which its intelligentsia and urban bourgeoisie were replaced after reunification by men and women – mostly men (there hasn't been a top level female Communist Party official in Vietnam since the 1940s) from the North who had spent 20 years in the jungles fighting and had no idea what a desk looked like, let alone what to do when given an official post sitting behind one. In true Maoist style, the South's own cultural and social leaders, if they were not already dead or imprisoned, were set to work in rural collectives.

The North–South problem is an ancient one disappearing back through the dark glass of pre-history. Although the victorious NVA (North Vietnamese Army) claimed in 1975 that they were 'reunifying' Vietnam, this was not strictly true. Vietnam had only rarely in its long history been a single, united country. One of the longest periods of 'unity' was of course the 95 years Vietnam spent under the discreetly brutal French regime, which ended abruptly in 1954 with the battle of Dien Bien Phu, when East trounced West and 13,000 French and an untold number of Vietnamese troops died, along with Indo-Chinese colonialism.

Observing the activities of my fellow travellers at the Sinh Café, I realized far more was going on than the mere provision of refreshment. The café proprietors had seen a niche and wholeheartedly leapt into it; their travel section, which covered an area something less than 6 square feet, was busier than most Thomas Cook's and offered almost as many services. The head-height plyboard walls separating the 'travel bureau' from the café, were covered in maps of Vietnam, the delta and the Ho Chi Minh City area. These in turn were covered by list after list of tours the café offered and sheets where you could write your name beside those of fellow visitors eager to see the sights of the south. The Sinh Café advertised various expeditions throughout the region, the longest being a week trip west, across the delta, to the 'fish sauce' island of Phu Quoc off the Cambodian coast which, to my disappointment, didn't fit with my timescale. I considered something a little more modest and was told by the vague and hyperactive person giving advice and taking bookings that the most popular tour combined the Cao Dai cathedral at Tay Ninh and the Cu Chi tunnels, both north of the oddly shaped dip in the Viet–Cambodian border called the 'Parrot's Beak' and within 60 miles of Saigon. I agreed to think about that one and went to sit on the raised pavement outside the café to drink deliciously cold coconut water from a green nut, breathe lead exhaust fumes and address myself to *A Dragon Apparent*.

Reading Lewis' account of travelling through Vietnam, I felt vaguely disappointed at the apparent impossibility of initiating independent travel in Vietnam, or from Saigon at least. The ex-pats and fellow travellers I'd already chatted to over water and coffee had confirmed my grasp of the situation – travelling alone or even in small groups was really not on unless one was prepared to cycle or ride a motorbike over huge distances and sleep rough. Over breakfast, however, I had met a young Frenchman – possessed of that startling blue-eyed, black-haired Gallic beauty which seems to fill Anglo-Saxon bosoms with delight and chests with envy – who had done just that from north to south. Lacking the Frenchman's muscularity of buttock, however, I was obliged to confess to myself, though it stuck in my craw, that I much preferred the sound of Norman Lewis' semi-hysterical colonial officials to a night alone and tentless amid the flora and fauna of Vietnam.

Having finished the coconut by scooping out the wonderfully slimy jelly lining the inside with a long-handled spoon, I reached my decision. The Cao Dai cathedral I decided to avoid on the grounds that any religion which worshipped on the set of a computer fantasy game and had canonized Lenin, Shakespeare, Descartes, Victor

Hugo, Pasteur and Jeanne d'Arc with such a shameless bias towards France and fame might offer limited enjoyment. However, another reason for deciding against visiting what is, after all, one of the main tourist attractions of South Vietnam was the perfect, if vicarious, satisfaction I had already found merely sitting on the street reading Lewis' unparalleled description of the building at the heart of Cao Daism. He writes:

> From a distance this structure could have been dismissed as the monstrous result of a marriage between a pagoda and a Southern baroque church, but at close range the vulgarity of the building was so impressive that mild antipathy gave way to fascinated horror. This cathedral must be the most outrageously vulgar building ever to have been built with serious intent.

I gave the Cu Chi tunnels more serious consideration, but decided against them for physical rather than aesthetic reasons. The tunnels, 45 miles north of Ho Chi Minh City, were part of the vital troglodytic infrastructure which allowed the Communists to wage guerrilla warfare so successfully against considerably more powerful enemies. Begun by the Viet Minh in 1948 as an anti-French measure, they were originally 3 feet high and less than 2 feet wide. They've been widened in recent years to allow tourists, better fed and less agile than the Communists, to pass through them. The tunnel system stretches 150 miles and is three-tiered, the deepest gallery being nearly 40 feet below the surface. By 1975 this underground network housed communities of up to 16,000 people with hospital, kitchen, conference and dormitory facilities. B52 bombers occasionally destroyed the first and even second galleries, but never reached the third.

The tunnels are increasingly popular as a tourist attraction, particularly, it seems, with Taiwanese, Japanese, South Korean and French tourists, of whom over 500 a day scrabble around in the dark and dirt. Despite the undoubted historical significance of Cu Chi, I persuaded myself that as I was on a restricted time schedule I really didn't need to crawl on knees and elbows through what were, after all, just long holes in the ground. Also, I wasn't entirely certain how I felt about seeing the guides dressed up in the black pyjamas that were the unofficial outfit of the Communist resistance (as well as being what pretty well what all peasant farmers wore) and encouraging tourists to shoot everything from AK47s to pistols at pictures of wild animals for $1 per bullet.

There was another less serious reason, too. I was slightly nervous of being mistaken for an American – American tourists are visiting Cu Chi in ever-increasing numbers – as I had read that a few of the less restrained Vietnamese guides apparently entertain themselves by luring unsuspecting tourists, US citizens being the victims of choice, into the narrowest parts of the tunnels. When claustrophobia has thoroughly set in, the victim is drawn towards harmless but heart-stopping man-traps in the tunnel floor. All this may well have been no more than a vicious rumour started by those who didn't quite fit the tunnels, but I wasn't prepared to risk it.

So almost by default the Mekong delta became my outing of choice. I bought a ticket for a day trip leaving the following day for My Tho and Phung Island, home of the 'Coconut Monk'. Included in the tour was a previously uninhabited island which, I was told in a serious and confidential tone, had been the secret headquarters of the Communists in that area of the delta during the war and was now a centre for the making of coconut toffee.

December is the start of the dry season in the south of Vietnam and the temperature in Saigon is at its most pleasant, like a hot Mediterranean autumn but with a stronger and more insistent sun. I set off the few hundred yards back toward the Hoang Vu to shower and take my rehydration concoction. After various visits to extremely hot parts of the world it was only while in Egypt with a former Green Beret and Vietnam veteran in 1991 that I had discovered the benefits of electrolyte salts for rehydration – clearly the military still had a thing or two to teach me.

Walking back along Pham Ngu Lao I felt pleased that I had secured a trip out of Saigon before my friends Grace and Nicholas were due to arrive, but was sorry that my view of the delta would be quite limited. My sense of relaxation on arriving hadn't lasted long and I was already beginning to feel the impulse to move on. One of the difficulties I have always found travelling long distances in short timespans is overcoming that urge to do and see everything, which is of course quite impossible. I had made up my mind before leaving the UK that I *would* get from Ho Chi Minh City to Ha Noi and beyond that to China and had set this plan in stone by getting my exit visa from Vietnam stamped with the exciting but unsettling words 'Lang Son'.

Lang Son is a north-east border village once flattened during the swift and brutal Chinese invasion in 1979 and now a centre for Sino–Vietnamese smuggling and banditry – politely referred to by the Vietnamese as 'unofficial trade'. This unofficial trade stocks many of the markets of Ha Noi with everything from CDs and pirated videos to electronic goods and machinery. It was only two years since the last shots had been traded across the Friendship Gate border crossing instead of merchandise and in my mind Lang Son was a place of permanent mist and heavily moustached men with eye-patches and bandoliers. More accurately, according to travellers' reports, it's a place with expanding numbers of tourist villas, plans for high-rise hotels, a faulty electricity supply and appalling food. It is also one of only two official overland crossing points into China. When I asked for a visa exiting into China, the Vietnamese embassy official in London only offered me one route, so I politely accepted what they stamped in my passport. As far as I knew 'Lang Son' meant 'Land Exit' or even 'Let This Woman Out'. Naturally, within moments of looking in my atlas I realized that in order to enter China heading in the direction of my first-stage destination of Kunming in Yunnan province, the crossing I needed was Lao Cai, far to the north and west of Lang Son. I swore I wouldn't be so lax in examining maps in future. Before leaving London I had contacted the Vietnamese Embassy and asked to change my point of exit, only to be told that it would now have to be done in Ha Noi. It was in part this uncertainty which unsettled me and made every day a day to be counted and a day to be moving.

As I stood under the delightful lukewarm water of my shower on the third floor of the Hoang Vu, small insects of all sorts ran along the high window-sill where I kept my soap and shampoo; occasionally one would make the mistake of slipping off the sill and into the water stream running down the stained, plaster walls below before getting swept into the flow around my feet and spinning down the plugless hole into insect-oblivion, whilst I tried not to add insult to injury by stepping on them as they drowned.

Cooled by the shower, I dozed for a time. The daytime heat made sleeping difficult, but after an hour or so I felt rested and decided to make a telephone call. My vigilance against spiders remained constant and I re-examined the underside of the desk before sitting down with my notebooks to retrieve a telephone number given to me by Tim Page. I had carried a bottle of Johnny Walker from Moscow to present to a former Communist activist, recently a general, along with a videotape of the documentary film of Tim's search for journalist friends Sean Flynn – son of Errol – and Dana Stone, both of whom had been missing in Cambodia since 1970, believed murdered by the Khmer Rouge. I had watched the video with Greg in Hong Kong and had found it difficult to believe that the few bones Tim was shown by helpful Cambodian villagers had once been part of Sean Flynn, the incredibly beautiful young man Tim's images had captured meditating naked or heading a charge of leaderless GIs, armed only with a camera and a great deal of front.

I called the General from the lobby telephone. The four receptionists were now reduced to three and they were most helpful with my attempts to use the rather creaky system, but I found the absence of any sort of privacy while speaking rather strange. My call was greeted with momentary bewilderment, followed by a courteous invitation to visit that afternoon at 5 p.m.

It was now 3 p.m. and deciding I was thirsty again, I set off up Pham Ngu Lao. I went to the café where I had eaten my breakfast and ordering yet another green coconut, sat and examined the map of Saigon in my guidebook. I looked for District 3 and found it immediately north of District 1 and the General's house not far from the railway station.

I finished my coconut, looked around for Nin the cyclo driver and saw him parked a few metres away at what was clearly his usual spot, sitting in the passenger seat reading a newspaper. It didn't strike me at once that the simple, everyday activity of reading a newspaper was something unusual in my experience of pedicab drivers. But walking towards him, I remembered that he had also read the map

I'd shown him of Cholon, the Chinatown of Ho Chi Minh City, where I intended to leave a message for Grace and Nicholas at their hotel. I suddenly realized I had taken for granted that Nin could read simply because I could, though I had never made that assumption anywhere else in Asia. I had never seen a Burmese, Thai, Indian or Bangladeshi rickshaw driver read a newspaper – they couldn't, the overwhelming majority being illiterate. This distinction made a great impression on me, which was partly a reflection of my own love of words and of written material; it was also a recognition of the similarities between this thin brown young man with bare feet and Khmer features and myself, beyond the merely human. In other places I had always been more aware of the differences between myself and those whose country I was in. This would not be possible here, a barrier had cracked and I sensed, with both pleasure and discomfort, that I would not be able to secure myself behind difference in Vietnam.

We set off at 4.30, the worst possible time of day, as the rush-hour traffic was at its heaviest. I clutched my small rucksack and a carrier bag with the whisky and video. Tim Page had suggested I take the General's grandson chocolate and I had bought some at Heathrow but eaten it before reaching Hong Kong, so the grandson would be chocolate-less. I was grateful that any small interest I'd ever had in Scotch had been thoroughly purged on a single occasion during my teens after drinking nearly a pint of 12-year-old malt as though it were water.

The roads we followed were jammed with bicycles, cyclos and the occasional car. There were several enormous junctions where there should have been roundabouts but weren't; everyone simply pedalled forward, looking straight ahead, like the short-legged dog. There was some shouting and ringing of bells, but compared to Milan or Paris in the rush hour it was all rather calm and very orderly. Nin suggested that I keep my bag on my lap or under my legs, as bag-grabbing from tourists was apparently a popular pastime in Saigon. I felt rather lost in a sea of purpose as men and women, sometimes three or four to a scooter, swerved politely past my vehicle, eager for home, the evening meal, families or lovers. I saw only two other Westerners throughout the journey, which confirmed the ghetto nature of Pham Ngu Lao.

The heat of the day had subsided somewhat by the time we reached District 3. The sun was getting low and dust particles in the air created a fine yellow haze through which people moved like actors in an old film on dirty celluloid. Friends have often laughed at me for following maps wherever I go, whether to Richmond, the Isle of Skye or Los Angeles. Now, I followed our progress through the jammed streets and was aware as we approached the General's house that this was it, the moment I was to meet a former Viet Cong² fighter, one of the people I had heard about on the red radio in all those years before.

American veterans I had met by the score, literally, during a sojourn at a Special Forces Base in Bavaria in the late 1970s. None of them ever talked to me about their time in Vietnam except to say they 'would have won if there hadn't been a goddamn anti-war conspiracy in Washington'. For all I knew at the time they might have been right about that; without understanding, I sensed it was what they badly wanted to believe. It was only two years after Vietnamese reunification and wounds both mental and physical were still fresh. This 5 p.m. appointment would be very different; I had never met anyone like the man I was visiting. The General was by no means your average soldier and never had been. In his youth he had been a student at leading Ivy League universities in the US, returning to Vietnam to work with words and the emerging Vietnamese nationalism which found its expression during the last years of French colonial rule through the work of Ho Chi Minh.

General Pham Xuan An's house was large by Vietnamese standards and stood in its own garden with a high metal gate. Nin had asked me whom I was going to meet and, showing no apprehension at the prospect of meeting a general ('Communism is a remarkable thing!' I mused silently), he strode up to the gate and started pulling

---

2   Viet Cong is a shortened version of Viet Nam Cong San, meaning Vietnamese Communist. It was also further shortened to vc and used perjoratively. us soldiers, confusing the Communist Party with the nva (North Vietnamese Army), often referred to North Vietnamese soldiers as 'Charlie', referring to the initials vc and radio-speak Victor Charlie.

on the bell rope. For a while nothing happened except a dog barked behind bushes which partly hid the house from the busy road we stood on. Then a small slender man in a dark shirt and trousers appeared and opened the gate. Bowing slightly, he extended his hand and said, 'You are Doctor Schramm-Evans? Please come in.' Turning, he asked Nin to wait and Nin, now slightly intrigued, hauled his cyclo to the side of the gate and sat down.

The barking dog turned out to be quite small but rather active and, though obviously intended as a guard dog, looked much like a corgi. Sitting very upright on the steps of the house I saw another dog, a large German Shepherd, ears pricked and tongue lolling. Realizing with surprise that it was a ceramic canine, an involuntary noise escaped me. The last time I had seen such a thing had been in a shop in Brixton, south London, which also sold ganja pipes and, I suspected, the fuel for them. I naturally said none of this to the General.

'How fascinating!' I exclaimed, looking at the dog and feeling I was learning to be discreet rather fast.

Pleased at my interest, my host, whose English was remarkable, replied, 'I am very fond of this statue. It reminds me of an old dog I had many years ago. I like to look at this now and think of him.'

He smiled and I nearly burst into tears; dog stories always make me sad.

I was shown courteously to a chair in the reception area, which also seemed to be a study, library and hallway. Left alone when my host went to make coffee, I looked around the large room with interest and remembered what Tim had told me about Pham Xuan An – that he had been a scriptwriter of the infamous President Diem who forced the abdication of Emperor Bao Dai in 1955 and had worked for some of the world's leading press agencies as a correspondent. Throughout this period he had also worked for the liberation and 're-unification' of Vietnam.

The walls were covered with a green paint which showed the plaster behind it in an almost Tuscan style; the ceiling fan gently ruffled the papers lying on the large desk at one side of the room. The whole place had an air of expectant tranquillity. Now I was here there were so many questions I wanted to ask about the General's own life and about the people he'd known, but felt I couldn't. I knew almost nothing at all about this man beyond what Tim had written in a letter before I left London, but discretion and politeness are highly valued in Vietnamese society and my natural tendency to dig deep would have to be thoroughly quashed. I would never have made a journalist.

We sat and drank the very strong black coffee from small cups. The General was courteous enough to sense any awkwardness on my part and maintain the conversation. He asked about Tim, his family and his work. I produced the video and the whisky, which I felt vaguely uncomfortable about. I had never given a gift to a stranger before and it felt in some way as though I were paying for my coffee. To deflect my discomfort, I said that Tim had suggested the whisky. The General thanked me and, smiling, said he was a teetotaller.

We talked about books, which my host said he loved and to which the bookshelves lining two walls testified. I was fortunate to be offered revelations without asking, as the General told me that while working for the Saigon government during the 1950s, one of his tasks had been to read the outgoing letters of foreign nationals. He did not use the word 'censor', but added that he had always thoroughly enjoyed reading Graham Greene's letters and had almost never found any fault in them, either political or artistic. Asked what I had read about Vietnam, I named my limited repertoire, all of which the General had read with the exception of *Saigon* by Anthony Grey. Asked about the story, I outlined it briefly, including particularly the parts about the 'Flying Tigers'[3] and Ho Chi Minh and General Giap planning the future of Vietnam in their cave at Pac Bo.

At the end of my short story my host stood up and went to a filing cabinet from which he took a document written on an elderly typewriter and now yellowing paper by a man called Charles Fenn. I knew that Fenn had been personally connected with the Vietnamese–American military co-operation, including the Flying Tigers, during the early 1940s. The document was partly about the Tigers and as I looked through Fenn's pages, I felt a surge of critical excitement. The

3   The Tigers were a command of American airmen based at Kunming in south-west China. They flew anti-Japanese missions into north-west Vietnam as part of the American co-operation with Ho Chi Minh, who was fighting the Japanese from a cave in the mountains on the Sino–Vietnamese border.

document was about Fenn's role as interpreter in the Vietnamese–American co-operation and the paragraphs describing the work of the American airmen were almost word for word as I had read them in *Saigon* only weeks earlier. I assumed that Fenn, now in his eighties and living in the west of Ireland, and Grey (the same Anthony Grey that spent two years in solitary confinement in a Peking prison) knew each other, but the General couldn't confirm that for me.

'Al Upstairs' had lent me *Saigon* and I had read it with no sense of its connection to anything beyond my forthcoming journey and now I held the work of a man who had himself been closely involved with the story that book told, a man who had known Ho in those heady days of the Pac Bo caves. The few corrections on the pages were in Fenn's own handwriting and I felt a bizarre sense of being linked to things in which I had no part beyond an uncommon interest.

After we had talked for about an hour, the General's son, who works for the Ministry of Foreign Affairs, and young grandson arrived. The little boy was delightful and I rather regretted having eaten his chocolate. As the son busied himself with more coffee, my host sat with his grandson on his knee and suddenly, my natural tendencies overcoming my discretion, I asked, 'When you look back are you ever surprised that you are here now, with your family around you? Did you ever think you might not reach this point?'

The General didn't answer me immediately but smiled once more and then said, 'I was one of the lucky ones. Many of my friends and colleagues did not live to see their families grow as I have.'

I replied, 'Is it about luck? It seems to me that you must be a tremendous survivor.'

This time I could see the smile was entirely genuine as he laughed and, tickling his grandson on the ribs, looked at me and said, 'No, it is always luck. Many people I knew seemed to have talent or to be natural survivors, but they are dead and I am alive. It is because my luck was good that I am here – no other reason.' He became serious again and said, 'I wanted to be a doctor when I was young, to mend people and make them well, but my luck was that I should be a soldier.'

The implication 'and damage people and kill them' was left unsaid. I realized that by 'luck' the General meant 'Fate' with a capital 'F', but despite a minor flirtation with Buddhism, my Western mind remained not entirely comfortable with the level of determinism my host clearly found entirely normal.

Shortly after that I took my leave. The sun was almost gone and I could hear that the level of traffic on the road outside had already fallen. Pham Xuan An walked with me to the gate. The corgi was out of sight and only the silent porcelain Alsatian guarded the house in its little oasis of trees and walls. Nin was waiting patiently and leapt up when he saw us approach; I had a vague notion that he had been enquiring from the passers-by who exactly it was I was visiting and he seemed marginally more respectful of the General than he had on our arrival. I shook hands with my host and wished him and his family well. I wondered what he thought about this woman who had appeared from nowhere and was now disappearing again – perhaps he was used to it, perhaps he had lots of groupies. Like Nin, he warned me about my rucksack and said that the city wasn't a safe place for people. I didn't know exactly whom he was referring to, but thanked him for his consideration. As we moved away I turned and saw him still standing at the gate, one arm raised, but whether he was shading his eyes from the last rays of the amber sun or saying farewell, I couldn't know.

The Sinh Café tour organizers had told me that there must be a minimum number of customers per trip for a tour to take place, so that night, curious to see whether numbers for the My Tho trip had been reached, I set off back to the Sinh. Walking along Pham Ngu Lao I passed a bar called the Long Phi. About 20 Westerners were sitting outside, some of the men dressed in pseudo-camouflage gear and wearing bandanas. From inside the deeper recesses of the bar Jim Morrison was belting out 'LA Woman'. The truncated beggar I had seen earlier that morning was lying in the gutter behind the customers' chairs; little girls were still pushing Graham Greene and still smiling at refusals. I thought of the General and his porcelain dog and the little boy whose chocolate I'd eaten without him ever knowing he'd had any and, not feeling entirely at one with myself, went for snake in lemongrass washed down with Seven-Up at the Sinh.

chapter three

INTO THE DELTA

The morning of the tour I was up, having a cold shower and doing laundry at 6 a.m., only to realize how entirely out of character I was behaving. Undeterred, I continued whistling away, washing woollen socks that almost skinned my knuckles, then remembered that due to an almost total absence of nightlife, I'd been in bed by 10 p.m. since arriving in Vietnam.

The departure point for the minibus that was to take me and four other people on our tour – I knew it would be no more than four from the list of names I'd seen on the wall of the Sinh's 'travel bureau' the previous evening – was in a nearby street at Sinh Café II. It was an easy matter to envisage a chain of Sinh monopolizing tourism across South Vietnam, Cafés I and II being just the start. Arriving at 6.20 a.m. for a 6.30 a.m. departure, I discovered 'SCII' – the owner was evidently fond of acronyms – already crowded with tourists, most of whom were attempting to scramble aboard the single minibus parked in the fenced-off lot. This scene of potential chaos was politely and quietly controlled by the SCII staff, some of whom were about to double as tour guides. I bought my water supply – I was discovering that most bottled water in Vietnam is distilled, not spring, and tastes appalling – and slid unnoticed into a window seat. Previous Asian travel had taught me that possession of a ticket is an irrelevance compared to the possession of a seat.

Whilst irritable to-ing and fro-ing continued around me, I sat chewing a banana, looking vaguely out of the window, and saw my first Vietnamese duck-transporter come squealing to a halt beside the minibus. The transporter was simply a woman riding a scooter with about 30 live ducks attached, by their legs, wherever attachment was possible. The whole effect was bizarre and I found it quite distressing to see the creatures panting from the vibration and the heat of the scooter's engine. During my time in Vietnam I rarely saw duck on a menu; ducks appeared to be kept for their eggs and chickens preferred for eating. I hoped the creatures tied to the scooter in the lot of the Sinh II were on their way to some pleasant pond home in the suburbs and not on an oriental tumbrel.

By the time the minibus left at around 7 a.m. it was almost full, the list on the wall at SCI clearly meaningless. Most of the passengers had a wary, early-morning look – a few were to keep that expression throughout the tour. A tall and very attractive young Vietnamese woman with excellent English and hair down to her waist had shepherded late-comers and the confused aboard the vehicle, sorted out minor upsets and sat by the driver as we left the parking lot. Driving through the already busy Saigon streets, the woman stood, her back to the windscreen, swaying gently as the driver continually sounded his horn and swerved to avoid dogs and cyclists, and told the passengers that she was a tour guide. Sloughing off their morning despond, the male passengers began to glow with hormonal anticipation until the woman confessed that today was her holiday and that she was just along for the ride out of town. As she introduced our actual guide, a smiling middle-aged man with just about passable English, the testosterone glow flickered and died.

Part of the excitement *I* was feeling came from the air of an 'outing'. I had never, apart from various school trips as a child, been on an organized anything. This first journey in Vietnam had the air of a magical mystery tour. I was a stranger among strangers in a strange land going none of us knew where, beyond the names of dots on a map. There were about 15 of us on the bus, of seven different nationalities: French, Danish, Sri Lankan, British, German, Japanese and Swedish. Watching my fellow passengers react to the pot-holes in the road, the food, the heat and the requirements of nature was to become almost as pleasurable an occupation as looking out of the windows at Vietnam passing by.

As we left urban Ho Chi Minh City behind us and headed southwest, the road, which was quite good, widened, allowing the driver to step on the gas while swerving continually to avoid the lone cyclists pedalling, slow and stately, about their business.

The landscape was changing dramatically, losing the uniformly dry beigeness of the cityscape and becoming green countryside dotted with clusters of houses and palms. Our road – National Highway 1 – ran between rice paddies, divided from each other by raised dykes and levees and occasionally by lines of trees and bushes. Deep green stalks waved lushly around tombs set at haphazard angles. Barefoot women in conical hats bent easily from the hip, planting or replant-ing rice, observed by the spirits of their ancestors, or perhaps the ancestors of those who had once lived on this land. The tombs were not recent, which made me wonder what this countryside had looked like in 1965 when American military strategist John Paul Vann, protagonist of Neil Sheehan's accomplished book *A Bright Shining Lie*[1], had been up and coming 'king' of the Mekong delta; and in 1975, when Vann and nearly 60,000 of his compatriots were dead and the NVA, sweeping all before it, was approaching Saigon, victorious.

Incomplete Vietnamese government statistics suggest that at least eight million Vietnamese people were killed or injured between 1960 and 1975. Driving along the My Tho road, which from Sheehan's account I knew had played a significant role in the war, over bridges built by American military engineers and blown up by the Com-munists, then rebuilt and rebuilt again, I began to have a sense of bodies lying beside the road and in the rice fields, under clusters of bamboo and below the floors of houses. This sensation of death all around was quite unsettling, particularly as the immediate picture was one of sunshine and cheerful cyclists waving at our minibus. Along, I suspect, with many northern Europeans and anyone subjected to too much Thomas Hardy at an impressionable age, I realized that I lived with the illusion that dreadful things only happen on dark, cold days when the wind and rain lash the trees and thunder and lightning are all around. On the My Tho road, I knew that dreadful things had happened in the full light of day, among the rice stalks, behind the tombs, perhaps feet or even inches from where I was sitting, and the dichotomy only made the knowledge more uncomfortable.

1   Pan, 1990.

The journey from Saigon to My Tho took almost two hours, with a brief stop for those with weak bladders, during which the four Frenchmen formed a line and had a public pissing contest over a roadside ditch, the Danes peed privately behind a clump of bamboo and I bought a half-pineapple from a woman standing alone at the side of the road carrying an usherette's tray filled with beautifully carved fruit 'lollipops'. We had been issued with a packed lunch by SCII which consisted of two small bananas, a bread roll and what I hoped was a hard-boiled egg, all in a brown paper bag. I thought this lunch was rather pleasant and prepared with consideration for Western tastes; the French contingent of four men and two women clearly disagreed with my interpretation, however, and demonstrated their gastronomic disapproval by waving the bananas at each other whilst the most disgruntled of the party remarked, '*Merde, qu'est-ce que c'est ça pour un repas, eh? Ca va seulement pour les singes en France, non? Mon Dieu, c'est merde, merde, merde!*'

'More for everyone else,' was my thought, but I felt sure that Gallic epicurism would succumb at the last to plain old-fashioned hunger.

My Tho, founded by Taiwanese refugees in the late eighteenth century, is a small city of less than 100,000 people which edges the bank of the upper branch of the Mekong River and faces across the wide brown expanse of water to Ben Tre Province, our destination, though none of us knew this.

The minibus driver allowed us a brief glimpse of grid-straight streets and pleasant palm-fringed riverside before driving slightly beyond the town to the Ben Tre ferry. The boat was out when we piled from the bus into the wide dusty street which led to the ferry dock. Most of the passengers, including myself, headed to the nearest café for liquid and lavatorial relief. I had drunk all my water after about an hour and was thirsty as we sat around in a eerily empty café that seemed to be there simply waiting for minibus passengers to arrive and provide custom. Small boys came round trying to sell Western brand cigarettes manufactured in Vietnam, without success.

Our guide eventually shepherded his flock out of the café and towards the docking area. The minibus, which I had assumed would accompany us onto the ferry, had disappeared and its passengers stood about looking slightly stranded. It was now about 10 a.m. and starting to get warm. About 200 people were gathered in the road-way under a large pillared area which reminded me of the Loggia in Florence, except that the statues were alive and comprised mainly of women in a variety of hats and Western cum Vietnamese cloth-ing, holding baskets and shopping bags. I wondered where these people were going, how they lived and what their homes looked like. Their clothes were very Westernized, but given where we seemed to be heading I couldn't imagine their homes or lifestyles matching their garments.

Bored standing in the heat, some of the passengers from the minibus began talking to each other. A tall blonde Danish couple started chatting to me and we discussed the things travellers usually talk about in such situations: 'How long have you been in the coun-try?' and 'What do you think of the people, the food, the other pas-sengers, the heat?' and 'Have you any bowel problems yet?' The Danes, like myself, were at the start of their journey.

Soon we were joined by a couple of British Sri Lankans who were at the end of their holiday, having already come down-country from Ha Noi. The rest of the time waiting for the boat passed pleasantly and at one point, just as the ferry docked, a quote remembered from my youth came to mind:

> When we talk it's not just idle chatter
> We talk about things that really don't matter.

The Ben Tre ferry was much larger than I'd expected, all sorts of two- and four-wheeled vehicles, including bicycles and cars, poured out of the hold, while foot passengers, their baskets empty, clam-bered down from a covered upper deck. The architecture of the boat reminded me of a light and sunny version of a Victorian British prison, with a central empty area surrounded by walkways.

Being slow to embark, the Danes and I stood throughout the journey across the Mekong. It took roughly half an hour. I soon saw my second duck-transporter – the central space between the walk-ways was filled by a large truck, the roof of which was completely covered in live ducks attached, who knew how, to the railing running all the way round it. I felt very sorry indeed for some of the ducks, which looked as though they were almost dead. A few were all heaving breasts and rolling eyes and by the time we were in mid-stream it had become a bizarre parody of science fiction with the unfortunate creatures fighting for space and oxygen. Under the deck roof, the air was cool as it blew off the muddied water and standing didn't seem so hard in comparison with the plight of the ducks.

I was separated from the Danes by three or four people, all of whom I topped by about a head. I wondered how we appeared to the seated Vietnamese – did we all look like strange aliens or were we already a commonplace, simply a new form of invader? Our cameras and conversation, shouted over the noise of the engine, raised no obvious curiosity, though a few of the younger men and women stole glances at us from time to time. I had certainly experienced none of the staring and following that is usual in many parts of the developing world. But then Vietnam doesn't consider itself as 'developing' in any but the economic sense, for although poor, its cultural infrastructures are considered extremely sophisticated.

I was enthralled by the sheer scale of the river we were on. The Mekong is the twelfth longest river in the world at 2,608 miles with a total basin area of 306,870 square miles. It rises in the Tibetan Himalayas, sweeping down through Yunnan Province in western China into Burma (aka Myanmar), through Laos, Thailand and Cambodia, to empty into the South China Sea among the delta islands of Vietnam. As it moves south from Laos, it supports 52 million people, almost 50 per cent of the entire population of the countries it passes through.

We were crossing the Mekong at one of its widest points, though the journey was not a straightforward process of moving from one bank to another. What had appeared solid land masses in my guidebook turned out to be islands of various sizes, separated by waterways, and this, combined with the fact that the ferry travelled in a curving rather than a straight line, made it quite difficult to follow a map.

Looking out through the boat's open sides I could see only a huge expanse of light brown liquid edged by a variety of trees, from high-rising palms and pines to the descending mangroves, roots poised like a pianist's fingers, reflecting in the murky surface of the Mekong. Gazing at the water as the stern wake foamed below me, I thought of the innumerable places it had passed through before reaching this point; the people who had drunk from it, washed in it, died in it. I wondered, as the ferry ploughed steadily across its calm water, how much longer the Mekong would look as it did. The governments of former Indo-China, already realizing the massive energy potential of the Mekong, plan to harness it. US companies plan, among other things, shrimp breeding projects *à la* Forrest Gump in the delta. In the northern districts dioxin poisoning is still a problem and defor-estation and pesticide use have reduced even the harvest of swiftlets' nests, a high earning luxury export, in the southern coastal regions. In Vietnam, which has a per capita monthly income of less than $20, who is in a position to speak up when former enemies return to the delta with concrete and steel?

Arriving at a small dock that seemed to belong to a fishing vil-lage, we disembarked and were immediately led to two small wooden craft for the next stage of our tour. Each blue-painted boat had an outboard motor and old truck tyre partially split and nailed to its prow, creating an effective and ingenious bumper. There was also a canvas awning protecting heads from the sun but causing stiff backs instead, being rather too low for Westerners. The boats held eight people each and getting in and out was facilitated by our guide, who so far had not been much in evidence, and the nimble young man and woman who were the boats' drivers.

We set off into the open river at a steady speed, close enough for friends who'd got separated to wave and shout to each other from boat to boat. We were moving westwards along the north side of Ben Tre Province; had we continued in this direction, we would have come to a much wider expanse of the Mekong and seen the narrow tip of Thanh Phu Island. Instead, our driver, a tiny young woman who handled the boat with all the skill of an old Yarmouth seadog, turned into a narrow channel and suddenly we were in Hollywood Vietnam. I didn't care that I hadn't got here all alone, that I was a tourist on a minibus outing, I didn't even notice at first that the other passengers had become silent. Sitting at the very front of the boat, all I could see was the tyre-bumper nosing its way through China-tea coloured water stained with shadow, towards a deep green corridor of parlour-palms that rose, like giant prehistoric ferns, straight up from the water's edge to line the banks. The waterway, being natural, wasn't straight and each bend seemed to promise some new mystery. This feeling of suspense was enhanced by the channel quickly narrowing to a width of only 10 feet until the palm-ferns met overhead, their leaves brushing together as though transmitting some secret by Braille.

Once again none of us knew precisely where we were going. I assumed we were heading towards the coconut toffee factory and was just beginning to wonder how my notion of a factory could possibly be accommodated in this jungle, when we had the excitement of realizing the other boat had totally disappeared. Our driver cut the engine and we drifted, listening for sounds of the other craft, which didn't come. Only an occasional splosh as the young woman punted away from the banks disturbed the green silence. I wondered vaguely how turning the motor off would help if the other boat were lost and likewise listening for us – and anyway, perhaps it was not they but we who were lost? After about 15 minutes, during which time a cathedral-like atmosphere had developed, appropriate to the Gothic-tropical charm of our situation, in which no one spoke above a whisper, the sound of an engine was heard and our driver immediately restarted our motor and began moving backwards at considerable speed. Within minutes we'd met up with the lost boat, which was coming up a different channel from the one we'd followed. After some hasty shouting in Vietnamese which seemed to satisfy anyone who could understand, we set off once more, our boat leading and the other following with what seemed to me, at least, a sheepish air.

About 20 minutes after this incident, the channel widened and we came to the first signs of habitation. A larger, square-sided, flat-bottomed boat was anchored beside a 30-foot wide 'bridge' made from a single palm plank supported by two logs sunk into the water. A small wooden house thatched with palm fronds and dwarfed by some of the biggest coconut palms I had ever seen stood beside the bridge and I wondered whether this was the factory.

We pulled up alongside the square boat and were encouraged to clamber up into it and thence to the bank; passengers of the 'sheepish' craft had to crawl through our boat before climbing into the square one and thence to the ground. When we were all assembled on the bank beside the building, our guide, who I decided looked more Tartar than Vietnamese, came into his own. Showing all his rather fine teeth in a broad smile, he launched into a potted history of the island we were on – the 'secret' island.

'This island,' he said, 'always uninhabited, no one live here at all until – ah – 1960s, when Communist forces make secret camp here. They have base in middle of US area and no one know; they have hospital and many special soldiers here who make training.' He smiled. 'But that was long time ago, now people live here and this very good place for fruit, especially coconut for toffee. As we walk I show you how we make fruit here in Vietnam.'

I found this story, which he must have told dozens of times to people like me, both interesting and rather moving. I liked to think of fruit growing in places where people once had their limbs amputated in field hospitals, and the guide's own interest and pride in the successes of his country – although I sensed some ambiguity around old allegiances – were self-evident. The guide's English wasn't the easiest to understand – much of what he said I inferred from context and gesture – but as an English-speaker I appreciated that he spoke my language at all. The French contingent, however, harboured no such sentiments. Bored because they couldn't understand the man's English, they soon started talking and laughing together loudly, which most of the party seemed to find irritating and impolite. Untrammelled by etiquette and, I suspected, embittered by the realization that their former colony might as well have belonged to Britannia for all the linguistic use it was to them, the French continued to interrupt and eventually wandered off, to the relief of all others present.

Kneeling carefully beside a small lemon bush, the branches of which were wrapped around with cloth and string, the guide described for us the process of grafting. He was clearly delighted at the cleverness of being able to make one very small tree bear large quantities of fruit before it had reached three feet in height, which also of course made picking much easier. I thought of the citrus trees I had seen in southern Europe and agreed with him, infected by his enthusiasm.

Walking on, we passed a stand of particularly large straight palms. Pointing up at one, he said, 'Here you see marks from bullet holes, in tree, fired from helicopter in war with Americans!' and, looking up, I saw, about two-thirds of the way up a tree trunk, large black holes with long vertical cracks running out of them. The tree looked as though it had been gored by a particularly large and savage elephant. I wondered who had made the bullet holes, assuming that was what they were, and found myself wishing I knew how quickly palm trees grow in order to judge the date of the marks. If the island was a secret, why would a helicopter have been firing bullets? Could it have been a foolish trainee, firing off his AK47 by accident? Who had told our guide that a helicopter had flown over this place one day, decades ago, firing at palm trees? I gave up. There were no answers to any of these things, but it made me acutely aware of the tension between my wanting to believe what I was told by courteous people and being aware that some at least of what I heard was what they thought would please or interest me. I had encountered this difficulty before, of course, but in other places I had found it blatant–being told, for example, in some remote outpost on the Burma–Bangladesh border that the Dakar train is coming in an hour when it isn't in fact due until next month. Here in Vietnam I was already conscious that the mix of economic hardship and cultural sophistication was a potent and potentially problematic mix for me, an ignorant visitor.

We walked on for about 15 minutes, along pleasant shaded paths. I watched in fascination as the three young Japanese women in our party tiptoed neatly across small bridges constructed from narrow logs, their high-heeled, open-toed sandals as immaculate as the rest of their dress. They seemed delighted by everything they saw and I was struck by the combination of neat femininity, quite different from that of Vietnamese women, and intrepid determination. Had the guide asked them to walk through the water-filled ditches that criss-crossed the island I felt sure they would have obliged, high heels and all, for the sake of getting wherever it was they thought they were going. I looked down at my Dr Marten boots and thick red wool socks and was glad I had no heels to teeter on and no bare skin to get bitten by anything. When one of the women spoke to me a little later I was completely taken aback by her voice. I don't quite know what I had expected, maybe I'd some ridiculous notion of a high-pitched geisha giggling, but her resonance and power reminded me of Henry Kissinger and certain Israeli politicians and I felt we should swap footwear.

The palms and occasional pines were interspersed by fruit trees of various sizes and shapes: bananas, longans, jackfruit and others I didn't recognize. Two or three small children darted among bushes of soft fruits; they were shy and playful at once, following us silently and hiding to get a better look. Their presence and the few huts I could see through the palms suggested we were nearing our destination. Then our guide, who had been chatting with the Germans, turned to us, a broad smile on his face, and announced that we had arrived at the coconut toffee-making factory.

It was, indeed, nothing like I had imagined when we set out that morning and I was relieved to find it far more interesting and picturesque than anything the word 'factory' suggested. Open-sided palm-thatched huts, which reminded me of a stable housing a nativity scene, formed three sides of a square. The home of the factory owner or manager – we never learnt whether this was a private enterprise or not – formed the fourth side. The factory itself was divided into three main sections. The power producing section, an area of about 10 square feet, was filled with neat piles of dried coconut husks, 18 carefully ordered car batteries and various articles of metal bric-a-brac. The relationship between the batteries and the coconut husks was explained, but I entirely failed to understand how the husks could be used to top up the batteries, and later when I saw husks being thrown into an oven, I realized that the words 'top up' had been slightly misinterpreted, probably by me.

The central section of the factory, an area just over 8 feet by 4 feet, consisted of a young woman in fuschia-coloured pyjamas stirring two enormous pans of bubbling coconut milk over a traditional knee-high clay oven. The heat was tremendous and the woman sat on a stool as far away from the fire as her stirring stick allowed. Her face was wet with sweat and had a rather peculiar glazed look; perhaps she already dreamt of swinging gently in one of the hammocks that hung nearby.

The final and most active section of the factory involved six young women, four separate activities and a plastic table about 20 feet by 4 feet covered in red, white and blue plastic sheeting. At the end of the table nearest the fire, the bubbling mixture, having attained the correct consistency, was slopped onto the plastic, where it was allowed to cool before a chunk of the still warm goo was cut off by a girl wielding an elderly plastic plate like a cleaver. The goo was then pressed into a corrugated metal mould from which it emerged after about 10 minutes in cold strips which the girl passed on to three women who formed the chopping-into-bite-sized-chunks stage. The final stage involved other women wrapping the little toffees in pink and white waxed paper then packing about a dozen of them together in polythene bags. They looked so innocent, those small coconut toffees.

Several local men, women and children stood around and watched this rural production line, which went from stage to stage with the confident ease of long practice. Some of the tour party asked questions; I took photographs and, walking around the factory freely, chatted with some of my companions of the day. I noticed a small altar clinging to the former tree trunk supporting the factory roof; joss sticks and fruit sat in front of small images I couldn't identify.

We were offered some of the toffee to taste and that was when it happened. As I unwrapped my toffee, I was talking to Pia de Silva, the British Sri Lankan woman, who was describing how her husband lost a capped tooth somewhere outside Ha Noi.

'Really, how dreadful!' I mumbled through a mouthful of coconut gunge, before biting down hard and painfully on a large gold filling that the toffee had instantly sucked from the back of my jaw. Pia was still discussing the cap when I put my fingers into my mouth and produced a piece of solid, rather sticky, gold.

I now had almost all my journey still ahead of me with a hole in my jaw, but the idea of visiting a Vietnamese dentist was simply unthinkable. Relieved I hadn't swallowed the thing and wondering whether there was any superglue in Vietnam, I spat out the remaining toffee, tucked the offending nugget into a corner of my money pouch and had a drink.

Leaving the 'secret' island many of our party, including myself, were visibly tired and hungry as we headed in the boats through further waterways into the wider flow of the Mekong for Phung Island.

This time I felt the river's full grandeur, being in a small craft low in the water, and all things seemed larger.

After about half an hour we landed beside a steep bank and were led up tiny steps to one of the strangest places I have ever visited in my life: the island shrine of the *Ong Dao Dua*, or 'Coconut Monk'.

Before venturing anywhere on Phung Island, we took advantage of a pleasant picnic area and little stall selling drinks and consumed our packed lunch. Faced with the reality of the boiled eggs, the French looked as though they wished the colonial guillotine were still available for culinary crimes. Bananas were thrown, eggs left unshelled and much banging of fists and use of the words *merde* and *cuisine du cochon* could be heard. The rest of us ate with conviction and began to revive.

Phung Island is only a few miles from My Tho, though I don't think any of us knew we'd described almost a full circle since leaving the minibus several hours earlier. The guide, still smiling though looking a little frazzled himself now, led us along what seemed like the high mud walls of a ditch, on either side of which were planted young palms and other small trees. I knew, from reading Norman Lewis, that South Vietnam had produced a number of bizarre local religions this century as well as having various brands of mainstream religions. In the 1950s the Catholic President Diem had to deal with the militia of the Hoa Hao Buddhist sect and the army of the Cao Dai 'Pope' at Tay Ninh. Buddhist monks have always been regarded as a thorn in the side of both pre- and post-war governments and in the 1990s Vietnam's treatment of its *bonzes* can still make international news.

In 1950, when Lewis visited My Tho, the Coconut Monk, Nam Thanh, would have been a new addition to the South's cults. Nam Thanh was a delta local, born in Ben Tre Province in 1909. He studied scientific subjects at various French universities in the 1920s and '30s, returning to Vietnam in 1935. Ten years later, overcome by religious fervour, he left his family and took up residence under a flag-pole – a testament to early twentieth-century French higher education perhaps? Over the next quarter century the Coconut Monk – so called because he apparently ate nothing but coconuts for three years – was the figurehead of a community on Phung Island which finally dispersed following his imprisonment for 'anti-Communist activities' during the 1970s.

Today the island is, in every sense, ghastly. Large ceramic dragons compete for the visitors' attention with live snakes, monkeys and other animals kept in pitifully small cages. The coloured lights and twisting flag-poles encircling the small area of worship overlooking the river reminded me of a fairground when all the punters have left. Christian and Buddhist symbols were all around, but my overwhelming sense was of the absent figure of the 'Big Coconut' himself. The guide led us to the small grotto where Nam Thanh apparently meditated night and day for years. It was made from the Vietnamese equivalent of stone-cladding: concrete, shaped, pricked and painted a dark blueish-green. We sat inside where it was at least cool, while the guide, sitting on the meditation platform, told us all about the Coconut Monk. The French were restless again and began talking over the unfortunate guide, who seemed uncertain how to address the situation without losing face. In the small space of the grotto the problem became impossible and eventually one of the Germans suggested the recidivists shut up or leave.

I found Phung Island depressing, though companions said they enjoyed its surreal qualities. My lasting memory was of a tasteless and vulgar monument to a very odd man whose island 'paradise' has become an eerie testament to the rise and fall of a cult.

Boarding our little boats for the last time, we sped back towards My Tho, where the minibus awaited us. It was about 4 p.m. and the guide told us we would be in time to see the spectacle of the Ho Chi Minh rush hour. It seemed very strange to be thinking of rush hours while in the Mekong delta; the peace of the waterways and waving palms was still with me and I was rather sorry to be returning to the city at all.

The atmosphere on the minibus was friendlier than it had been in the early morning, the wariness gone now. Even the French chatted with their neighbours and laughed about the boiled eggs. Approaching the city I scarcely noticed the rush hour, used as I already was to the bicycles and cyclos. I also realized that there are rush hours and rush hours and the guide had never seen Earl's Court, London, at 5 p.m. on a Friday afternoon or the Lincoln Tunnel any evening, as it descends into the bowels of New York's Lower West Side.

By the time we reached Saigon, everyone was very friendly indeed. The British Sri Lankans Pia and Kosh de Silva, the Danes Birta and Morten, and I decided to eat together that evening. Leaping from the minibus at around 6 p.m., we thanked our relieved-looking guide and headed immediately for cold beer and hot noodles at the Sinh Café I. That night, for the first time in a week, I had no need of Dr Lo's blue pills.

chapter four

SAIGON

The food of Vietnam reflects its diverse cultural heritage as well its current economic situation. As a single nation, Vietnam has existed only since the early eighteenth century, by which time the cultures of the Chams of the central region and the Khmers of the south had been gradually overcome by the Vietnamese pushing down from the north. The historical Vietnamese were ruled by the Chinese for 1,000 years and the Chinese influence is perhaps the most obvious to a foreigner eating in Vietnam today. There are, however, over 500 traditional regional dishes and although the Chinese influence is strong, there are obvious Thai and less noticeable south Asian undercurrents, leftovers of the Hindu Champa kingdom of south-central Vietnam.

One of the most striking things about Saigon was the constant availability of food. People eat anywhere and everywhere, at all times of the day and into the night. The food is mostly rice, with interesting-looking additions – meat, vegetables, salads and herbs. *Pho*, a large bowl of noodle broth with the same additions as the rice, is a staple throughout Vietnam. Desserts don't much feature in South East Asian diets and in Vietnam traditional desserts were dishes like *che dau xanh*, a sweet soup made from green peas, or *dau hu*, soya cake, neither of which activated my tastebuds. The alternatives were a selection of the fabulous fruits, custard apples, jackfruits and longans, or French-style pastries.

My first bowl of *pho*, breakfast on the morning after the delta excursion, was a broth with chicken and lettuce, and after I'd added a fair bit of soya sauce it tasted very pleasant. Most fellow travellers seemed to find Vietnamese cooking rather bland compared with the sophisticated cuisines of Thailand and China, but I found its lack of excessive spices – chilli in particular – a relief.

The half-empty tooth was concerning me. I knew I would have to go to the dentist and was scarcely allowing myself to contemplate it. My father spent four years in a Japanese prison camp and occasionally recalled with masochistic relish that the fillings the brutal camp dentists had put in were still intact after 30 years. No occidentist could match up in his opinion, but I'd have given anything to avoid putting his opinion to the test. The prospect of searching for a dentist who would do the business painlessly and hygienically was daunting. I decided to call on some of the contacts that Dwayne had left pinned to his kitchen noticeboard in Hong Kong.

As I finished my *pho*, a cyclo driver who had been parked up near the café approached and handed me a piece of paper. I had seen him looking at me as I ate but had thought nothing of it. Now as he held out his hand I hesitated, my scepticism momentarily overcoming my curiosity. Seeing my hesitation, the man put the paper on the table in front of me. Looking down, I saw a drawing of myself on a small piece of paper torn from a pharmaceutical company's advertising pad. In semi-profile I looked out at Pham Ngu Lao, a pink and yellow logo crossing my face like a port-wine and custard birthmark and the words 'Rocephine – ceftriaxone' over my throat. Though not an expert drawing, it was most definitely me, but wearing an unfamiliar tight-lipped and gimlet-eyed expression. The artist had signed the corner 'Hien Dich Lo'. I looked up at a wiry, self-consciously smiling man of perhaps my own age and had no idea what to say to him. My role as observer had been usurped and I had unwittingly become the object of another's observation. It was a salutary experience. I thanked him and wondered if he hoped for payment, but he had already turned away, smiling. Perhaps my disconcertion was payment enough. Looking at the drawing once more, I wondered if the expression the artist had captured was truly mine or whether all Westerners had the same wary look.

Armed with the address of one of Dwayne's contacts, I found Nin the cyclo driver and we set off the short distance to the home of Ho Trung Chanh. We found the house at the bottom of a spotlessly clean alleyway. Leaving me in the cyclo, Nin leapt from his saddle and rang the doorbell. At signs of life within he beckoned me and we stood together waiting for the door to open. A very elderly man with white hair, long beard and a strong resemblance to Confucius opened the door and I asked him in English if he were Mr Chanh. It became plain, when he responded in French, that he was indeed Mr Chanh and that he spoke no English, both of which facts I found confusing, as Dwayne had written that the man was fluent in English and young. I showed the man Dwayne's piece of paper and he immediately smiled, showing remarkably few teeth. '*C'est mon fils*,' he said, looking relieved, and invited me into the dark interior that I had glimpsed over his head.

My French wasn't really up to much of the conversation that followed; though I understood most of what was said, my replies were of the most basic kind. I established that Chanh junior would be home very shortly and that I should wait. I was astonished at the hospitality and trust that the old man demonstrated. I wondered whether I would entertain a complete stranger just because they showed me a piece of paper and thought I probably would. Halfway through my glass of iced water, Chanh junior returned, pushing his scooter into the room where we were sitting. He was an attractive, open-faced young man of about 23, though, as usual, he looked considerably younger. He seemed very pleased to have news of Dwayne and most willing to help me out of my dental distress. He said that he was busy for a few hours but that he and another friend of his, a girl, would meet me at my hotel later that afternoon. I was extremely grateful but slightly uncomfortable at suddenly appearing and taking up his time, however he made it plain that he would be glad to help me out and for the first time since my arrival I felt that I was not just a visitor but a tiny part of the lives of the people around me. The feeling was good.

He asked, 'What have you seen in Saigon? You have seen the war museum?'

I said I had not, that in fact I had seen almost nothing as yet.

'Then we will go there, this afternoon, yes? Then you will go to the dentist!'

I wasn't entirely sure that looking at pictures of war crimes was the very best thing to do immediately before going to a Vietnamese dentist, but I said I would love to go. Thanking the old man for his kindness in the best French I could muster, I left, pleased at the prospect of the afternoon, even the thought of the dentist less fearsome now.

To fill the time before meeting Chanh and his friend, I decided to go to Cholon and find the Hanh Long Hotel, where I hoped Grace and Nicholas would arrive from Singapore that evening. Having no confidence that the telephone messages I had already left giving my whereabouts and phone number had been understood by the receptionist, I decided it was best to go in person and leave a written message. It would also give me the opportunity to see something of Saigon other than Pham Ngu Lao.

'Cholon,' I said to Nin, having a clear idea from the map of where that was, but not how far.

'Very far,' he said to me, looking rather downcast.

'How far?' I asked.

'Over four miles,' he replied.

'Too far?' I asked, at which he reluctantly shook his head.

It was about 12.30 p.m. when we set off and the sun was very hot. I hadn't thought to buy a hat and after only 10 minutes the V of flesh where my collar was unbuttoned was already beginning, ever so slightly, to burn. Forty minutes later Nin was still pedalling – and I could tell that even his slender, hard-muscled legs were beginning to flag. When I looked back and up at him, he and his flimsy clothing were soaked in sweat. Some of the roads we went down were barely metalled, pitted with holes and ruts, the old French cobbles sticking like warts through the surface of the rotting tarmac. I tried to suggest to Nin that we stop and have a drink, but he either failed to understand me or simply didn't want to. I bought a green coconut and sat drinking the clear sweet milk through a straw as we jolted along. The General had told me that the Vietnamese believe drinking coconut milk makes you tired, but I never found this to be so.

The streets were relatively busy despite the heat. Women food vendors lined the narrow roads, their bunches of herbs or bowls of eggs arranged neatly in front of them on newspaper or cloth. One more permanent stall stood in a cloud of flies attracted by the fresh meat suspended from hooks and as we passed Nin pointed and said laconically, 'Dog.' On closer inspection the haunches did look remarkably as though they had once belonged to a Spot or Rover. Certain that Nin had an expectation of my reaction, I made the appropriate noises of horror and disgust that he evidently hoped for and which made him break into a smile that lightened his normally rather severe face.

Cholon, Chinatown of Ho Chi Minh City, means 'Big Market', indicating the vital role the Chinese have played in the economic history of Ho Chi Minh City and Vietnam itself. Cholon and Saigon were neighbouring but separate cities until the twentieth century, when urban sprawl finally united them. Cholon, which was established in the late eighteenth century by Chinese merchants setting up home and business, is still the largest ethnic Chinese community in Vietnam, though it is far less Chinese than it once was.

In the late 1970s, after reunification, the Communist government began a systematic 'anti-capitalist 'campaign against its large ethnic Chinese minority, during which several hundred thousand inhabitants of Cholon and similar districts fled in tiny boats across the South China Sea to anywhere they thought might accept them. Many Vietnamese 'boat people' were and are ethnic Chinese. With them, of course, the Cholonese took their economic and business skills as well as their money, if they were able to extricate it in time. The tragedy of these refugees still continues. In places such as Hong Kong they remain penned in camps; the youngest have never known any other life. Some, however, found true refuge and 20 years after fleeing Vietnam are being called 'the world's newest major global tribe' and a 'diaspora phenomena'[1]. In the '90s *viet kieu*, 'overseas Viet-namese', are returning to their former homeland armed with foreign passports to set up business once more.

We passed only two other cyclo-driven Westerners between downtown Saigon and Cholon, reconfirming the impression I'd had on my way to visit General Pham Xuan An of District 1, and Pham Ngu Lao in particular, as Western ghettos. I did, however, see several white stretch limousines carrying oriental people clearly not

[1]   Joel Kotkin for Reuters News Service 21 September 1994.

Vietnamese who I guessed were businessmen and their ladies from maybe Taiwan, Singapore or Hong Kong. Some may have been *viet kieu* and I wondered later with what feelings they viewed this, their former country, as they sat on the inside of luxury looking out. The plate glass was not so dark that it entirely hid the indiscreet flash of diamonds and gold from within the vehicles' depths and as heads turned to follow the cars' progress, I looked at the road-sweepers and water-sellers and tried to imagine their feelings which, after all, may not have been so very different from my own.

Each town or city in Vietnam has, I discovered, a limited number of street names. Every place I visited appeared to have an avenue, street or boulevard named after Le Loi, or Nguyen Trai, or Ly Thuong Kiet. The Hanh Long Hotel was on Tran Hung Dao Street, named after one of the greatest of all Vietnamese heroes. Tran succeeded in doing what a number of Western nations in the mid-fourteenth century signally failed to do: overcome an encroaching half a million strong Mongol army. At the Battle of the Bach Dang River the invading horde was overcome and its ships captured or destroyed though being impaled on steel-tipped bamboo stakes sunk into the river bed. As in many such historical episodes of Vietnam's history, Tran's force was far outnumbered by that of the Mongols and the parallel between this and twentieth century Vietnamese history is striking. If, one wonders, any of the American military and political executive of the '50s and '60s had troubled to read and take seriously a history of Vietnam, would they still have felt so confident about their chances of success? They probably would have; after all, the Great Khan didn't have God and the B52 on his side.

I found, as I suspected, that the Hanh Long Hotel had no record at all of my having telephoned three times with messages for Grace. I had already learnt that there was no purpose to recriminations in such a situation and wrote out a careful message, explaining that Grace was arriving from Singapore that evening and that it was most important that she contact me. Yes, they did have her name on their list – I had the right hotel at least – and yes, they would of course give her the message as soon as she arrived.

I asked Nin to take me back by a different route so that I could see more of Cholon and buy a much needed hat. We stopped at the

Andong market and after several homilies on not getting lost and how to find him again, only a fraction of which I understood, Nin let me loose to wander into the vast and overwhelming space that was a temple to humble materialism.

Four storeys high, the market is not the largest in Ho Chi Minh City but is probably the most compact and has the most amazing range of goods I have ever seen under one roof. Brilliant green and yellow *ao dai*s hung next to plain white and black shoes from Europe; multi-coloured shirts from Hong Kong lay in heaps next to plain, straw-coloured conical hats. Food and live animals, both in baskets, jostled for space on the stalls of one floor, while in the basement below, the same animals were later eaten by shoppers in the largest selection of restaurants I was to see in Vietnam.

I ventured down alley after alley inside the market. Not all were adequately lit and in the semi-darkness I began to wonder how I would find my way out and back to Nin. I didn't want a conical hat, it seemed embarrassingly stereotypical – the foreigner in local gear. But after hunting for about half an hour, I had come up with nothing besides a baseball cap or two – which was stereotypical in an even less acceptable way – and a few woolly tam o'shanters in red and yellow tartan, made in China. There was nothing for it but a conical hat or burn; so, having beat the vendor down from 10,000 to 2,000 dong, I grasped my acquisition gingerly by its rim and set off back to Nin.

After spending 20 minutes trying to find someone who spoke enough English to direct me back to the front entrance, I eventually found my driver dozing on his vehicle. He laughed when he saw the hat and told me it was very good, though I harboured a strong suspicion he was being politic rather than truthful. I knew I resembled a mollusc with legs. He asked me how much I'd paid and when I told him, he seemed genuinely surprised that I hadn't been ripped off for more. The double economy, one for Vietnamese and one for tourists, can be quite problematic at times because it's unofficial; the price of a bottle of water may vary from one vendor to another, with stalls less than 6 feet apart. The price is whatever the tourist will pay and while I always struggled to bring down the price to somewhere between the local rate and the tourist one, I observed some Westerners paying whatever they were asked and occasionally even more, which I thought was probably a disservice to everyone in the long term – locals, low budget travellers and the wealthy tourist alike. I was also surprised at the lack of enthusiasm a lot of Westerners seemed to have for the entertaining pastime of bargaining. Vietnam is a tough place to bargain – women vendors in particular are quite ruthless – but it is, after all, one of the poorest countries in the world and though it was clear I was being over-charged much of the time, everything is relative.

Driving through Cholon's crowded streets was a very different experience from moving through Saigon. The faces were different, the voices, even the gestures. People looked at me differently as Nin pushed his way past them. The faces were neither hostile nor indifferent, but they were not welcoming either. Wary is perhaps the best description, but if Hien Dich Lo's portrait was anything to judge by, my own expression was little different.

Moving slowly was actually a bonus, as I got to look at my exotic surroundings more closely. Shops selling gold and jewellery seemed to be everywhere and men in suits and shiny shoes stood in their doorways, looking much like my fellow passengers on the flight from Hong Kong. Talking to a Australian ex-pat engineer over a beer the previous evening with the Danes, I'd been told that although Cholon has seemingly eschewed opium dens, red lanterned brothels and mahjong parlours in favour of karaoke and brandy, there is still a hidden life in the place which is gradually reasserting itself. Looking around the streets I could well believe that interesting things went on behind the glitzy Taiwanese-style exteriors. In traditional medicine shops it is possible to buy technically illegal animal parts such as tiger bones and balls. Windows filled with exotic fish flashed past me and animals squealed and screeched from inside 'pet' shops. Cholon is apparently one of the few places left in Asia where if you've got the money your more unusual tastes can be indulged. The Australian engineer told me that Cholon still has women's 'baths' where it's possible to smoke opium and be massaged all day and all night. Apparently, older ethnic Chinese women use 'baths' much as Mediterranean crones use the local church as places to pick up gossip and avoid the husband. I would have given a lot to see the inside of such a place, but the risks are high for naïve and ignorant foreigners, and

I was advised against trying.

The general feeling in Cholon was one of energy and expansion; buildings were being renovated, repainted, rebuilt. The improvement of economic relations between Vietnam and the West has clearly given confidence to Cholon as it recovers from the economic, social and personal devastation of 1975 and its aftermath. But the ethnic Chinese of Cholon are still wary – hence perhaps their facial expression. From British and Singaporean businessmen drinking in some of Saigon's fancier bars, I learnt that the Cholonese are careful to work with their Communist government, who apparently watch and manage new trends and changes in the district very carefully indeed.

We arrived back at the Hoang Vu Hotel just in time to meet Chanh and his friend. Nin was exhausted and looked as though he'd lost about 5lb in weight. My guilty Western conscience overcoming my economic judgement, I paid him $6, the equivalent of 10 days' wages. His face when I handed him the notes was a study in cool; I caught his pleasure at the amount from only a small flash in his eyes which was there and then gone, replaced by a nonchalant and quite appropriate acceptance that his work was worth what I had given him.

I then dashed into the beige lobby, explained to the several seated receptionists, who at that moment reminded me of the Royal Crescent at Brighton, that I was expecting friends and rushed to my room to wash and change into undamp clothing.

Chanh and his friend Phuong, a very pretty young woman of 22 and a student of English at the university, proved to be excellent companions. I was surprised at how easily they fell into being with a total stranger and foreigner, and recalling that only a few years earlier that contact would have been impossible made it all the more surprising.

I hadn't considered beforehand that going around Saigon with two locals meant riding on motorbikes, but I soon overcame my nerves at the prospect of riding into the Highway Codeless mêlée of Saigon streets without a helmet. Sitting pillion behind Phuong, I put my hands on her waist and was amazed at her smallness in comparison with myself. I closed my eyes on a few occasions as we steered into what seemed an impossible tangle of cyclos, cycles and scooters and once made the mistake of leaning forward and telling her I thought her a very good driver. To which she replied over her shoulder, amusement in her voice, '*Now* I very good driver. A few years before I have accident with car. My leg is smashed very bad, I in hospital six months. No fun. Now I drive very careful!'

I said, half joking, half pleading, 'Please don't tell me that now! I don't want to hear!' which made her laugh even more as we headed into yet another traffic maze, following the tail of Chanh's scooter.

An old iatrogenic disability in my left foot was proving problematic. I'd hoped the hot weather would improve the condition but it didn't and walking was often uncomfortable, so I was particularly grateful for the ride and also for the companionship. Being with people, even strangers like Chanh and Phuong, made me realize how much time I'd spent alone since leaving London and it felt particularly good to be with people who were not Westerners, who belonged here in this place. I thought myself fortunate to be going to the famous War Crimes Museum with two Vietnamese, feeling certain that it would be a very different experience from going with fellow Westerners, and I was right.

The 'Exhibition House of Aggression War Crimes' is on Vo Van Tan Street in District 3, a mile or so due north of Pham Ngu Lao. Chanh, a relaxed and jolly person, had explained that he would enjoy coming to the museum with us but afterwards he must return to his work as an interpreter; Phuong would take me to the dentist later. It was with a visibly light step that he approached the Exhibition House. I wondered how often he had seen it all before. Not knowing exactly what I might see, but having a pretty fair idea, I hoped it wouldn't be more disturbing than my imagination had already devised. Some of the images that I would see were well known: the massacre of My Lai, GIs setting houses on fire, napalm victims, B52s carpet bombing Ha Noi and planes spraying Agent Orange. None of these things would be new to me, yet I still felt apprehensive as we approached the building which nestled among tanks.

The museum experience was pretty gruelling and the images not, as I'd expected, confined to American war crimes. They included the torture and confinement of opponents of the Diem regime which succeeded the fall of the French and the deposition of puppet Emperor Bao Dai and which ran South Vietnam from the mid-'50s. It was in support of the sleazy and corrupt Diem government that the CIA openly intervened in Vietnam from the late '50s onwards; and it was the CIA which fomented the military coup which brought about the political destruction and subsequent assassination of the Diem brothers in 1963, 21 days before the assassination of President Kennedy. After the demise of the Diems, the President and his brother, a series of military leaders took power, each one increasingly indebted to US military assistance for their continuing existence, each one graphically represented in the war crimes exhibition.

But it was American activities in Vietnam which held the centre of this gruesome stage: bodies littering roads; bodies dragged behind tanks in a bizarre Homeric parody; semi-naked prisoners roped together by their necks like slaves being prodded by bayonets; women and children dragged screaming along jungle paths by grinning Marines; living bodies photographed falling through the air, thrown from helicopters presumably to induce others, still inside, to speak.

But worst of all, most disturbing of all, I found a single photograph of a youthful, grinning GI holding the head and shoulders of a Vietnamese man by the hair, presenting it to the camera. The rest of the body lay mangled on the ground. For some reason I noticed that there was no blood and wondered how that was possible when everything was such a mess. Balzac's Colonel Chabert said, 'Death is red, then blue…' Maybe the photograph had captured the blue stage of death; maybe the GI had cleaned up the pieces for the photo, so that there could be no mistaking their identity. It was, I think, the grin that did it. He could have been any young man holding up a big catch at some fishing competition in Alabama or Georgia, but he held parts of a man's body and laughed. He looked quite sane, but in such circumstances who could be certain of remembering the definition of sanity? It was vile, as was the recollection that such brutality was not one-sided.

My companions seemed to have none of the squeamishness of the many Western visitors to the exhibition. Passing a photograph of an appallingly malnourished man, imprisoned for many years by the

South Vietnamese government, Chanh pointed at the image and, giggling quietly, said, 'He was fat once!' My first reaction to his comment was to want to laugh hysterically, but I controlled myself. Passing pictures of the My Lai massacre, Chanh asked me what I felt when I saw these pictures and at a loss for suitable words, I said I was disgusted. He nodded in agreement and said, 'Yes, it was very bad.' But there was no conviction in his voice and I wondered how many times he had seen such images, whether he had been force-fed them at school, at home, in youth groups? Maybe he simply didn't want me to feel uncomfortable and tried to lighten the mood. Phuong, too, showed very little emotion at the exhibits. I wondered how it was possible for Vietnamese youth to make sense of all that had happened so recently and yet so long ago.

Later, reading the closing lines of the leaflet given to visitors to the exhibition, I thought perhaps I understood it all a little better. On the page facing the photo of My Lai the text ran:

The Americans were deeply shocked at the war in Vietnam. In consecutive years protests against the war were staged by different walks of life in the US as well as in other parts of the globe. The Vietnamese have been grateful to the people around the world, especially to the Americans, for having helped them struggle for independence, freedom and happiness in Vietnam.

I subsequently read an article commenting on the death of Richard Nixon which was further enlightening. It read:

'May he rest in peace,' a [Vietnamese] Foreign Ministry spokesman said... 'Morally speaking he may have done bad things while he was alive – we never relive the bad things – we only speak about his good deeds.'
Reuters News Service, Ha Noi, 23 April 1994

Outside the exhibition I said goodbye to Chanh and thanked him for his kindness. He smiled and shook my hand before jumping on his motorbike and riding off, waving as he went.

I asked Phuong whether she had any time constraints and she

said she had none, then asked me if I would like to see the Water Puppet Theatre. Perhaps I looked in need of light relief. We checked the performance times and found one starting in 15 minutes.

The War Crimes exhibition is part of a rather surreal visitor complex with a peculiar range of 'attractions' which includes tanks and other military hardware, the Water Puppet Theatre and a souvenir shop selling, without any apparent awareness of irony, Rolex and other watches which had belonged – ostensibly – to dead or captured US troops. Such souvenirs can be found all over Vietnam and by my reckoning there were never enough US soldiers in Vietnam – dead or alive – to account for the number of watches they left behind them, but the fakes look quite good. The shop also displayed a selection of poor quality Russian amber and US army dog tags which the sales assistant assured me, in response to my questions, were definitely taken from the bodies of dead GIs. I found it all rather unpleasant, even though I assumed the tags were as fake as the watches. Perhaps the assistant believed them to be genuine, in which case to profit from the effects of the aggressor might be no more than poetic justice; on the other hand, if she knew they were fake, then what would it matter if the gullible are foolish enough to part with money they clearly have too much of anyway?

The entrance to the Water Puppet Theatre was behind a tank. A show, which is free for Vietnamese, costs $2 for foreigners and is worth every cent, being the perfect antidote to the previous gruesome half hour. Water puppetry, *roi nuoc*, is part of a wide theatrical tradition dating back to the Chinese–Mongol influence of the medieval period. It is unique to Vietnam, however, and legend records that it developed as a result of the Red River flooding a traditional puppet performance during which the brave puppeteers continued with their work, submerged. The north of Vietnam is said to produce the finest water puppetry, but I was delighted with what I saw in Saigon. The show took 45 minutes and was a marvellous combination of *naïveté* and incredible dexterity and skill.

Phuong and I were the only audience the puppeteers had and I was amazed that such an exhibition would be put on for me and my $2. Halfway through, a man and his small child came in and sat near us eating nuts and laughing at the antics of the puppets.

The 'stage', which the raked seating overlooked, was a shallow tank of rather dirty water, probably about 12 square feet in size. The backdrop was an elaborate Chinese-style 'house', with roof and eaves and plastic plants. The water tank was surrounded by a low fence and the overall impression was of watching a performance in the water-filled front garden of someone's home. The 'ground floor' of the 'house' was formed by three overlapping green plastic screens. Behind this four semi-submerged men in grey pyjamas manipulated dozens of different puppet characters from Vietnamese legend on the ends of sticks. The puppets seemed to walk on the water, swim, run and even fly through the air. Smoke appeared from the mouths of dragons as they chased maidens round and round the grimy pool; traditional dancers in gorgeous gold and green costumes moved in perfect formation, their heads and hands re-creating ancient ritual gestures; fishermen and their spouses caught leaping fish in baskets. Best of all I liked the courting birds, their red and gold plumage vivid against the muddy water and green plastic backdrop. The female bird, a mixture of coyness and allure, sped round the pool followed by the enthralled male to the strains of a haunting Vietnamese melody played over crackly loudspeakers which echoed tinnily around the empty auditorium. She finally gave in and they mated politely, before disappearing under the turbulent waters of the pool.

At the end of the show, the four puppeteers, their clothes cling-ing darkly to their slight bodies, emerged from behind the green plastic to bow to their audience. I clapped enthusiastically, having enjoyed the whole thing enormously, though still trying to work out how it had been done. Despite concentrated attention I hadn't been able to see how the puppets had been controlled or how they had moved as rapidly and realistically as they had. Phuong wasn't able to enlighten me; she seemed to find my enthusiasm rather surprising and indulged my childlike questioning. It all remained a mystery, which was of course part of the charm.

From the exhibition complex we went to the History Museum. It was now after 4 p.m. and the museum was closing but Phuong persuaded the security guards to let us in for a brief visit. Exhibits represented cultures from the Bronze Age to the Chams, Khmers and Vietnamese. All seemed in excellent condition and had brief descriptions in English as well as Vietnamese. The time constraint made seeing very much impossible, but I got at least a flavour of what else there might be and the extent and incredible variety of Vietnamese culture since BC was astonishing.

The dental moment had been put off long enough and Phuong said that the dentist she had in mind would now be open for his evening practice. We set off once more through the tide of vehicles, swollen by the mild rush hour, arriving some 15 minutes later at a wide dusty boulevard where Phuong parked the motorbike and I saw the dentist leaning against the door frame of his surgery. I decided he looked OK, not particularly brutal or sadistic, and with nerves firmly under control, I stepped into the gloom of a 1950s French dental practice. From my single experience of it, Vietnamese dentistry has remained untouched by the professional progress of the last three decades. Approaching the chair was like a *déjà vu*. I was once again in Mr Morgan's dental practice in Ross-on-Wye, at a period contemporaneous with the American landings at Da Nang. The upright chair, the round white glass instrument tray; everything was reminiscent of my extreme youth, when I could bear fillings without injections. On the instrument tray lay a few pieces of dental digging equipment and the customary mirror. My eye leapt immediately to the enormous syringe, half-filled with what must have been luke-warm novocaine, and the needle, curved and entirely blunt looking, lying there like a sentence.

While Phuong hovered, the dentist, who spoke no English, waved me to the chair. I pulled out my gold nugget and after laying it next to the needle, opened my mouth and pointed to the offending molar. He poked and prodded around for a few seconds before seizing the drill, pumping vigorously with his right foot and giving it a quick whirr. I was appalled. The drill looked like it had been used to excavate at Cu Chi and was of the ancient revolving band type that I hadn't seen since the days of Mr Morgan, who at least spoke English and kept aged pit ponies in his back garden. Shaking my head vigorously, I tried to explain via Phuong that I only wanted it glued back in and had no interest in being drilled. She told me that he said it would glue better if some of the old glue were removed. I was quite sure he was correct about that but I really didn't care. As long as it got me home it would be just fine. So he mixed up a fuschia-pink rubbery solution on a glass slide, dried the cavity with a piece of cotton wool – not an air blowing machine in sight – and glued it back, pressing down hard into my jaw with his rather big hand. Of all the Vietnamese men I had met, the dentist was undoubtedly the largest. Through Phuong he explained that I shouldn't eat for an hour or so and after thanking him and paying $2, we left. I felt elated. It was all over; I had survived and no longer had a hole in my jaw.

We drove back towards Pham Ngu Lao, the evening traffic still busy, but I was relaxed now and confident of my companion's skill. A few times we passed rather close to a cycle and my leg brushed the leg of another rider, but nothing could bother me now that the dental distress was at an end.

We sat at my breakfast table and had a mineral water together. The key-ring to Phuong's motorbike, a plastic glass slipper, hollow and filled with small gold and silver beads, lay on the table between us. It made me think of the story of Cinderella and I asked her if she had ever heard of this children's fairytale. She shook her head and briefly I outlined the rags to riches story of the glass shoe and the handsome prince. Phuong said that it was a very nice story, but I wasn't absolutely certain that I'd explained it any more clearly that she had understood it. I already knew that people often appeared to understand when they did not and vice versa, simply to maintain the appearance of harmony.

Following on from the romance element of Cinderella, I asked Phuong if she had a boyfriend. She blushed and said, 'No, but – ah – I will have boyfriend next year when university finished and I get job.'

I was rather taken aback at the planned nature of her potential relationship, but remembering that it is impolite to pry too much in Vietnam, I asked no further questions, though I would dearly have loved to. I remembered, too, that when we had been in the History Museum earlier that afternoon, Phuong had coloured and giggled slightly as we looked at the *yoni*, the female objects of worship, and had stared with no apparent recognition at the *linga*, the phallic representations of godhead.

I was extremely grateful to Phuong for her help and thoughtfulness, but was aware that it would be inappropriate to offer money for her kindness; she was well-off by Vietnamese standards and would rightly feel insulted. But it seemed wrong that she should pay to drive me around, so, hedging cautiously, I offered to pay for petrol. She refused and said it was her pleasure to help visitors. Having a better idea, I pulled out a new pen that I'd bought in England and not yet used and said I hoped she would find it useful. She was delighted and accepted it with genuine pleasure. Then she picked up her bike keys from the table and removed them from the slipper key-ring. 'I would like give you this,' she said, smiling, 'and when you look it and think of Cindamellor, you think of me.' I was very touched that she wanted to reciprocate my small thank-you gift and wanted to be remembered.

Shortly after that, she left, waving to me from the motorcycle as she headed for her home and family dinner. As with the General, I knew almost no more about her than I had done four hours earlier when we met. I knew nothing of her life except that she was a student who drove a motorbike and had once had a bad accident to her leg. But her kindness and willingness to help me, a complete stranger, told me more about her and her family and her culture than any words she might have said.

Grace and Nicholas didn't telephone that evening. At 10 p.m. I called the Hanh Long and was told that the Singapore party had arrived and was now out at dinner. I asked whether they had received my note, but of course, nobody could answer that question.

I walked up Pham Ngu Lao, past the bars and cafés, the beggars and children, and ordered squid and beef which I cooked at the table on a hot grill then wrapped in rice paper. A young street girl, seeing me grill badly, came over and without looking at me, stood and cooked it all while I ate. She said not a word and asked for nothing and when I had finished I gave her money because I wanted to, not from discomfort or guilt or embarrassment, but because she had done something for me without my asking.

Later I met Morten and Birta, the Danes from the delta, and we drank beer together for a few hours, talking about London and Denmark and ourselves, and it seemed both strange and a relief to talk and ask questions without hesitation. Together we planned our escape from Saigon. The day after the next we would leave by car for

Nha Trang. It would mean spending only a little time with Grace, but I had had enough of cities: London, Hong Kong, Saigon. I wanted air without lead and no building bigger than a house. I wanted to head north.

chapter five
UPWARD TO NHA TRANG

Grace Lau and I finally spoke at 6.30 the next morning. She had received none of my messages, not even the one I'd delivered personally, and this time I was disappointed and irritated; but it was good to talk to a friend and any chagrin I experienced at learning that she and Nicholas had been in Saigon a day and unable to contact me soon passed. She invited me to join their tour of Saigon that morning, but I had things to do and people to see if I were to make possible my northward journey with the Danes. We arranged to meet in the beige lobby of the Hoang Vu that afternoon and reluctantly I told Grace of my intention to leave the next day. My timing had been bad all along; Grace, a photographer, and I had planned for many weeks to meet in Vietnam and perhaps work together. Now, that wouldn't happen.

I was reading about Nha Trang and eating *pho* when Birta and Morten joined me at my usual breakfast table. We sat and ate together, talking about the projected journey and looking out for Nin and any news he might have of a car and driver. The previous day we'd asked several travel and tour operators about hiring a car. The results were at best ambiguous, at worst hopeless. To hire a good car would take two or three days to organize and be prohibitively expensive at around $150. The new cars I had seen driving through Saigon belonged to private operators and foreign tour companies, so when I approached Nin it had been with hopeful rather than certain expectations of success.

'A good car,' I had said to him the previous day. 'A new one, with good wheels.'

'A Japanese one.' Morten had been more specific and Nin had smiled a rare but encouraging smile.

'Toyota,' he said. 'Two year old, very good wheels. Tomorrow 6.30 in morning my friend come here, take you Nha Trang.'

We relaxed a little.

'How much?' Birta and I spoke together. This was the crucial moment, having already decided our limits.

'Sixty dollar,' Nin said, the words slipping easily off his tongue.

It seemed too much to hope for and of course, it was. But infected with Nin's certainties, we continued our breakfast.

The rest of that morning passed in the hallways and waiting areas of government offices as I tried to change the exit point of my passport. Knowing it might be some weeks before I arrived in Ha Noi, I hoped to resolve the problem in Saigon and, following up the names of officials given to me by An Pham, the General's son, I sat in several waiting rooms and met with much politeness but no success. The exit would remain Lang Son until I reached Ha Noi.

At 2 p.m. I was summoned from my writing by the telephone – a visitor awaited me in the lobby. Seizing my bag and hat, which now sported a black hanky as a chin strap, I ran down the stairs, stepping over the corpse of a cockroach on the first landing, and into the arms of Nicholas, who seemed very much taller than I remembered him. Looking past his elbow, I saw Grace sitting in the back seat of a long white limousine waving to me.

I got in fast, half-convinced that the water and baguette sellers encamped around the entrance to the Hoang Vu, having seen me get into a 'serious' tourist vehicle, would charge me double in future. It was marvellous to be with friends and chattering happily we headed for the Nghia An Hoi Quan pagoda in Cholon, the next stage on Grace and Nicholas' itinerary. This itinerary, I soon discovered, was set as stonily as the Ten Commandments and their guide, despite his youth and rather camp cuteness, was nothing less than an oriental Moses.

The pagoda was a great disappointment from the outside, being brown brick, but the bizarrely contrasting roof was completely tiled and panelled in ceramic bas-relief. Small life-like figures from Chinese legend capered under and over the eaves, chased in and out of trees and houses by dragons in bold primary colours. It was rather vulgar and ill-conceived in its resemblance to an over-decorated public lavatory. The interior was quite different and much more pagoda-like, being all red, black and gold, with slender pillars surrounding an open courtyard.

The Nghia An Hoi Quan pagoda is famous for its carved woodwork, but what struck me particularly were the enormous coils of incense which hung everywhere. Large enough to cover a tall Western person from head to knees, the incense spiralled like scented hoop corsets or delicate, bottomless birdcages, but the perfumed smoke given off was rather nondescript and faint, having none of the crusading, throat-catching vigour of Roman Catholic incense. The shape charmed me, however, and I made my first serious purchase in Vietnam: two round boxes filled with smaller versions of the incense spirals, gifts for friends in England.

The open courtyard held two large bronze bowls, one square, one round, both filled with sand and hundreds of joss sticks which burnt as tributes to the dead. The scene reminded me of lighting small thin candles before graven images as a child at the convent in Ross-on-Wye; but that had stimulated the eye and this, however delicately, seduced the nose.

In a side area we found the tiny pond of the sacred temple carp, a large silvery-pink fish with the hyper-thyrodic eyes of its genus. In this creature the good fortune of the temple resided and I was a bit surprised that it was in such a small and dingy pool. It seemed very good-natured, however, and enjoyed being stroked and tickled under its chin.

Dingier still was the sacred tortoise enclosure which, from the foetid dark brown water of the pond and the concrete slabbing around it to the brown plastic tray that held the creatures' food, bore every conceivable resemblance to a hastily deserted public urinal. I sincerely hoped that the smallness of their brain permits a tortoise no aesthetic sensibilities, or the pagoda would surely have been cursed. On the far wall of their enclosure was a gaudy pale blue ceramic of a mustard-coloured tortoise walking on water, with a little package on its back. The image reminded me of a Terry Pratchett plot and looking more closely, I noticed that the mustard tortoise appeared to be spitting a fountain of something white up and over a lotus plant. I couldn't blame it for wanting to spit – not at all. I wasn't certain about the purpose of the tortoises – something perhaps to do with longevity or wisdom? Or was that the carp? The guidebooks were very scant on information and no one in the pagoda spoke sufficient English to explain.

It was a very strange sensation looking out from the cool dark interior of the limo between the shoulders of the driver and the guide. Sitting in the back of that car with my friends, I suddenly felt perspectives change momentarily; I had become those people flashing past Nin's cyclo the previous day. I saw more of the bustling streets, shops and population of Cholon in half an hour of driving than in the hour I spent with Nin on the cyclo. However, the means of observing and the observation itself needed to be at one for me to have any real appreciation of what I saw, and the sense of divorce that I felt looking out from behind dark glass reduced my limousine experience to the purely cinematic.

The War Crimes exhibition was on the itinerary too, but Grace avoided it, using me as an excuse, and she and I were conducted to a very cold, very European ice-cream parlour where we were induced to sit while Nicholas and the disapproving guide visited the exhibition without us. Going from one cold place to another, I realized how truly different the experience of being a traveller and being a tourist is in a country like Vietnam. There is a growing argument that developing countries need the real money and business that tourists bring in, while travellers merely create change without contributing to significant growth. There may well be an economical legitimacy to this argument. Travellers take themselves – not always a benefit, no doubt – but most hope to learn or teach something. It's not an exchange that builds railways or rehouses people, but it allows each side to appear human to the other, to meet with at least a semblance of equality. The tourists I saw, particularly, but not exclusively, from other parts of South East Asia, seemed to me to be in Vietnam for a good time on the cheap. They expected to be treated deferentially and be provided with facilities similar to those of a developed nation; most travellers I saw hoped to be treated politely and had a far more realistic expectation of what Vietnam could provide. As Grace, herself British-Chinese and well-acquainted with the intricacies of the oriental lifestyle, pointed out after staying in a hotel full of Taiwanese businessmen, 'The men are here for sex and their wives are here to stop them having sex.'

Our strange afternoon ran appropriately into the evening as we went to Maxim's restaurant in Dong Khoi Street, heart of tourist Saigon. The tour guide had been very upset that we weren't sticking to the itinerary and eating in some Chinese restaurant in Cholon, but we refused to be terrorized and Nicholas, a very 'British' solicitor, indicated politely but firmly in his best legal manner that we *would* do our own thing that evening. We were dropped at the Hoang Vu and within minutes of finding Nin, all three of us were heading by cyclo towards Dong Khoi. Nicholas had a vehicle to himself and Grace sat, nervously at first, on my lap. It was great to be in the air again and although the money I paid Nin was making only a microscopic contribution to the overall wealth of Vietnam, I hoped we both enjoyed the exchange; though if asked, he might well have preferred to be driving a limousine.

Before eating, we visited the Q-Bar, most modern and exotic of all Saigon's many bars and situated under the Opera House. I had read about the place in a magazine supplement back in London and seen photos of the *viet kieu* owner and her American husband. The woman, a former model in California, had transported '90s Soho to Saigon. Familiar with London's Soho, I was not unduly impressed by the twisted wrought iron candlesticks, distressed walls and gothic-clinical bar, but the service was impeccable and the cocktail the best and strongest I'd had since shaking my own for officers of the Green Berets in Bavaria in the late 1970s. The owners were absent, but their barmaid was perfect in a way that entirely outstripped the homespun beauty of the Vietnam Airlines stewardesses. This was glamour, this was the ultimate oriental sex-symbol; this was also cold as ice, with none of the pliancy that occidental men fantasize oriental women possess in abundance. I didn't even wonder where she lived, whether she had a lover, an ageing mother, children. She had none of those things. She didn't live anywhere. She was soldered to her steel workstation in the most tasteful bar in Vietnam and that was that.

After the Q-Bar, Maxim's was a sad let-down, or maybe the *mauvais ton* of the latter was more noticeable after a visit to the former. I was perfectly happy, however, having just bought a bi-plane to add to my collection at home in London from a vendor outside the Opera House. I found a vast childlike pleasure in this purchase, which was amphibious and made from recycled beer cans. Billed by *Lonely Planet* as 'the best restaurant in Indo-China' – which has an immediately exotic ring – and '*the* place for power dining', Maxim's could hardly fail to disappoint. The food was almost the worst I ate during my entire journey and undoubtedly the most expensive at $16 for half a dozen exceedingly shrivelled frogs' legs and not much else. Grace and Nicholas fared no better, Grace being especially uncomfortable with the atmosphere, which she said reminded her of many tedious Chinese restaurant parties of the '6os. The gastronomic disappointments of Maxim's were, however, entirely outweighed by the entertainment, which was pure kitsch. The largely oriental clientele seemed enormously appreciative of the shows, while the foreigners looked vaguely bemused at renditions of 'Jingle Bells' interspersed with a Grade 4 level performance of Beethoven's 'Für Elise' on a piano badly in need of tuning and bits of an Elgar concerto played hesitantly on the cello. The 'Jingle Bells' particularly was utterly memorable for being danced by a troupe of graceful but dispassionate young men and women wearing miniature Santa outfits and fixed grins.

The entire experience was oddly synchronous with a passage of *A Dragon Apparent* I'd read under the mosquito net only the previous night. In it, Lewis describes visiting a Saigon theatre:

> [It] had been an appalling fiasco, although cruelly funny in its way; a pathetic attempt at a Wild Western musical, inspired perhaps by reports of 'Oklahoma'. It was acted by fragile, slant-eyed beauties in chaps, wearing ten-gallon hats and toting six-shooters; their cheeks heavily incarnadined in representation of occidental plethora. The cowboys had coloured their top lips and chins bright blue to suggest a strong Western growth of beard. Provided with guitars which they were unable to play, they shrilled a strident version of hill-billy airs...

Despite the coy rendition of 'Rudolph the Red-Nosed Reindeer' there was a particular atmosphere to Maxim's, and I fully expected a striptease at any moment. Apparently the restaurant has a nightclub section where much more *exotique* carryings-on take place, but after the frog, I had no stomach for such things. Instead, we headed for the much-heralded Apocalypse Now bar, a place I had studiously avoided during the previous days and which turned out to be just another bar for Westerners that belted out the Doors and sold American beer. This one did have bar girls, though, or perhaps I was cynical and they were customers too.

That night I said good-bye to Grace and Nicholas in the middle of the street before heading back to the Hoang Vu to pack my few belongings. Though sorry to part with my friends, I was glad to be on my way at last. The rest of Vietnam lay before me and I was eager to see it.

At 6.30 a.m. the next morning I was sitting in an almost deserted Pham Ngu Lao Street eating a baguette and *pâté* – an unnaturally pink and greasy substance of dubious origin – when Birta and Morten joined me. None of the cafés were open but the few bread-and-water street vendors were plying a good trade out of their glass-box trolleys. At 6.45, Nin arrived, looking faintly anxious but trying to be reassuring. At 7.15 an elderly Renault which had to be a minimum of 25 years old pulled up. Memories of Tan Son Nhut airport rushed at me and I felt angry with myself and with Nin that this had happened. I said, 'What is this? This isn't a Toyota,' to which Nin, visibly more anxious by the second, replied, 'This very good car, you go Nha Trang no problem,' at which Morten said, 'This car is very old, we don't want to go to Nha Trang in an old car. You said new Japanese car.'

The driver, a dark thick-set man with a serious skin problem, spoke no English at all, but seeing our dislike of his vehicle immediately and understandably became surly. Nin was talking desperately with the driver, trying to calm him and us simultaneously and failing miserably on both counts. Although anxious and annoyed, a part of me sympathized that his attempts at entrepreneurism were proving so unfortunate. I had no idea how much money he was making out of the deal; I hoped it was worth the anxiety he was experiencing. Birta and

Morten talked quickly together in Danish, the driver and Nin rattled on in Vietnamese and I stood and wondered, doubtfully, if this vehicle would carry us the 280 miles to our destination.

We were in a no-win situation – if we refused the car then we would have to start again and risk the same problem. Deciding that we would only get what we paid for, I said we might as well take what was on offer and try and reduce the price to compensate for the loss of the fantasy Toyota, but the driver was angry now and, via Nin, adamantly refused any reduction. The desire to be gone was greater than our fears about the car and the surliness of the driver and we finally gave in. Nin couldn't look at me and I didn't want to look at him, but I was sorry to part from him in such a way.

The ordeal lasted almost 15 hours and if it hadn't been for the good company, I would have stopped somewhere along the road and found other means to continue. The seats had once had springs but, along with the entire suspension system of the vehicle, they were long since destroyed – with crucial consequences for the coccyx. The vibration was constant and unrelenting and the engine blew visible fumes back into the car after the first five miles and continued to do so for the rest of the journey. This meant that the windows had to be open at all times, which allowed the lead-laden fumes of all the other vehicles using the road to enter the car too. Soon both Birta and I were wearing scarves over our faces from the eyes down because breathing had become difficult.

About 20 miles out of Saigon our driver decided that the car would go no further as there was some problem under the bonnet that was not solvable. By sheer coincidence no doubt, the lay-by we had stopped in also held a minibus with the words 'Nha Trang' writ large on a sign in the back window. We didn't believe that there was a single thing wrong with the car that hadn't already been wrong at 7 a.m. that morning and by gesture and grimace refused to get our belongings out of the boot or pay a single dong until we reached Nha Trang. Nha Trang, the name was already beginning to sound like a knell.

I don't know what I expected the countryside to be like; drier certainly than the Mekong region, interesting in a different way perhaps. It was not at all as I had envisaged Vietnam. Immediately north-east of Ho Chi Minh City, the dusty white-yellow road rises away from the flatlands of the delta to be lined with pines and rubber trees for many miles. Semi-distant hills occasionally showed startlingly bright red soil emerging like bloody cracks in the earth, clashing violently with any green around them and reminding me of the old rhyme 'Red and green should never be seen, except upon an Irish queen.' I had seen vividly coloured soil in other parts of Asia but never so bright and vibrant a red as this.

Later we passed newly built church after newly built church, which surprised me, as I'd seen very few such marks of Christianity elsewhere. I was later told that when the French were obliged to recognize the Communist North Vietnam as a separate state after 1945, most of the North's Roman Catholics moved to the South, hence communities of them in unexpected places. Each church seemed larger than the previous one, with no evidence of villages or towns near or large enough to fill such a building. I pondered which international Christian groups had donated the money for such buildings in an area where water was scarce and the roads off the highway still made of dirt.

Later we passed a few small towns, all with the same dusty, beige uniformity which would occasionally be broken by a crocodile of beautifully dressed young schoolchildren wearing white shirts, the red scarf of Communism tied neatly under their chins.

Leaving the tree-lined roads behind, we drove for several hours between Bien Hoa and Phan Thiet. This region reminded me of the Balkans, particularly Croatia. The road was fairly flat now, the higher ground being far away to our left. The road itself, the most important highway in Vietnam, was quite dreadful – a narrow two-lane road, mostly without any sort of dividing line, which encouraged drivers to keep to the middle of the road at all times, regardless of which direction they were travelling in or what other traffic might be on the road. Many drivers in Vietnam have never taken a driving test and have no licence. As the driving test itself consists of driving a moped through a figure-of-eight, the difference between having a licence and not is probably rather marginal, but may be a reason for the high number of road accidents. The other reason is simply the literally crumbling infrastructure. We saw our first serious crash shortly before Phan Thiet and I wished I could ask our driver where ambulances came from and where they went to.

While looking out of the windows, the Danes and I began a series of long and involved conversations which included discussion of the linguistic similarities of Danish and English, the differences between the voting systems of Denmark and Britain, and the Vietnam war. Morten was a great conversationalist and I was constantly reminded of my own linguistic feebleness when I was able to express complex ideas and be understood by someone who regarded his English as limited. Birta, sitting in the front seat to stave off travel sickness, sometimes joined in. The only occasion when she felt impelled to actually turn around in her seat and look at me was during a conversation on voting when I admitted to voting in elections only rarely. Both my companions voiced their disapproval of this, saying each vote counted.

'It may do in Denmark,' I replied, 'but in Britain we don't have proportional representation.'

This took some further work and as the lakes, huts and distant hills of Vietnam passed us by, I tried to explain Britain's voting system, which I wasn't entirely clear about myself. After a few minutes, what I was saying fell suddenly into place and as Morten exclaimed in disbelief, Birta turned round sharply in her seat.

'No!' she said, looking genuinely horrified. 'You mean that people vote but that each vote won't have an equal representative weight?'

I wasn't sure that I would have put it quite like that, but it sounded OK. 'Yes,' I said, 'that's about it. The most I can hope to achieve in voting, if my choice isn't elected, is to be counted as a number and it would need a bit more than that to get me into the voting booth, I'm afraid.'

'No, no!' they both exclaimed. 'We understand now what you were saying about not voting. It's unbelievable that it should be like this in Britain, it's so...what is the word?...archaic.'

I agreed, naturally.

The further north we drove, the higher the hills on the distant left-hand horizon became, until we were looking at the southerly ranges of the Central Highlands. These highlands are the start of the interior of Vietnam, the place that even in 1950 was marked

'Unexplored Territory' on Norman Lewis' map. Beyond those mountains lay more mountains, forests and the homes of *Montagnards*, the original Vietnamese peoples. The relationship between the Vietnamese government and its minorities is not always entirely happy. As in northern Burma and Thailand, there are ethnic groups in Vietnam which do not wish to integrate. Organizations like FULRO (acronym for the French words 'United Front for the Struggle of the Oppressed Peoples') provide a refuge for the disenchanted or disenfranchised of such minorities.

Looking over at the far distant hills, I thought of Lewis driving through them with his French and *Montagnard* companions and felt sorry I wouldn't be going there. That was a decision I'd made on two counts: no other travellers I'd met were going through the interior, which would mean travelling alone; I could not, by myself, afford to hire a vehicle and driver for long periods of time and public transport was out of the question.

I'd come to the decision about public transport after a conversation with the de Silvas in which they'd told me about their journey by local bus from Da Nang to Nha Trang. The 17-hour trip was mostly at night and the bus driver, clearly anxious about carrying foreigners, kept trying to put them off in the middle of nowhere. At one point, uniformed men came onto the bus and began threatening and intimidating the couple, handling them roughly and pulling at their clothing. There were serious problems with language and communication, and clearly there were underlying issues which neither traveller understood. Though very nervous following this experience, both told me how much they had enjoyed being in Vietnam and that they looked forward to coming back. Having experienced similar situations in other countries, I knew how unpleasant it could all be and had no interest in placing myself in such a position alone.

The fields alongside us often seemed barren and the soil, even in this, the cool season, looked dry and parched. The villages became fewer the further we drove; occasionally a single man or woman could be seen bending over a hoe, weeding lines of tobacco plants – splashes of green in an otherwise yellow-brown world. Small herds of animals – goats and hump-shouldered Asian cows – were carefully tended by children in bright clothing and once the Ho Chi Minh

City–Ha Noi 'express' train moved alongside us for several miles before being left behind at a small stop in the middle of nowhere as a handful of people got in and out of its long line of coaches pulled by an obsolescent steam engine made in China or Czechoslovakia. Vietnam's 1,900 miles of railway is one of the prime targets for foreign investment in the '90s and by the new millennium it's quite likely that the century-old French tracks and locomotives will have been replaced by American, New Zealand or German models, with India providing cash for new carriages. The rail track and the Ho Chi Minh–Ha Noi highway run parallel the entire length of the coast of Vietnam; for foreigners, using the railway is still a slow and unusually expensive experience, though first class is reported to be extremely pleasant.

By 1 p.m. we were very hungry. The one packet of 'antique' biscuits Morten had bought had been eaten and our three bottles of water had been drunk. We had wrongly assumed that there would be plenty of places to get food and water along the way. The driver, his surliness entirely unabated, seemed without bodily requirement. We had already made one bladder stop, which involved peeing in someone's kitchen garden observed by several black fowl with red eyes. As we approached a small village, Morten made it clear to the driver that we would stop to eat. We found a reasonably pleasant-looking café overlooking the road which, for some unknown reason, appeared to fill the driver with disgust. Although he sat at our table, he refused to eat or drink anything and I had the feeling that this was not so much irritation with his passengers as some secret knowledge about the place and its food that he could not share with us. The meal consisted of a bowl of soup made from dried packet noodles with large lumps of pig fat floating greasily. The meat made me hesitate but only momentarily; then it went the way of all pork. Asking the direction of the toilet, I was shown to a very pleasant courtyard full of young pigs which I viewed apologetically, having almost certainly just eaten one of their relatives. The driver looked appalled that we would eat such stuff and indicated as much by turning his back on the rest of the restaurant.

The café was quite full, though few people seemed to be eating. Most simply sat and chatted quietly or stared at us. It was the first time since arriving in Vietnam that I felt a true outsider. No one spoke English, or if they did, had any desire to do so with us, and the driver communicated with no one. Birta, a vegetarian, ate nothing, but Morten, a chef and restaurateur, ate as fast and as thoroughly as myself.

As we ate, we were observed closely by four girls on their way home from school. They stood tentatively round a nearby table and stared politely, clutching their textbooks to their chests. All were very pretty, their dress a mixture of the ubiquitous '60s frills and a firmer, 'Communist' style. The hats, which they all wore, ranged from a white straw 'church fête' style to broad-brimmed baseball caps and an green alpine type lacking only the feather. As we were leaving, they showed us their books and I was surprised yet again to realize that they must be considerably older than they appeared, judging from the level of their school work. They had been studying the human alimentary tract and I hoped that this was not an omen.

As the afternoon wore on, we passed relics of the Cham civilization: broken brick towers with grass and small trees growing in profusion from their crumbling faces. One particularly large tower brought the car to a standstill as the driver waved us encouragingly out of the car and towards the ruin. Wondering what his real reason might be for stopping, I noticed him race behind a bush to take advantage of the natural facilities and reappear dragging desperately on a cigarette. Birta had told him before we left Saigon that smoking in the car was not allowed and though he was not a likeable man, I felt sorry for him shut up hour after hour in a dodgy car with three people laughing and complaining around him in a language he didn't understand and, to top it all, unable to smoke. The tower was particularly unremarkable visually and with no information either on site or in any guidebook to explain its historical significance, we learnt nothing. But the driver had proved himself human and the workmen shovelling away around the base of the tower seemed to find our presence very amusing. The Vietnam tourist authorities are keen to encourage foreigners to visit sites of historical interest; foreigners are keen to do so, if it is both possible and worthwhile.

At about 6 p.m., the driver attempted to dump us for the second time. On this occasion he flagged down a passing car containing two men and talked them into taking us the remaining 90 miles. They agreed after some discussion. We, naturally, disagreed, refusing to travel with two strangers, the three of us squashed into the back of yet another small, though less elderly, car. Perhaps realizing that because we had given in on Pham Ngu Lao didn't mean we would continue to do so, the driver slammed his way back into his seat and with a great clash of gears we set off on the last stage of the journey.

It was dark when we passed Cam Ranh Bay, which I regretted as I would have liked to see the place where the Russian fleet, or what remained of it, sheltered in 1905 after its defeat by the Japanese – the first defeat of a major Western power by an Eastern one. The Japanese used the bay during World War II and in the '60s the Americans turned Cam Ranh into the busiest harbour in South East Asia, backed by a vast military 'city' and serviced by an enormous airfield. During the war years it also contained one of the largest ice-cream making factories in Vietnam, one of 40 such units spread across South Vietnam and run by the US military, who seemed to have had great faith in the anodyne qualities of frozen dairy products. When I passed Cam Ranh Bay on the night of 22 December 1994, the Russian fleet, unable to pay the rent, had all but given up its occupancy. In 1989 the Vietnamese, fed up with their Russian tenants, had offered the place once more to the Americans. But the Russians are hanging on; had it been still daylight I might have seen a supply ship or perhaps even a destroyer anchored in the bay – but not much else.

Two hours short of Nha Trang it started to rain and became relatively cool. The fumes continued to pour into the car, making it impossible to close the windows, so we got wet. Our faces were now dark grey above the scarf line and Birta and I were feeling decidedly unwell. Approaching the city, I felt an enormous sense of relief – which was to be short-lived.

Nha Trang in December was a wet place. The dirt roads were holed with enormous puddles and the rain continued to drift sleepily, turning everything to dampness. The driver had never been in Nha Trang before and was clearly tired and even more irritable than previously. He had almost certainly never intended to bring us this far and was showing his temper, an unusual thing for a Vietnamese.

Perhaps he didn't want to stay overnight in Nha Trang, perhaps he had work the following day back in Saigon. Whatever his problem, it began to overcome his judgement as he drove round and round the poorly lit and wet city.

After some time we found the hotel we each agreed sounded best from the guidebook; unfortunately, everyone else reading the book had had the same thought and by the time we arrived at 9.30 p.m., it was completely full. The driver now began to lose whatever control he'd clung to throughout the day. By gesture we were told he'd brought us to Nha Trang and had fulfilled his part of the bargain. He made it clear he had no intention of helping us find a hotel and we refused to pay him until he did so. It all threatened to turn nasty once or twice and although we knew he would be very careful because he was operating outside the law, we didn't want to involve the authorities any more than he did. At this point, Morten and Birta decided to have a disagreement and I began to shrink into the seat and wish I was anywhere else in the world but Nha Trang on a wet night with a driver from hell, nowhere to stay and two marauding Danes in close proximity.

Three hotels later, we eventually found rooms. When I got out of the car and stood up I realized to my surprise that I was shaking; almost 15 hours of constant vibration and the inhaling of lead and dust, combined with the sudden onset of serious pre-menstrual sickliness made me feel very bad indeed. Morten, who was a true gentleman, did all the manly things such as sorting out the driver – who began to demand extra money – and carrying most of the bags. The young woman behind the reception desk of our Soviet-style hotel was wearing a fuschia-pink parka jacket with fur trim collar, which I found most depressing. I was glad I had followed the intuition which told me to leave my conical hat in Saigon. Sitting in my small and depressing room, damp, cold, hungry and unwell, I began to wish I was back in the warmth and bustle of Saigon, or even – and this was hardest to admit – in my own home in London, or with friends in front of a fire, a Christmas tree, a decent meal.

Washing my face quickly and swallowing a cold beer that I found in the mini bar, I went to join my travelling companions for dinner at a fish restaurant Morten had set his heart on, having been told about it by Pia and Kosh de Silva the evening after our return from the coconut toffee factory. The restaurant was pleasant, the rain had almost stopped, Morten and Birta had made up, the driver was long gone, but my enthusiasm had foundered along with my oestrogen level. Returning to my room later that evening I unpacked nothing beyond my toothbrush and soap. There was an in-built mosquito net which I enjoyed playing with as it swung away from the wall and over the bed rather like the sails of a boat dropping from the yardarm. Bored with that but still agitated, I took one of Dr Lo's few remaining blue pills. Before the anaesthetic seized and dragged me down into oblivion I had already decided that I was leaving Nha Trang the following morning.

I was awake at 8 a.m. and showered and ready by 8.30. Having located the Vietnam Airlines office, which opened at 9 a.m., I set off to buy something in which to carry my bi-plane and incense spirals. I found the perfect solution in a shop that sold wigs, shell suits and perfume in bottles containing plastic flowers. The bag was quite small but by an ingenious series of zips could be opened out and out to become larger than my original travel bag. I was most impressed. As my purchases increased, so would my bag. 'How marvellous Communism is,' I said to myself yet again.

I was the first customer at the airline office and with no difficulty at all bought a $36 ticket to Da Nang for the 11 a.m. flight. The weather was warm and pleasant with no sign of the previous evening's downpour beyond a little dark shadowing of the pavement.

I bounced back to the hotel. The receptionist, still in her pink and fur parka, was most helpful and, having paid my bill, I knocked on Birta and Morten's door. They were surprised and seemed disappointed that I was leaving. I was sorry too that I had made friends and was leaving them so soon. I liked them both very much. They had been easy people to be with, thoughtful and generous. We exchanged addresses, wished each other well for the rest of the Vietnamese journey and said goodbye. I was alone again and it felt good. A small part of me was sorry to be seeing nothing of Nha Trang, but the urge to move on was stronger than the desire to stop and look about.

The best part of being in Nha Trang was the journey to the

airport. I hailed a cyclo, driven by the same thin elderly man who had taken me to the airline office. He spoke some English and had a wicked sense of humour. The ride took me along the beach and seeing the place in daylight confirmed my decision to leave. The beach at Nha Trang is pleasant enough, but something about the arrangement of hotels, road and seashore made me think of Brighton or Eastbourne – in the Middle Ages.

Situated on the outskirts of the town, the airport is at the end of a long shaded road much like the drive to a private house and is the most delightful I have ever used. The waiting area was an open-air colonnade on the roof of the building. In a tiny dark refreshment shop nestling amid the columns, a woman wearing a thick winter coat sold warm soft drinks and cold beer. The passengers were mostly foreigners, with a large proportion of Americans, the first I had seen in any numbers. One older man pointed at the runway and remarked loudly that it had been built with American tax dollars.

Standing at the check-in I had the misfortune to queue immediately behind a European man reeking of alcohol and sweat. Every time he lifted his arm to move a bag or swat a fly I ducked slightly in the forlorn hope of avoiding the wafted odour. I should have realized that queuing behind him could mean sitting beside him, but it was still early in the day. 'The Flying Dutchman', as he came to be known, was to affect the next few days of my life quite markedly, as were several other people on that flight, each in their different ways.

The sky had clouded again as we took off, but I had time to glimpse the white Buddha of Nha Trang. Forty-six feet high and seated on a lotus leaf, he was spectacular even from the air.

Then the Buddha and all the streets, houses and pagodas of Nha Trang disappeared into a mist of cloud as the plane turned over the sea and headed north for Da Nang and my next destination.

chapter six

HOI AN

The 20-mile route from Da Nang airport south to Hoi An was one of the most actively rural I had yet seen in Vietnam, though the freshness of its pastoral scene was somewhat marred by the continuing presence of the odorous Flying Dutchman. Having hired a taxi from Da Nang airport to Hoi An with an American couple, I was congratulating myself on escaping the Dutchman when I saw him ask my co-passengers if he could share our car. He clearly had thought better than to ask me following a little contretemps on the aircraft when I'd suggested one of us sit elsewhere. Being kind people and unfamiliar with his personal problem, the Americans said, 'Yes.' With a sinking heart, I watched him load his bag into the boot of the taxi and immediately got into the front seat myself.

The fields bordering the road were alive with women and girls cutting the wheat crop. The road itself had been turned into a threshing device, with the wheat laid, ears pointing inwards, along its edges, waiting for vehicles to drive past. At first I thought the trucks and taxis seemed unaware of the hard-won crop they were so carelessly driving over; it took a little while for me to realize the effortless work that each passing vehicle did, tyres acting as a threshing wheel, separating grain from stalk, to be gathered up at leisure, or at least before it rained. This bizarre mix of the modern as an unwitting instrument of the archaic was pure Vietnam and once more I was amazed at the ingenuity behind so much that was seemingly simple.

We passed 'Marble Mountain', a conglomerate of five rock stacks standing squarely out of the ground like old teeth from dry gums. Our driver, who spoke some English, told us that Marble Mountain was famous for having been a VC hospital and intelligence centre during the war. Smiling as though at some private joke, he told us that the Communists had maintained the hospital in a chamber at the heart of one of the stacks throughout the war, literally only a few hundred yards from the US military using the road from Da Nang to Non Nuoc Beach, the R&R 'playground' which the GIs using it renamed 'China Beach', since made famous by a Hollywood war film and TV series of the same name. I knew I would have to pass this place again on my way north and resolved to have a closer look at Marble Mountain.

Driving into the town of Hoi An, I was immediately struck by the lack of '60s buildings, cars and other symptoms of twentieth-century living. Hoi An is one of the few towns in South Vietnam undamaged by the war with the US and even at first glance, its houses, bridges and streets reflected a very different Vietnam from anywhere I had yet seen. A small, slow-moving, riverine town with a long history of trade and merchanting, Faifo, as Hoi An was formerly known, was spared the ravages of the US war, avoiding the fate of Da Nang, which American bombers almost eliminated in fierce fighting. During the earlier anti-colonial war, this tranquil town had also remained undamaged because, ironically, the French had made it the administrative capital for the region. Much of Hoi An looks little different from how it must have appeared over two centuries ago. There was something immediately comfortable and relaxing about the place and the driver told us it was a good town and popular with foreigners, which might be a mixed recommendation, but I could quickly see why Westerners or indeed anyone coming here might like it.

We drove along the street which edged the riverside, past tall full-leafed palms and long wooden rowboats pulled up onto the sloping shore. Open-fronted restaurants faced onto the water and we passed between plastic tables crowned with colourful parasols on both sides of the street. Being the day before Christmas Eve, there were quite a few Westerners making merry in what, at first glance, seemed a semi-European environment, until we almost ran over a piglet which had ensconced itself in the dirt of the road and appeared both startled and indignant at our approach.

Patti and Skip Weisser, the Vermont couple with whom I'd shared the taxi, had been told by travellers in Saigon that there was a great hotel in an old house in the centre of Hoi An. The driver took us there directly and we walked confidently into the wonderful lobby of the Vinh Hung Hotel – so newly able to accept foreigners it wasn't in the *Lonely Planet* guide. Heavily carved black wood pillars rose up out of the marble floor to support roof beams. The lobby, which was filled with elegant black wood furniture carved with the same dragons and birds as the pillars, had a reception desk and bar. The woman receptionist was most pleasant and helpful as she told us that there were no free rooms at all in the hotel, nor were there likely to be because of the Christmas holiday. She thought the Hoi An Hotel had rooms – but we already knew that this large state-run place charged $35 per room and smaller private hotels like the Vinh Hung only $8–16. Seeing our dilemma, the receptionist offered us beds in the upstairs corridor at $3 per night each, which seemed very reasonable indeed.

There were six beds in the corridor, two of them already taken by an Italian couple, which meant that the four remaining were for Patti, Skip, the Dutchman – who, having seen the lobby bar, was already keeping his alcohol level up – and me. Dumping my bags, I sought out the bathroom and on my return found that the beds had already been allocated, leaving me last in the line of six, between the Dutchman – who had left the bar long enough to stake his claim – and the balcony. I began to seriously consider paying $35 at the Hoi An Hotel, but Patti told me it would all be all right and I wanted to believe her.

We three sat on the carved black balcony which drooped gently over the road and watched the occasional bicycle pass below us. Small groups of young Vietnamese people wearing baseball caps and T-shirts waved up at us from time to time and I thought how strange the modern clothing seemed against the backdrop of centuries. I relaxed again, as I had on my first arrival in Saigon. Vietnam had beckoned all my life and now I was here I wanted very much to respond as fully as possible, but it had proved far harder than I'd imagined to shake off London and simply let go.

After an hour or so of casual chat I'd learnt that Skip was a kind of high-class gothic jack-of-all trades – 'an inventor' was his own description – and Patti an acupuncturist. Visions of an instant cure for PMS (a problem which some of my friends refer to as Permanent Menstrual Syndrome) sprang to mind and I thought with a kind of perverse pleasure of the dozens of brand new needles lying in my medical kit – a going away present from my regular acupuncturist in London. I regretted not bringing my Tarot cards with me but wondered whether Patti might be interested in swapping a past-life regression for an acupuncture treatment.

As the afternoon wore on and more Vietnamese beer was swallowed, we were joined on the balcony by another American couple, Paul and Anna, who seemed to have cycled everywhere and whose utterly solid thighs shouted, 'I've pushed this body across Asia.' Legs could certainly remove the problem of cars and drivers I thought, as I considered the seriously hefty pairs in front of me. We talked the usual traveller talk, about the war in Vietnam, the places we'd been, where we hoped to go, how long we'd stay in Hoi An and what was uppermost in the minds of many of the travellers I'd talked to over the past few days – what we would do for Christmas. It seemed strange to be away from the Christian world and yet still talking about its most important festival. The previous year I'd spent alone on a beach in Catholic south India, frying in the sun and reading a biography of Roman dictator, aristocrat, murderer and debauchee Cornelius Sulla. On Christmas Eve, I'd been to midnight mass in the usually deserted chapel of the sixteenth-century Portuguese fort, now a government resthouse, on the border of Maharashtra and Goa where I was staying. Christmas Day I'd been fed fresh-caught pomfret and a magnificent *crème brûlée* which I ate in the cobbled courtyard in company with a life-size statue of Christ; together we watched the kitchen staff slowly and methodically pick microscopic grit out of the handfuls of rice scattered across a table. The afternoon was spent fishing, picturesquely but ineffectually, and pondering how Sulla, one of the most powerful and ruthless men the Western world had ever known, was obliged to conceal his sexual preferences from a censorious society which adored his brutalities.

Reading about ancient Rome while in India taught me that it's easily possible to be somewhere in body but not entirely in spirit; that for many people – judging by the reading material of my fellow-travellers

– it's impossible to leave the familiar behind entirely – even if that familiarity comes in the shape of Cornelius Sulla. I didn't want to do that in Vietnam, I wanted very much to be able to just *be* there, but already I could feel that I was drawn towards the comfortable society of other Westerners, which I both enjoyed and strangely resented, as it seemed to highlight the difficulties – logistical and personal – of travelling alone.

We were discussing Christmas when the Dutchman suddenly appeared among us wearing nothing but a pair of red underpants and a drink induced smirk. He immediately began to hold forth on the pleasures of Amsterdam, particularly the sexual ones, more particularly the bisexual ones. As a former academic researcher on the topic of male bisexuality and sexually-transmitted disease, I found my professional self responding to his ill-timed outpourings by wanting to reach for a clipboard and a tape recorder. My normal self responded by jumping up and saying I was extremely hungry – which was true – and heading for the door.

My new companions, Patti and Skip, joined me for late lunch at a marvellous restaurant on the waterfront which sported a rattan ceiling, with yellow and green balloons vivid against the blue washed walls. Christmas decorations included paper chains and a melancholic and truncated Santa Claus which in some unfortunate way recalled the 'Skateboard Beggar' of Pham Ngu Lao Street. The shrimp were large and wonderfully fresh and the *cau lau*, the flat heavy noodles which are a speciality of Hoi An, were delicious. I began to feel less concerned about the coming night in the corridor.

After eating, we walked along the waterfront, now hung with lines of coloured electric lights, to the large indoor market-place and wandered through the silent darkened stalls which by day would be bustling and vibrant. There'd been a light rain as we sat on the hotel balcony, which had freshened the air and brought out the cagoules. Most of the cafés and restaurants we passed were full of Westerners, many French and Italian from what I could hear, but the character of Hoi An, its quietness and simplicity, seemed as yet untouched by the invasion of foreigners.

In a shop selling prints and ceramics, I met a shaven-headed Frenchman sitting at the shop's desk practising Vietnamese writing.

He told me he spoke seven languages and that he'd lived in Hoi An for many months, learning Vietnamese and unofficially teaching French and English. His English accent was decidedly Clouseau-ish and I had visions of the youth of Hoi An speaking English with a pseudo-colonial flavour, but said nothing in deference to the Frenchman's linguistic abilities, which far outstripped my own, or indeed those of almost anyone I knew.

Away from the waterfront, Hoi An street lighting wasn't good and by nightfall some people were using torches to negotiate the dirt roads and ward off angry barking dogs and rooting pigs. Few of the bicycles had lights on them and I wondered how people avoided accidents. We walked slowly back along the riverside to our hotel; there was a low whirr of activity in the streets, but generally it was quiet and for the first time since arriving in Vietnam, I crossed roads without thinking each move might be my last. The rowboats were still in the moonless dark and the pigs snorted gently under the trees. I had drunk just enough beer to feel all might be well with the world after all. Little did I know that the nightmare was only beginning.

I could hear the rantings of the Dutchman before we reached the hotel. He was still on the balcony in his knickers alternately singing in a vile tenor and laughing to himself. Reaching our corridor, we discovered that every other hapless foreigner who'd asked for a room following our arrival had been shown the same kindness as ourselves – literally. The number of beds in the upstairs corridor had become 10, not counting the mattresses on the floor. Whilst from a democratic and compassionate perspective I felt it quite right that everyone should have been shown the same hospitality, I also knew I couldn't bear it. Normally I wouldn't have had any problem with the arrangements, but my current hormonal condition couldn't cope with sleeping in a dormitory with at least 15 people, next to the now raving Dutchman. Just my luck, I thought, for him to have some sort of alcoholic attack or DT hallucination in the night. Skip kindly offered to exchange beds with me, but seeing Patti look forlorn, I declined and, taking the initiative, asked the management if they had any solutions to the bed difficulty, but they said sadly they did not.

Overhearing my discussion with the manager, Tuan, the young bar/bell boy, immediately offered his nightly resting-place – his and that of the other two young male staff.

Taken aback, I said, in what I hoped was a polite but firm tone, 'Thank you, but I couldn't possibly take your room.'

'No problem,' said Tuan grinning, 'is not room, but same-same as room; small bit different.'

I realized after this that things were going badly. I was getting into a situation where I would be unable to turn down what was, after all a very kind offer and, I felt, a terrible imposition on my hosts.

'You look, is here, my room.'

Moving towards a door beside the bar, Tuan opened it and gestured me inside. Once in, there was almost no space to turn round and go back out again. I was in the hotel's linen and toilet-roll cupboard and Tuan was proudly patting a large box-like chest and saying, 'This my bed and my friends' bed, is very good, you very OK here!'

With a heart as heavy as the proverbial lead I stepped gingerly forward and felt the top of the chest, which was the same solid black wood as the pillars and lobby furniture. Not wanting to seem ungracious, but with visions of rigor mortis the next morning, I tapped the top of the chest and said, 'Hmm, very hard!'

It was the worst thing I could have done. Tuan, who had the same rather unnatural hyperactivity I'd noticed in many Vietnamese men his age, leapt into action. 'No problem, no problem,' he said gleefully and opening the chest pulled out seven thin cotton sheets, laying each one carefully over the chest. Finished, he stood back and admired his handiwork.

Not quite believing what was happening, I lost what reserves of tact were left to me and, leaning forward, tapped the chest again.

'Still very hard,' I said ungratefully.

'No problem,' Tuan said, smiling broadly and pointing at my haunches, 'you very fat.'

I tried to splutter but gave up and laughed instead – it was that or punch him, but I remembered just in time that it was caddish to hit people smaller than myself and that temporary insanity caused by crashing hormones might not stand up in a Vietnamese criminal court. And after all, it was true, I was bigger than him by several inches, both vertically and horizontally. In reality I was grateful to Tuan and having recovered from the 'fat' allegation, thanked him profusely, glad to be alone with Norman Lewis and Dr Lo's pills, both of which I decided would be required to get any sort of rest in the linen cupboard.

The two American couples piled, separately, into my cupboard and congratulated me, though I wasn't sure what for, except perhaps having escaped the Dutchman who was now hanging over the balcony waving his limbs like a demented marionette to the discreet delight of the Vietnamese passing below him. I hoped he wouldn't vomit before he passed out; if he vomited *after* he passed out then there would be a good chance he'd choke to death.

By 11 p.m., everything had ground to a halt, the bar was closed, guests had returned to sleep and even the Dutchman was quieter. The narrow street beyond the large wooden doors of the hotel was almost silent as I retreated into my boudoir, suspended my mosquito net off a peg already hung with men's shirts, tucked it carefully and pointlessly around and under the seven sheets and generally made myself comfortable. I realized, as I made my nightly spider round, that the planks making up the cupboard didn't always meet, which meant there were gaps of several inches on both 'walls' that faced into the lobby area, giving a clear view in, especially if the cupboard light was on. I decided to undress with the light off, which was easy, as light from the lobby poured in anyway, the cupboard being merely a box without a lid. I thought it unlikely that I would be disturbed by other guests' comings and goings as there was no nightlife in Hoi An unless one made it oneself. I was topless when the door opened suddenly and one of the young bar staff whose 'bedroom' I'd usurped came into the tiny space and, grinning at me as I sat on the chest/bed, turned on the light and began to undress slowly and to my mind quite deliberately.

A cupboard *and* a striptease, I thought as I covered my breasts with a T-shirt and my confusion with a stiff upper lip. 'He can't be doing this on purpose, he just can't,' I said to myself; but despite the culture differences and the language barrier, I knew well enough that the youth was enjoying himself and I looked at his rather-too-thin-for-my-taste body in a new light. After what seemed like hours but was only minutes, he finished changing and, smiling, left.

Alone at last, I lay reading Norman Lewis' account of his meeting with the last emperor, Bao Dai, during an imperial hunting trip to Buon Ma Thuot in the Central Highlands, the furthest extent of Lewis' journey in Vietnam. In 1950 Buon Ma Thout was an even more remote destination than in the '90s and one which Lewis had reached with some difficulty. The area immediately below it, reaching south and west towards the Cambodian border, is marked on Lewis' map as 'Unexplored Territory'. I envied my fellow Welshman for having been in a country when its maps still held such magic words; it all conjured up images of Victorian explorers hacking their way through dense jungle towards the cooking pots of unfriendly tribespeople. This image was actually not so far from the truth in 1950, when large numbers of the various tribal peoples living in this area of Vietnam were still predominantly animists, despite the best efforts of French and other missionaries. Tribes such as the M'nong, Rhades and Jarai maintained interesting and reprehensible practices which they contrived to hide from the censorious eyes of the foreign men of God. Lewis had great respect and concern for the minority peoples he met and wrote about; less so some of the missionaries, one of whom he described as collecting the souls of the tribe '...with the not very fierce pleasure that others collect stamps'.

Sitting in my cupboard holding a torch to the pages of *A Dragon Apparent*, I particularly envied Lewis his ability to disappear into remote areas of Vietnam, only to be offered a flight out on the Emperor's own private plane.

'Those were the bloody days,' I said to myself just as a strange noise sounded in the lobby. Closing the book, my decision to swallow one of the few, now precious, little blue pills was made urgent by Tuan and his guitar striking up a fearful rendition of 'Hotel California' only metres away. The whole experience was becoming quite surreal and as I thought of the words of the song – which I had to recall from memory as I couldn't quite make out Tuan's version – I began to have paranoid imaginings about hotels where one could check out anytime but never leave, and Sartre's 'No Exit' vision of hell began to form in my mind. I saw myself forever in the toilet-roll cupboard with the Dutchman repeatedly slurring, 'Amsterdam is the best place in the world for having a good time with men and women,' whilst running on the spot and flapping his elbows up and down like a flightless bird to ensure maximum odour dispersion. All the while Tuan would be singing, 'Don't worry about the hardness, feel the fat,' to the tune of 'She'll Be Coming Round the Mountain'.

'Just take the pill,' I commanded myself, 'take the bloody pill.' Very quietly I began to unscrew the cap of my mineral water bottle, but the plastic container popped with a sound like a Colt 45 backfiring which escaped through the slits in the cupboard walls and echoed round the lobby. The guitar paused and went silent, everything was suddenly absolutely still and I held my breath. Then I heard a gentle scratching on the unlockable door of my retreat, followed by Tuan's jolly voice whispering, ' 'Allo. You want man?'

I froze, unable to decide whether to laugh or scream. A man was the last thing on my mind at that moment and Tuan didn't quite fit the category anyway. There's young and there's young; I'd always thought paedophilia unpleasant and though I guessed Tuan to be about 17, he looked not a day over 12. I sat clutching at my water bottle and stiff upper lip again until I heard soft steps moving away from my door and the voices of the three youths outside joining the guitar for the umpteenth massacre of the Eagles' classic song.

Mercifully, Dr Lo ensured a reasonable period of sleep, which was disturbed at 2 a.m. and 4 a.m. by the separate entrances of two exceedingly butch Frenchmen I'd noticed earlier in the day breasting their way around the lobby, each an *alloyage* of Querelle and Beau Geste. Then I passed out again, only to be woken permanently at 6 a.m. by Tuan and his companions, who had slept on the marble floor of the lobby, setting about their daily chores. I have subsequently read that Midazolam, the drug in the blue pills, induces short-term memory loss, which is why they're used for pre-ops and anaesthesia. This was a side-effect which I never had the good fortune to experience.

The next day Tuan was all polite smiles, the night's experience never referred to by so much as a glance. But I'd had enough of the cupboard and also felt genuinely uncomfortable at seeing three other people sleeping on marble when I was merely on wood. Before any of the guests had a chance to leave their rooms, I darted from door to door enquiring whether anyone was moving on that day; no one was. The last door I knocked on opened very, very slowly and by only a few inches to reveal the handsome cropped head of the larger of the gay Frenchmen. The room behind him was dark and steamy and I had the distinct impression I'd interrupted something, if the face of the other man peering out from the shadows was anything to judge by. When, shortly afterwards, sitting in the lobby drinking tea, Tuan explained to me, with a nudge-nudge-wink-wink smile, that the noises at 2 a.m. and 4 a.m. had been the Frenchmen returning from a visit to *girls* at the Hoi An Hotel, I smiled right back.

I breakfasted with Patti and Skip, who told me that their night had been even more eventful than mine, with the Dutchman talking and singing to himself while staggering back and forth to the bathroom throughout the night. I'd noticed him as we left the hotel for breakfast, sitting very quietly on a stool at the lobby bar looking rather shrunken and unwell, his face probably reflecting the pulpy and discoloured state of his liver, and felt slightly sorry for him.

Later that morning, I met Annalena, a Swedish woman who was looking for someone to share her room at the Hoi An Hotel. Convinced after my earlier explorations that there would be no rooms free that day at the Vinh Hung, I agreed to share with Annalena at the Hoi An, which after all was only about 500 yards away. I was sorry to be parting from Patti and Skip, but our Christmas plans together were already laid. Now I had yet another companion.

The Hoi An was a 'proper' hotel. Large and with several wings set around open plant-filled courtyards, the central building was in a late colonial style. There was something rather compound-ish about it all which was at odds with the rest of the town and I wasn't particularly surprised to read that it had been a US Marine base during the war. I found it difficult to imagine large numbers of GIs walking round the quiet streets of Hoi An and wondered what the town had thought of them and them of it. Perhaps some were reminded of remote share-cropping homes in Arkansas or Kentucky.

The room was small but comfortable with the same built-in mosquito nets I'd used in Nha Trang and a large white tiled bathroom with the miracle of occasionally hot running water and a large porcelain bath – the Marines may have been surrounded by VC while in Hoi An, but at least they'd avoided the rigours of the toilet-roll cupboard. I was relieved that I was somewhere comfortable for

Christmas, and having put all my dirty laundry in the bath, to soak out the dried-in dust, I set off armed with a camera and water bottle to explore Hoi An with Annalena.

chapter *seven*

AN UNTOUCHED TOWN

Some guidebooks suggest that a day is sufficient time to spend in Hoi An, but that's misleading, underestimating the town's attractions and ignoring its hidden treasures. My entire Christmas holiday was spent in Hoi An, sightseeing with Annalena and meeting up to eat, drink and generally make merry with the two American couples. We all agreed that for such a small place Hoi An has many charming architectural and historic secrets worth discovering, not least because there may be few other places in Vietnam which will so richly repay such interest.

Hoi An, to use its modern Vietnamese name, was a seaport nearly 2,000 years ago and central to the kingdom of Champa in which it lay. Recent archaeological finds suggest that by the third century BC, the region was already inhabited by the Late Iron-Age Sa Huynh culture which was related to the Dong Son culture of the Vietnamese north. Arab and Persian ships stopped at this town when Rome still held sway over the known world and by the middle of this millennium, Faifo, as it was then known, was one of the busiest ports of South East Asia.

The military successes of Vietnamese hero and subsequent emperor Le Loi against the Chinese in 1428 initiated a period of calm and relative prosperity in the north and allowed expansion south into Champa and west into Laos. By the sixteenth century, central areas of the country were under Vietnamese control and seaports like Faifo flourished. By the seventeenth, eighteenth and nineteenth centuries, the height of its mercantile significance, the port, which was contemporary with Macao and Malacca, was an almost obligatory stop for ships from across the globe. Traders from Holland, Portugal, China, India, Britain, Japan and North America came for the numerous luxury goods that Hoi An could provide. All across the world, merchants' eager wives waited with excited anticipation each time the Faifo ships came in. Bales of the high quality Chinese and Japanese silks, muslins and locally made cotton sold in Faifo became gowns and underclothing for the rich and famous of Europe and its colonies; during the fifteenth and sixteenth centuries paper bought in Faifo fed the presses of the newly invented printing machines of Caxton and Manutius; porcelain almost as thin as paper held the teas that the city also provided; nuts, pepper and other spices were for delicacies and special occasions in palaces, castles and manor houses; opium and other plant extracts provided a sophisticated herbal unknown to many European and New World physicians; mother-of-pearl and ivory made enviable decorations and jewellery; fine beeswax supplied candles far sweeter than suet-scented tallow, while sulphur and lead were vital to the arms trade of a continuously warring Europe.

Vietnamese ships based at Faifo during the fifteenth and sixteenth centuries voyaged throughout the South China Seas and the Indian Ocean to Burma, Thailand and the islands of Indonesia, returning with their wooden hulls filled with goods that would pass, in time, still further westwards. As in Europe and the Middle East during this era, trading companies maintained their own quarters and compounds, and merchants arriving in Faifo in the spring would stay until summer, competing for the best wares available. Some came and stayed permanently; the Chinese and Japanese presence from that period is evident today in the architecture I saw in and around Hoi An. About 1,500 ethnic Chinese still live in the town among their 60,000 Vietnamese neighbours. Following the 1633 *sakoku*, the xenophobic decision of the Japanese ruling dynasties to close their country to outside contact, especially with Westerners, international trade was forbidden to Japanese by imperial decree and no more Japanese junks visited Faifo. The tombs of some of their number, dating from the 1620s to '40s, are still there, standing under twisted trees, surrounded by the ubiquitous ducks and their keepers. I looked at the stele of the merchant Yajirobei and for a few moments thought of this man who had never returned to Japan after his home-land had shut out the world and who had died here in Faifo, a for-eigner among foreigners. I was moved to see that despite his exile, which I guessed to be self-imposed, his tomb faced north-east, towards Japan and home.

It was not easy to imagine the activity of earlier centuries as I walked along the present-day waterfront of Hoi An; fishing and tourism are what engages most of the small boats plying in and out of the town today. My imagination wasn't helped by the fact that around 100 years ago, the river Thu Bon, at whose mouth Faifo was built, silted up, making the port unnavigable for deep-water ship-ping. The result of this geological phenomenon was the rise of Da Nang as a port and centre of commerce, eclipsing, and paradoxically preserving, the literally stranded Faifo.

Hoi An has a multiplicity of historic buildings, one of the oldest being the small but delightful Chuc Thanh pagoda. The history of its making is written across one of the ceiling beams, but it was in Chinese lettering and so I never discovered anything beyond the fact that it was built in 1454. Compared with the pagoda I'd visited in Cholon, the Chuc Thanh was almost primitive, but I preferred its quiet simplicity, its archaic bells and gongs, some many hundreds of years old. Looking almost as old were the few elderly Buddhist monks who still tend and live in the pagoda. I watched them sitting cross-legged or strolling contemplatively within the small compass that was their home and wondered who would take their place when they were no longer in the physical body. Were there young monks eager to live in this pleasant spot, away from the bustle of the cities? Would the pagoda fall into disrepair and finally disappear, or would the government maintain it simply as a tourist attraction? There was no one to answer these questions.

With the exception of the pagoda and the Ba Le well, which has two claims to fame – it's believed to date back to Cham times, a period roughly equivalent to the European Dark Age and medieval periods, and is also the well from which all water used in the prepa-ration of the Hoi An noodle speciality *cau lau* must be drawn – most older construction in Hoi An dates from post-1780s. Between the 1770s and '80s the town was rebuilt following its virtual destruction during the Tay Son Rebellion, an event which completely changed the political structure of Vietnam, ushering in a new imperial dynasty. The ousted ruling family, nominal descendants of the wonder-worker Le Loi, appealed through French Jesuits in Thailand for French assistance against the revolutionaries. Ironically, the king appealed to in 1787 was Louis XVI, shortly to lose both throne and head in a revolution of his own. But this marked the beginning of serious French interest in Vietnam and within 100 years of its rebuilding, Hoi An had become the regional administrative centre for the French colonial government, which ironically ensured its continuing importance despite the loss of its harbour.

Walking along Phan Boi Chau Street which borders the waterfront, I looked at the block of attractive French colonial buildings still maintained in shades of yellow and white, their roof terraces and balconies nestling among the high palms, and thought that, with a slight leap of the imagination, this could be almost anywhere from Martinique to Antibes.

On Christmas morning, Annalena and I decided to hire a rowing boat from the Phan Boi Chau dock to take us around the An Hoi peninsula. It was a mistake. Scarcely had we set foot on the small harbour than about 30 screaming harridans seized us from all sides and began literally dragging and pulling at us and our clothing as an inducement to go in *their* boat, rather than their neighbours'. My first thought was to walk away and forgo the ride, having learnt in the past that there's little pleasure to be gained from such situations. But eventually we allowed ourselves to be half dragged to the large wooden canoe of the most persistent woman and her co-paddler and stepped in, glad to be out of the worst of the mêlée which was continuing in our wake.

The woman pushed off immediately, keen to escape the Furies still pursuing us. I was quickly fascinated by the way the two women handled the boat as though it were a toy. Sitting with one leg outstretched and the foot of the other leg pressing into the extended knee, a position which recalled the Hanged Man of the Tarot, each woman paddled with a single light oar and, with only a few strokes, the boat darted away over the olive green water. No sooner were we away from the shore than the vociferous woman in the front turned and, holding out her hand, asked me, I assumed, to pay for the trip. The narrowness of the craft meant we were sitting in single file, the two paddlers fore and aft with Annalena and me in the middle. I turned to Annalena and we agreed that we shouldn't pay until the end of the ride. We'd settled on 2,000 dong and I explained as best I could to the woman that she'd get it when we returned to the shore. She seemed to accept this and leaving her colleague to paddle, lolled idly for the next few minutes. But we had only gone another few hundred yards when to my annoyance she again asked me to pay her. She did this regularly for the next 20 minutes, leaving all the work to the unfortunate woman paddling away at the back and turning to face me with bony hand outstretched.

Despite growing irritation, I was loathe to turn back because there were fascinating sights to be seen. As we moved south, keeping the shore of the An Hoi peninsula close to our right, we passed several sampans moored to poles sunk into the muddy bottom of the river. Looking at them closely, I found it difficult to believe that whole families lived in what were, in effect, wood and rattan baskets. Spotlessly clean clothes hung on mooring lines and smiling faces peered out at us from under the woven eaves of the sampans' roofs. Beside one, a beautiful young woman washed her hair, standing fully dressed in the water which, I was surprised to see, reached only to her breasts. One or two sampans had aerials on their roofs and I wondered what sort of generator they must have to power a TV. The boat-dwellers seemed to live in a permanent crouching position, the roof of the boat being no more than 3 feet at its highest point. I tried, unsuccessfully, to imagine myself in a continual squat.

Because the woman in front had decided paddling was beneath her, our movement was very slow. After about 20 minutes we reached a cleared shore area on the peninsula, where two quite large wooden boats were under construction. Hoi An has a long tradition of wooden boat-building and I was fascinated to get a glimpse of how things were done before the days of steel and fibreglass. Each boat was about 20 feet high and supported by wooden scaffolding. A man sawing at something while standing between the boats was dwarfed by his own constructions. Unlike much workmanship I'd seen in Vietnam, these boats looked perfect; their prows curved down to the swell of the mid-section and on the deck of each stood a multi-windowed cabin. Everything was still in natural wood, unpainted, and I could smell the wood resin as we passed. Though I couldn't identify the type of wood being used for certain, it had the colour of teak. When finished, these boats would be red or blue or green, with vigilant caricature eyes painted either side of their prow to protect the craft from the dangers of the seas. The eyes recalled pictures seen in books, as a child, of Jason and the Argonauts. Medea had thrown the carefully chopped pieces of her brother's body over the side of a ship such as these. Watching the boat-builders, the sampan-dwellers and particularly the fishermen whose canoes raced with such skill, skimming across the calm surface of the water to drop a line into its depths, I was aware that Hoi An's extraordinary combination of tranquillity and vibrancy made it far more than merely the sum of its considerable history.

As we approached another boatyard further around the peninsula, the woman in charge gestured towards it and turned our craft, clearly intending to stop there. Annalena poked me in the back and said we should go on. I completely agreed, as a ruffianly collection of men had assembled on the shore in front of the boats and I could see no purpose to us stopping there beyond some devious notion in the woman's head. I pointed forwards, gesturing away from the boatyard, and again, the claw-like hand shot out to clutch at my knee while the woman whined, 'You give dollars. Yes?'

I could stand it no longer and, turning to Annalena, said so. We turned and headed back, both of us annoyed and disappointed that our trip had been spoilt. We had a small and simple revenge on our return, however, giving 1,000 of the promised 2,000 dong to the woman who had irritated us so much and 2,000 to the woman at the back who had silently and patiently done all the work.

That afternoon we met Skip and Patti and had lunch in our favourite waterfront restaurant. The big Christmas blowout was planned for that evening when we would meet up with Paul and Anna for dinner. When I'd moved to the Hoi An Hotel, Skip and Patti had found a room in a private house in the heart of the market. This was illegal, as only registered, tax-paying properties were allowed to rent rooms to foreigners in Vietnam and there was much anxious whispering and clandestine carrying-on before the deal was struck. I had considered taking the second available room myself before meeting Annalena, but I had found the cramped, windowless space and dark green walls a little depressing. Because the owners feared prying eyes seeing foreigners going in and out there were restrictions which meant Patti and Skip had to be out of the building throughout the day and couldn't return before dark. The combination of dark room and restricted movement made up my mind against the place, but I enjoyed seeing the inside of an average urban Vietnamese home.

In the early afternoon Patti walked up to my room at the Hoi An and there I finally swapped a past-life regression for acupuncture. Patti was a wonderful subject for regression and I thoroughly enjoyed her former life story, which was as positive and vibrant as Patti herself. Annalena joined us in time for my acupuncture. She'd asked to watch and I'd agreed. Patti was very good at her work; the needling was mercifully painless and her manner soothing but professional. Left alone in the dark while the needles did their job, I half listened to the voices of my companions as they sat outside my window in the hotel garden. Patti had sensed I needed to be alone, if only for 20 minutes, and it did me good – the quiet and the feeling of being cared for, however briefly, was a good Christmas present.

We walked back towards the waterfront together, three blonde women from very different countries and different walks of life and yet in some ways so very similar. Annalena had a cool Scandinavian detachment and Patti the warmth of the best of America. And me? I was still discovering what the phoenix had to teach me. I wondered briefly, as we walked side by side, whether we all three looked the same to the local people sitting eating or playing in their doorways? A photograph taken an hour or so later with Anna shows four blonde women smiling under the reflected light of a red and yellow sun-umbrella.

Leaving Patti to rejoin her husband, Annalena and I walked past hibiscus-hung houses and restaurants draped in pink and white bougainvillaea, vivid against the bright blue of the sky, to the marketplace which lies between Tran Phu and Bach Dang Streets and edges the waterfront. Though Hoi An had fewer street food vendors than

I had seen in Saigon, eating still took place with the same regularity and vigour, and it was there in the market that the process began. We watched young women and girls sort and carry endless bundles of leaves, grasses and herbs for flavouring, wrapping and baking in. It appears that almost all market traders are female; I don't recall ever seeing a single adult male stallholder. The principle behind this one-sided arrangement as far as I could see was that women are masters, or mistresses perhaps, of the hard sell; and of course, of the hard bargain. The only males to be seen in markets were the offspring of the vendors and shoppers, as yet too young to be truly male.

I had noticed that animals in Vietnam, up until the point where they ceased to be viewed as living entities and turned into a prospective meal, seemed to have a rather pleasant life. The Hoi An pigs, unruffled by the dangers of passing bicycles and ignorant of their impending demise, dug themselves into the roadside dirt with grunts of ecstasy, their small wary eyes peering shortsightedly at tourists who pointed and laughed, unused to this juxtaposition of urban and rural. The ubiquitous brown and white ducks meanwhile hung from bicycle handlebars in Hoi An as they had hung from the scooter handlebars in Saigon and the roof of the delta ferry truck.

We walked first through the butchery stalls where women who could have been any age up to and including 100 sat motionless in front of small heaps of flesh from which even the flies seemed to have absented themselves from lack of enthusiasm. A closer look revealed the flesh to be little more than lumps of yellow fat with particles of pinkish tissue adhering tenuously. The antiquated weighing scales had globules of fat stuck to them, as did the greasy fingers of the vendors, who wrapped their sales in used writing paper. I imagined quite a few Hoi Anese must have eaten the imprint of a shopping list or a maths lesson along with their pork.

Not being squeamish, I found the meat stalls quite interesting and wished I could ask what animal the bits of fat and meat had once belonged to, but Annalena wanted to move on, so we made our way towards the deeper recesses of the building where ancient crones, older even than the lady-butchers, sat behind twinkling dirty brown globes which I was told were sugar. Others guarded piles of white powder, possibly salt, which might have resembled a giant haul of cocaine had the crones been more animated.

Under their conical hats the cheeks of the oldest women were so completely sunken they looked like silent wizened babies. A few women spoke to us as we passed and once, when a wrinkled but extraordinarily powerful hand shot out and gripped my arm, I turned to find myself staring into a cavernous mouth, lips stained dark red from betel juice and the few remaining teeth coated in the black enamel which was popular with the middle and upper classes of the East for tens of centuries. Enamelling was held to reduce the animal appearance of the human mouth. In *A Dragon Apparent*, Lewis records a marvellous story of seventeenth-century European merchants visiting a Vietnamese emperor, who apparently almost fainted with horror when he saw the traders' white teeth as they bowed and smiled ingratiatingly. The Emperor is reported to have remarked to his courtiers something along the lines of, 'Who are these barbarians who dare to come before me with the teeth of dogs?'

Enamelling the teeth went out of fashion during the colonial years, which gave me a rough idea of the age of some of the stallholders.

The remotest and darkest corridors of stalls held some of the most entertaining goods. Beautiful conical hats, of far better quality than my Cholon purchase, were plain outside but inside were decorated with brightly coloured patterns of incredible intricacy. How very different from Western culture, I thought, to put all the beauty on the inside for the mind of its wearer to take private pleasure in. Plastic toys vied for space with face cloths and towels; sweet rice cakes wrapped in bamboo lay piled on trays next to scarves and rolls of fabric. Plain earthenware bowls stood in neatly stacked rows untouched by bicycles and close passing feet. A very beautiful and elegant old woman sold great clutches of incense sticks and what I supposed to be some kind of medicines, along with containers full of suspicious-looking substances. I tried asking in French what the boxes and bags held, but either the woman spoke only Vietnamese or my linguistic skills were rubbish, or possibly both.

Before leaving the covered part of the market we found the sellers of silk and cotton. Silk is not locally produced, but cotton is still woven in Hoi An; I heard but never saw the clacking cotton looms which many of the town houses seemed to possess. An astonishing range of fabric was available from the many stalls we passed, most of which had seamstresses cutting patterns with large blunt scissors and stitching hour after hour at ancient French treadle machines. As I watched them peering at the rhythmic motion of the needles in the half-light, I wondered how much the stallholders paid the women who worked for them and guessed it wasn't much. We were promised 'a new wardrobe overnight' for almost nothing by a particularly insistent woman whom I thought of as 'the Hatted Claw' because she wore a bizarre velvet creation on her head and had the rather unpleasant habit of reaching out and grabbing the wrists of prospective customers. Having pulled us into her lair, where she sat hung about with swathes and bales of beautiful fabrics, she proceeded to stroke my wrist with long curving fingernails which set my teeth thoroughly on edge while ingratiatingly and forcibly doing the hardest sell I've ever come across. When the HC thought my attention was lapsing, she recovered it with a swift dig of the fingernails. I had always known that Western men make grave errors of judgement when they perceive Eastern women as placid and accommodating, now I felt it – literally. Annalena, more utilitarian in her attitude to such things than I was, had two garments made; I agreed to a black silk suit, but after initial sartorial misunderstandings, gave up in despair and decided against it, to the enormous pique of the Hatted Claw, who was obliged to return my deposit.

We exited the covered market towards the open air fruit and vegetable stalls. In a different way, the exotic colours and fresh smells that greeted us were almost as overpowering as the dead meat on the butchers' stalls had been. The heat of the sun penetrating the cloth awnings of the stalls caused the various fruits to render up their scent even more powerfully than usual. The sugary odour of pineapples, rambutans and jackfruit mingled with the stink of durian. The vivid reds of tomatoes and chillis, unaffected by chemical treatments, was a wonder next to the emerald greens of *choy sam*, spinach and watercress which rested on large leaves carefully arranged in wide flat-bottomed baskets. Lemongrass lay in bundles tied with the stalks of other plants, and cabbages, sweet potatoes and spring onions jostled for space on the stalls with white-green duck eggs and plastic washing-up bowls filled with ready-made salads of beansprouts and green and red peppers. But most exotic of all I found the pale orange heaps of candied kumquats, some of which I bought, only to find they looked far better than they tasted.

That evening, Christmas night, Annalena and I met our American friends as planned at our favourite restaurant on the Bach Dang Street waterfront. Annalena had been uncertain whether she would spend her evening with the Swedish contingent a few restaurants along, but at the last minute she decided to stay with the English language crowd and there were six of us as we sat down to our Christmas dinner. Hoi An had some of the very best food I ate in Vietnam and our five-course meal was the epitome of this. I even got used to the dead reptile in the corner of the restaurant. It lay as though asleep, curled for all time – or until the alcohol surrounding it was exhausted, anyway – at the bottom of a large glass jar. It looked like a small python, but suspended in alcohol the unfortunate creature had lost the distinctiveness of its markings, which had become blurred and brown. I was told by the restaurant owner, a very pleasant and helpful man who took great delight in seeing his customers clear their plates, that the alcohol became impregnated with the essence of the snake and when drunk would impart healthful properties to the drinker.[1]

One of my enduring memories of Vietnam was the sight of the naked buttocks of this restaurant owner's two-year-old child disappearing up a winding staircase, giving a juvenile but very fair rendition of the Euro-techno number 'No Limit'. He had the refrain, 'No No, No No No No, No No No No, No No…' off rather well and only lost his way on encountering the words 'There's no limit', which he mumbled in a suitably unintelligible, technoish way not too dissimilar from the original. Make way Coca-Cola, I thought to myself, forget Robusta coffee futures, discotrash has hit Vietnam.

During the meal we were joined by a number of the street children whom we had come to know over the previous couple of days. One boy in particular seemed very attached to Paul and I'd noticed he'd always gravitate in Paul's direction whenever he came across him

---

1   I was subsequently informed in a letter from Patti and Skip in Vermont that it was cobra wine.

sitting in one of the numerous waterfront restaurants. On this occasion, the boy sat between Paul and myself and it became impossible to avoid noticing the child stroking the thick hair on the American's arms, then drifting to his chest and from there to his nipples. Paul seemed to find it all a grand joke and though it made me feel uncomfortable, for once I was at a loss for a comment. I turned to my food, only to discover a small light hand on my knee which speedily moved up to my thigh. I grasped the small wrist and placed the hand on the table where I could keep an eye on it. The child – he was probably about 12 or 13 years old and looked nine – was evidently related to an octopus. I found it curious that he thought that men could be groped publicly, but women only under the table. Discussing the incident later with Annalena, I said that I had been at a loss for words and with typical Scandinavian incisiveness she replied, 'Do you think Paul would have behaved like that in public with an American boy?'

'No, I'm sure he wouldn't,' I said.

'Precisely,' was Annalena's final comment.

The courses kept coming: shrimps in lemongrass and coriander on crispy pancakes; shark with lime, baked in bamboo leaves; chicken with rice and tender green vegetables; prawns, bigger than my hand, grilled with garlic and spices, lay temptingly on a bed of noodles. We were beginning to bloat, but the beer and Vietnamese wine kept coming. The dessert was pure French, a delicious *crème caramel*, which reminded me of the Portugese fort in India. All this was devoured to the repeated playing of 'Jingle Bells', courtesy of Pinky and Perky, a pair of plastic pig puppets beloved by British children of the 1960s. No one at the table but me understood the cultural significance of hearing Pinky and Perky singing in Hoi An. Suddenly I wished some of my friends from home were with me, just to share the tacky magic of the moment.

I had a moment of anxiety regarding the restaurant when I went to look for the toilet, which I found situated in the middle of the kitchen, its door literally inches away from the place where the women squatted on the floor washing plates and cutlery. So far, my journey had been problem free in the gut department. Looking at the dish-washers as they smiled up at me, I wondered if all that was about to change.

By 9 p.m. we were all suffering a gastronomic collapse, but the waterfront was just coming to festive life. Parties of foreigners strolled along the pavement between the parasolled tables or ate and drank amid the increasing noise and smoke of long ribbons of firecrackers. Boys who had been trying to sell us postcards for days seemed to give up all thought of sales and flung themselves into the spirit of the thing, which must have been almost exclusively aimed at foreigners, as the Christian population of Hoi An is largely confined to the European missionaries buried in the churchyard. Dignified elderly women emerged from the depths of restaurants, houses and shops to sit on the steps and observe the goings-on. Looking at their faces, ancient yet serene, I thought of all the things such women must have seen during their lives – not merely the ordinary events of the years since the turn of the last century, the births, deaths and marriages, or the natural events, the annual floods, famines and plagues, but the interminable wars, against French, Japanese and Americans, all of whom were represented in Hoi An that Christmas night and all of whom had sought to subjugate these people whose guests we now were. Taking a photo of one such woman who, her grandson informed us, was 93 years old, I noticed that despite her age and slowness of movement she retained a delicious vanity, removing her headscarf and smoothing her beautiful white hair into place while she waited patiently for me to focus on her.

Tired, not entirely sober and deafened by the sound of the firecrackers, which, after the excitement of the first dozen or so began to resemble an artillery barrage at close quarters, we left Bach Dang Street and headed for the roof terrace of the Vinh Hung Hotel where Paul and Anna still had the room beside the balcony. We put candles around us, avoiding the washing line where garments from across the globe hung to dry, and bringing out the remains of our duty-free purchases, carried on the Christmas spirit. It was all very pleasant indeed, relaxed and relaxing. Around us, rockets and firecrackers continued to light up the night and create a pall of lead fumes which hung, dispersing only slowly in the still, mild air. Even the occasional shooting star could be seen moving across the sky. Our conversation was simply a continuation of the first day's chatter on the hotel balcony, but the day and its festivities made it all seem more significant, more intimate. We told each other small secrets then smiled with embarrassment. At about midnight, we went our separate ways, Patti and Skip to their room in the now silent market, Annalena and myself to the Hoi An Hotel and shades of long departed GIs, Paul and Anna to their room beside the eventful corridor.

The following day Annalena decided was to be a shopping day. I was perfectly happy with this suggestion as Hoi An was the only place I'd yet seen in Vietnam where I could have happily spent quite a lot of money. Shopping there turned out to be a marvellous experience. Annalena was of the 'I shop therefore I am' school of thought and she successfully hustled me around innumerable houses and places of interest I would simply not have seen except on a spending safari. Many shops were in the beautiful old merchant houses whose owners, elegant and sophisticated women clearly used to dealing with a cosmopolitan public, were a mine of fascinating information about the products, the house and the town itself. In one particular old wooden house we were shown around by an elderly lady who spoke excellent, though somewhat antiquated French, liberally quoting from works of literature, some of which I recognized, to her great delight. I saw how several generations shared the same quarters and became aware that I was being shown people's lives, not merely their business property, and this privilege was added to by the gift of French biscuits which the same very genteel old lady had baked herself.

Other Hoi An houses we visited or passed by. The homes of barbers, carpenters and bakers were similar to those all over Vietnam. Many resembled small neon-lit billiard halls, some sported karaoke machines (a great favourite throughout Vietnam), all had TV sets at varying degrees of loudness. This was one face of the new Vietnam, homogenous, colourful and youthful, but it seemed to me too much part of Western culture to warrant closer investigation.

The detailed construction of the antique buildings, however, repaid close scrutiny. The same black wood as in the Vinh Hung Hotel was everywhere, in pillars, roof beams, joists, screens and furniture. I realized that I was seeing the interior of middle-class houses, not typical merely of this part of Vietnam, but probably, with minor differences, of the whole of South East Asia a century or two ago.

Perhaps the best preserved building in Hoi An is the Tan Ky house, which was built for a wealthy Vietnamese merchant shortly after the Tay Son Rebellion. The building is a perfect amalgam of Chinese, Japanese and local styles. The Escheresque roof beams are of Japanese design, but the inlaid poetry hanging from the columns is Chinese, with each perfect character formed in the shape of a moving bird. I didn't know what particular style my favourite piece of the Tan Ky house reflected, but for me, the carving of crossed scimitars wrapped in silk ribbon depicted the essence of Vietnam: strength within flexibility. It reminded me of a story I'd read as a child, concerning the mythological twelfth-century trial of strength between Richard Coeur de Lion and Sala-ah-din. The story tells that Richard who, despite, or perhaps because of, his homosexuality, knew how to be macho, roared loudly and swung his massive broadsword at an anvil, splitting it asunder. Sala-ah-din merely smiled at this display and, drawing a scarf of silk so fine as to be almost invisible, laid it over the blade of his scimitar. So sharp was Sala-ah-din's weapon that the silk cut itself, divided by its own weight. I don't think the look on Richard's face was recorded, which I always felt was a great oversight.

Near the Japanese Bridge, which reflects the simplicity of Japanese style in a sea of Chinese and Vietnamese flourish, we found another beautiful building, the Phung Hao house. For the first time in Vietnam, I became aware of class and class distinction. The women who lived in these houses were perhaps not wealthy, but belonged to a very different social class from any I had yet seen. They had different faces, hands and body shapes; their mothers and grandmothers had almost certainly never done menial work. Educated, cultured and graceful, the woman of the Phung Hao house, as part of the business of selling the beautiful cotton embroidery for which the region is famous, gave us tiny cups of strong black tea, the equivalent, I suspected, of ristreto coffee. The small candied kumquats she offered us were divine and bore little resemblance to the large tasteless ones I'd bought in the market; it was all I could do not to impolitely eat the plateful. All the things we were shown were beautiful. I particularly liked the exuberance of the white tablecloths covered with heavily embroidered dragons, chrysanthemums and characters loaded with symbolism.[2]

Later, sitting in our favourite bottled python/cobra restaurant, Annalena and I drank beer and observed the most discreet prostitution either of us had seen. A very pretty brother and sister couple (we were told this by the restaurateur), both dressed in traditional white Vietnamese dress, picked up Western men on the waterside and rowed them presumably to a sampan or perhaps merely to a discreet island where the transaction took place. Together the pair had it all worked out, I thought, providing mutual protection and offering services to cover most tastes. It all looked so simple, quiet and even dignified, a million miles from the back streets of King's Cross or Earl's Court in London.

Annalena and I had talked of when and how we would move on. Both of us were heading north to Hué and we agreed to find and share a car. I believed I'd learnt my lesson with transport after the Saigon-Nha Trang fiasco and, having been told that the scenery between Da Nang and Hué was some of the most spectacular in Vietnam, I was loathe to travel any way other than by train or car. I would have liked to take the train the relatively short distance from Hoi An to Hué, but as Hoi An is not on a railway line, there was small chance of that.

Directly opposite the Hoi An Hotel, we saw a sign advertising tours and trips by car and minibus, and feeling luck was with us, we arranged with the two professional-seeming women who ran the business from their sitting room for a car to Hué the next morning. We were told that for $16 we would be taken to Hué and have three 'tourist stops' of our choice. We decided to stop at Marble Mountain and Lang Co, a beach peninsula exactly between Da Nang and Hué. The third stop, we thought, we could simply take as it came. It all sounded very civilized and straightforward and we were told that the car would be new and Japanese, which gave me a slightly sinister sense of *déjà vu*. I had told Annalena all about the Nha Trang episode, but she reassured me that things would be fine and, of

2 Some months later I saw the saw the same embroidered pieces in a leading London department store, priced at more than 20 times what the gracious saleswoman at the Phung Hao house had suggested.

course, as usual, I wanted to believe it.

The following morning we were outside the 'travel bureau' at 8.30 with all our bags. There was no sign of a car, but the woman in charge said the driver would be along very soon. I had diarrhoea and nausea and the PMS problem was beginning to peak; getting out of bed had resembled the clash of the Titans as my mind and body refused to co-operate.

At 9 a.m. a large black Pontiac hove into sight. I viewed it with a sinking feeling. This was undoubtedly our chariot. I was livid with hormonal temper and gastric disturbance. Did these people not know that Japan and America were different places; that 'new' meant within the last two years, not the last two decades? Any American car *had* to be a minimum of 20 to 25 years old. I was either going to kick something, burst into tears, lose control of my bowels or all three at once. Summoning all my reserves of tact and pleasantness in order to maintain face, I demanded to know what the company was playing at – this was not what we'd agreed to pay for. Despite my tales, Annalena was rather taken aback by it all, 'inefficiency' not being a common word in the Swedish language, and when we were told that it was this car or nothing, I was tempted to stay in Hoi An. But I'd checked out of the hotel; perhaps I would be reduced to the toilet-roll cupboard again?

We got in and I found that the car was in fact as different from the Nha Trang Renault of ill-fame as it was from a 1992 Honda. There was air-conditioning that still worked and the enormous seats had some springs remaining. Part of me thought it was a rather nice old car and probably more fun than a boring Honda. But the other, hormonally bitter and twisted, part of me remained bitter and twisted, refusing to be placated as I set off with yet another irritated driver on the next stage of the journey north.

chapter eight

NORTH TO HUE

From Hoi An to Hué is 66 miles of some of the most beautiful and varied scenery I was to see in Vietnam. The reasonably good road careers giddily down from mountain passes, crossing waterfalls and ravines before strolling gently alongside beaches and lagoons.

All things have a beginning, a middle and an end, and so too our journey; the middle was very good, the end was not too bad, but the beginning was a disaster. Having accepted the Pontiac, I'd assumed that everything else would follow smoothly, but it was not to be. Within minutes of setting off from Hoi An things got difficult with the driver when we asked him what road we were on.

'Very good road, very fast,' he said, smiling at us toothily in the rear view mirror.

'This road to Marble Mountain?' I asked, slipping into the ludicrous pidgin language that all foreigners seem to adopt in any country not their own. I knew that there were two roads from Hoi An to Da Nang and that we needed the Korean Highway, the route I'd taken from Da Nang airport to Hoi An on my arrival. The other road, National Highway 1, which I'd followed from Saigon to Nha Trang and which winds the entire length of the Vietnam coast from the delta to the Gulf of Tonkin, avoids Marble Mountain.

'This National Highway,' the driver replied. 'Very good road!'

'I'm sure it is,' I said testily, my hormonal aggravation beginning to crawl up and peer over the edge of the abyss into which I'd thrust it, 'but it doesn't pass Marble Mountain, does it?'

This last was a statement, not a question and the driver answered in the same vein. 'We go Hué, we no go Marble Mountain. You say you want go Hué, yes? This road very good Hué.'

At this point Annalena chipped in to remind the driver about the three 'tourist stops', but he merely shook his head bovinely and smiled the inane smile of the perfectly intelligent who have decided idiocy is the smarter part of valour. With an almost calculated synchronicity, the creature from the abyss hung poised to leap up and out of its pit as my oestrogen level plummeted down, down, down to an all-time record low. I said, teeth clamped firmly together to keep my voice steady, 'We are going to Marble Mountain, then to Lang Co, or we get out now and we do not pay you.'

The driver continued smiling and shaking his head, then made the fatal error of giggling. Something in me snapped and the creature leapt, grinning from ear to hideous ear like Grendel's mother on a bad day. Quite suddenly I didn't give a shit about 'face', I would in fact have been delighted to shit on someone's 'face' at that moment. I grabbed the driver by the shoulder, entirely careless of such minor problems as steering, and yelled, 'Stop the car now!' and as he ground to an abrupt halt I slammed my *Lonely Planet* guide – which Annalena and I had been using to illustrate our proposed route during the more amicable stage of the conversation – down beside him.

As I watched the blood begin to drain from his face, I felt it rushing into mine and using all my powers of voice projection – the efficacy of which I'd discovered on a BBC World Service programme about Churchill – in the enclosed space of the car, I bellowed, 'What's funny, eh?' I almost said 'mate', but recalled this wasn't Streatham. 'Go on, tell me what's funny!'

I knew perfectly well he didn't understand, but it made me feel better; it was tears or rage and the situation called for a bit of rage.

For the first time since I'd known her, I felt Annalena hesitate, uncertain of the route I was taking here, but I continued unabated, 'We *are* going to Marble Mountain and you *are* going to take us. Now!'

The driver's manner changed immediately, he became very amenable and instead of shaking his head, began nodding vigorously and saying, 'You want go Marble Mountain, ok, no problem, we go.' And so we set off.

I was completely exhausted. Any reserves of energy had been

sucked out of me by the temperamental display. I knew just how Sarah Bernhardt must have felt having wrapped a sword round her wooden leg during a particularly trying performance of *Hamlet*. I sat back in the enormous seat and wished I'd brought the sal volatile or at least a feather to burn. But we were going to Marble Mountain and I felt a mixture of emotions, some more base than others. There was triumph at having not allowed myself to be coerced and a rather crass satisfaction at getting my own way with a stranger through brute means, a satisfaction largely denied women in Western society. I considered whether perhaps PMS wasn't such a bad thing after all; perhaps it was merely suppression of the feelings it engendered that made me feel bad? But there was also sadness that in order to obtain what I had anyway been promised, I had been obliged to compromise myself and humiliate the driver, or possibly the reverse. I had had to assume a 'memsahib' role which I guiltily resented. I realized, on consideration, that the driver hadn't laughed at myself or Annalena, his nervous giggle had been merely a way of concealing his own agitation, a common enough response in the West but much more common in Far Eastern countries where the maintaining of face is so important. Perhaps he was embarrassed *for* me. Who can say?

We arrived at *Nui Ngu Hanh*, or Marble Mountain, at about 10 a.m. Close to, the five stacks, which are the only high ground for miles around, seemed to merge into a single stone. In shape, the white-grey marble hillocks resemble the stacks of the New Mexico and Arizona deserts, the flat-topped Dolomites of northern Italy and even the squared-off hills of the Lake District of north-east England. In scale, however, they are very small, perhaps not more than several times the size of London's Royal Albert Hall in circumference and a few hundred feet high.

The driver, now the epitome of amiability, dropped us at what we subsequently realized was the exit, but we set off up the long and extremely steep steps which led to the shrines and caves at the heart of the stacks. We had gone only about five yards when every street child and crone in Vietnam descended on us offering themselves as 'guides', though none of them knew any English other than the word 'guide' itself. If they had offered to carry me at this juncture I would probably have agreed to any sum they named, the hormonal temper having now converted to physical feebleness, but I hadn't quite reached that point of mental decrepitude that I needed to be led up a set of steps scarcely wide enough for two people to pass each other. This was one of the few places in Vietnam where I found that 'No' was not understood. Regardless of what we said, they kept on coming, fighting and clawing at each other in a desperate attempt to be chosen and therefore paid. I longed to be alone, or at least to have a space of more than a few centimetres around me; I longed to be lying in a cool room on a comfortable bed. The unpleasant combination of nausea and PMS was making me feel profoundly unwell, both physically and emotionally, and it took every ounce of mental fortitude to press on up the steepening steps in the blazing sun, tugged on and surrounded by screeching women and children. I wondered vaguely why I had struggled with the driver to come here and remembered something a good friend had said to me many years before, something about not asking for what you want because you might get it and then realize you didn't want it after all. But I knew the struggle hadn't been about coming to this place – not at all.

Each stack represents an element of the Vietnamese canon and as I staggered up the marble cliff face of Thuy Son, the stack representing the Water element of the universe, I wondered vaguely how they must live, these women. All day they waited for people like me to come along and hopefully give them a small amount of money that, having changed hands, would immediately become a large amount of money. What hopes and dreams did they cling to as they pounded up and down the stone steps of Thuy Son? I imagined dreams like jigsaw puzzles in which people like Annalena and myself were tiny pieces forming the outside of the picture, from which the central point, the heart of the puzzle, might one day be assembled, given enough clawing and guiding.

At the top of the steps we found ourselves among miniature stone canyons with further steps and paths leading on and on in a series of complex upward and downward movements. After passing bullet-holed gates, we came across two small cave shrines with ancient seated Buddhas guarded by aristocratic stone warriors who may themselves have been objects of veneration, as each had incense burning at his feet. On closer inspection, I discovered that the warriors looked rather like benign caricatures of Dr Fu Manchu. They had once been painted, but the red of their cloaks and the blue of their helmets now clung to the stone in traces only. These shrines were very simple indeed, merely stone plinths, with the figures blending into the natural surroundings of jagged rock.

The light was poor and the general greyness of the rock gave the whole scene a rather dejected and gloomy feel, so it was quite a shock to walk out of a shrine into the bright light once more and see an outrageously garish hexagonal ceramic gazebo nestling in a stone dell, surrounded by green trees and brilliant blue sky. No one was able to tell me the name of this gazebo and none of the guidebooks that I read either then or since have referred to it, but it was certainly the most colourful thing I saw in Vietnam and in its own way was very pretty. The colours were so vivid that it seemed newly painted. Over the base colours of white and pale yellow, green and blue dragons coiled and twisted themselves round six columns which sprang up from saffron plinths. The inner dome of the structure was covered with swirling forms, also in different shades of yellow. In the centre of the gazebo, which measured no more than 13 feet in diameter, was an above life-size Confucian statue. The plain white of the figure contrasted powerfully with the brilliance of its setting and drew the viewer's eye away from the colour and towards the white. I wondered whether this was deliberate and assumed it was. The subtlety of what had at first glance seemed truly vulgar was proving to be fascinating.

As Annalena forged ahead up the path that led to other paths and other stacks, I sat and rested on the low wall surrounding the pool immediately in front of the gazebo and on closer acquaintance realized that the colours which had at first seemed so loud were in fact a subtle mixture of shades and tones. The pillared dragons were not merely green and blue, but several different shades of green and blue highlighted with russets and blacks. It was clearly Chinese in style, but I spied blue key-patterns edging between the columns. Each side of the smaller second tier of the square-domed roof was illustrated with ceramic pictures of seascapes and mountains, lotus flowers and lilies, which recalled the Cholon pagoda I'd visited with Grace and Nicholas. But unlike the Cholon designs, the work on this gazebo, while perhaps inimical to most Western tastes, was very fine indeed, from its plinths to the lion acroteriae poised to leap out from among the teal-coloured roof tiles.

Beyond the gazebo, through its columns, I could see the grey seven-tiered spire of a very small Buddhist pagoda and thought how few places in the world would tolerate such literal religious closeness. We never got to the heart of the mountains and I never saw the cave which had housed the military hospital. But what I did see, I enjoyed very much and finally, despite the lack of peace, I was glad I'd come.

As Annalena and I descended the same steps we'd come up such a short time before, we could see the sea lying over to our left, beyond the hamlet of Non Nuoc which lay at the southern base of the Thuy Son stack. There is considerable dispute over where *the* China Beach actually was, much like the Darling Café disputes I was later to encounter in Ha Noi. The sandy shore of this China Beach was obscured by trees and outcrops of rock not important enough to be designated mountains. I thought with apprehension of the planned US development of the long unspoiled stretch of sand which would include not only the renovation of the existing hotel but the creation of a major new resort complex and championship golf course. I wondered who would play golf in such a place and had visions of ageing Vietnam veterans returning down this road to wave a nine-iron instead of a rifle. I would almost certainly never again look down at the dirt-track road that ran through the hamlet. In a year, maybe slightly more, this place would be gone in its present form, replaced by asphalt and concrete.

I had been desperate to find a toilet since leaving the car over an hour earlier, but an absence of facilities and failing that, privacy, had meant I was obliged to practise bladder control for far too long. As we reached the bottom of the steps, I rushed to the nearest villager's house, a small stone-built affair, and asked if I might use their toilet. Bemused, the woman pointed to the bushes at the back of the house. I couldn't know whether she had no toilet or whether I wasn't welcome to use the one she did have, but by now I didn't care. Having been given permission to urinate anywhere I liked behind her house, I proceeded to do so on a carpet of fallen leaves, only to discover at the very end of the event that I had relieved myself on someone's grave. The offended spirit punished me, I suspect, by putting a very nasty stinging plant within easy reach of my naked right buttock. I didn't sit easily for two days.

The driver had arranged to meet us at 11.30 a.m. and we walked towards our rendezvous past shop after open-fronted shop lining the single dirt street of Non Nuoc. The air was filled with the voices of shopkeepers summoning us to view, and the sounds of banging and scraping as the local stone-carvers chipped away at objects large and small. The main designs were either Buddhas or Hindu statues of dancing women and gods, designs dating back to the early medieval Hindu kingdom of Champa. There were also large bird and animal statues beautifully carved but far too heavy to be carried by anyone not permanently chauffeured. Annalena bought a sizeable Buddha statue for her mother. I bought a very small Cham head for a friend and an even smaller primitively carved piglet, weighing about an ounce, for myself. The saleswoman smiled on Annalena approvingly as we left the shop; I got nothing more than a cursory glance.

The driver was nowhere to be seen when we reached the meeting-place. We waited half an hour, during which time we considered and reconsidered whether we were in the right place, whether he had absconded with all our luggage and was even now in the business of selling it; what we would do if he never reappeared. As I sat in front of a deserted café drinking my third soft drink, Annalena walked in the direction we thought the driver would come from. Ten minutes later, as I wondered whose bushes I could use next, I saw the car drive towards me with Annalena in the back seat, smiling. I was so relieved to see the man and his bloody car that I didn't even think to remonstrate when Annalena told me he'd thought 11.30 and 12 noon were pretty much the same thing.

As we headed towards Da Nang, only 7 miles away, I felt we were setting off in earnest. Since 8.30 that morning we'd covered only 12 miles. We would bypass Da Nang, a large port city of 400,000 people which neither Annalena nor I felt the least inclination to visit, and drive directly to the Hai Van pass which, in my mind at least, was a gateway to the north. I subsequently discovered that it had indeed been a metaphorical gateway. Until the fifteenth century, *Deo Hai Van* had been the dividing point between the Hindu kingdom of Champa to the south and the lands of the Vietnamese to the north.

Passing signs to Da Nang airport, Annalena told me she had heard that its runway area was one of the most potentially dangerous in the region. Apparently US military aircraft frequently dropped their loads of dioxin, also known as 'Agent Orange', before making forced landings, and former military airstrips like Da Nang and Bien Hoa are currently still affected by the chemical, which is known to have caused hundreds of thousands of poisonings and birth defects.

After passing the suburbs of Da Nang we drove along the coast, the sea a perfect limpid turquoise broken only around the edges by the inevitable frill of white. There were almost no boats of any kind on the expanse of brine stretching away to our right, nothing, except distance, to interrupt a view of the Philippines. The sense of vast emptiness created by the sea was reflected on our left-hand side by the apparently deserted and featureless scrubby landscape. There were very few houses alongside the road, though occasionally a few goats or Asian cows could be seen grazing in the distance and once or twice I saw the bright red dot of a child's shirt as its wearer herded sheep. Apart from the occasional truck and even more occasional car, we were the only vehicle on the road. After being in towns and cities, this seemingly untenanted world was wonderful. But, like China Beach, I knew it was unlikely that its tranquillity would be long-lasting. The *Vietnam Investment Review* Grace gave me in Saigon commented with modest pride on the 205 industrial, agricultural, marine and tourist projects worth over a billion US dollars scheduled for central Vietnam between 1995 and 2000. Looking at the surrounding landscape as the road began to draw us steeply upwards about 9 miles after Da Nang, I felt that Lewis' words 'never again in its present form', which had been relevant in 1950 as he visited places unchanged in generations, had little meaning in 1995. I couldn't know how this road had looked before the war with the US, or during it. I only knew how it was now, at the moment of my observing. Who knew when it would be changed again and then again? But in the peace and quiet of now, away from noise and pressing crowds, I saw the landscape and was happy.

The Hai Van pass is spectacular. It cuts across a salient of the Trung Son mountains and gives panoramic views north along fabulous shoreline towards Hué and south towards Da Nang. East is the nub of the salient, west the 3,845-foot summit of Ai Van Son. As we parked on the metalled circle of road that marks the highest point of the pass, the car was immediately surrounded by biscuit vendors and children selling badly made cigarettes. A row of shabby shops and cafés sat against the landward side of the road and the uncomfortable overall impression was of a remote trading post in Colombia or Venezuela. We hadn't asked the driver to stop, but he must have needed to relieve himself as he disappeared immediately, leaving us to the mercy of the mob, which had a subtly hostile air.

Ignoring the plaints of children and the ubiquitous clawing hands, I strode purposefully – at least that's how I hoped it appeared – off to look at the views. It was a strange sensation, strolling a few yards in one direction and looking down at a beach stretching away left and north, then retracing my steps and looking at another beach reaching right and south. It would have been disconcerting had I not known that I was on a spur of land cutting the coastline in two. Near where the car was parked, I saw the old colonial fort described in the guidebook and wanted to climb up the few dozen feet to look at it, but decided it would be pointless. Hands were already pulling at my clothing, stroking my camera and, something that had never happened anywhere else in Vietnam, grabbing my backside. Fortunately for all concerned, I didn't see the party guilty of that particular affront. But my happy mood of less than half an hour earlier had evaporated, to be replaced once more by irritation at never, ever, having even a minute to take uninterrupted pleasure in where I was and what I was seeing; or even to have another pee. It had taken me half a year of dysentery and anaemia in other parts of Asia to become as fed up and tired as I was in Vietnam after just a few weeks. I wondered whether it was merely hormonal paranoia or whether perhaps, as *Lonely Planet* so tactfully put it, Vietnam simply was more 'challenging' than other places? Perhaps, as usual, it was both.

The three soft drinks at Marble Mountain were making their presence felt and I couldn't face the 'trading-post' latrines. 'Give me the free fresh wind in my hair,' I hummed to myself as I hunted for a suitably private spot, in vain naturally.

Annalena was about to be throttled with an out-of-date packet of biscuits when I returned to the car. By the time I left Vietnam it was with the firm conviction that the whole country was involved in a Bennettesque conspiracy to get rid of past-the-sell-by-date biscuits on unsuspecting foreigners. The antique biscuits were coconut and always the same make, resembling a type called 'Nice' – or 'Neece' if you fancied yourself a cut above the average – familiar from my childhood. To silence the throng, Annalena had bought a packet, which naturally signalled a general rush, the collective thought evidently being, 'If she's silly enough to buy out-of-date biscuits she's silly enough to buy cigarettes, distilled water, blurred postcards and fake dogtags' – for they were there, too. PFC Elmer J. White and SSgt George R. Massie must have been killed and/or captured with monotonous frequency when they were 'in country'. We got back into the car and sat with the doors locked, the faces around us pressing against the glass, until the driver came up, his long undertaker's face wreathed in smiles.

As we set off, I looked down at the stupendous view below me, at the forests, the winding roads and the long, long line of sparkling beach, and knew there just had to be *one* place a Welshwoman could pee in private and that I would find it.

But there wasn't. For mile after mile the road was solid rock on one side and sheer drop on the other. My bladder was whispering, 'Why are you doing this to me? What have I ever done to you, etc. etc...' As I stared from the window with rapt attention, it was less from admiration and more from desperation with every passing minute. Finally I saw a place, a lay-by leading to a forestry track.

'Stop! Stop!' I yelled, but we had already raced past the point and were on dangerous ground once more. I cursed and a few minutes later decided that awkward or no, I would have to go. National Highway 1 was hardly Piccadilly Circus on a Saturday afternoon and I really no longer cared. If Uncle Ho himself had walked down the road and asked me why I was peeing in public I would merely have smiled with relief. Clambering over large boulders that had once belonged to the overhead cliff, I realized that for reasons entirely beyond my comprehension the driver was following me. But in the process of waving him away, I got entangled in a giant bush with finger-length thorns which seemed to leap up and grab me from all sides. Whichever way I turned, I got more firmly stuck and was eventually very grateful when the driver, hearing my plaintive swearing, turned back and unhooked me. I was lucky to have been attacked by nothing more assertive than a thorn bush. Apparently deforestation in central Vietnam has caused wolves and tigers to alter their habits, forcing them nearer to habitation; domestic animals and even people have been eaten in the absence of the predators' usual diet. So much risk and effort, just to pass water.

As we swept down from the heights towards the coast once more, the distant coastline was scalloped by inlets and fringed with sandy beaches and palms. The sky was unbroken by clouds and looking at the horizon, I counted at least eight shades of the colour blue, from deepest azure to palest turquoise, as sea rose to meet sky.

Approaching the small peninsula of Lang Co, the deserted rocky coast of the south became just a memory superseded by picturesque buildings perched on low dunes. Palm-thatched roofs overshadowed nets spread to dry on the sand and boats were drawn up along the white shoreline. I was fascinated to see the Vietnamese equivalent of the ancient Celtic coracle alive and well in the waters around Lang Co village. These circular tarred baskets, used for crab fishing, were big enough for only one person or perhaps two very small people but even from a distance I could see that balance was of the essence, as the baskets were manoeuvred from a standing position. I should have liked to get in one simply for the experience, but instead merely watched as a fisherman propelled his coracle with exquisite skill across the flashing water before settling to sit in perfect stillness under his conical hat, his line piercing the skin of the sea.

I would have loved to get closer to this particular spot, but it was not to be; the driver swung away from that direction – I was past questioning now – and headed a mile or so further on to a 'tourist' hotel and restaurant where we had lunch, looking at the dunes and admiring the large electricity pylons which, interspersed by tall elegant palms, completely dominated the scene. I found it almost unbelievable that one of the most attractive places I had seen in Vietnam should be thus disfigured. I guessed it was at least partly the presence of foreigners which created the demand for power, but I couldn't believe that the pylons needed to bestride the beach in quite such a colossal manner.

After a simple lunch, Annalena and I strolled along the seashore. Close to, the waves were high and strong and there was a fierce wind blowing diagonally across the shore which whipped up the water into a froth. A small girl and boy attached themselves to us and we all four walked hand in hand along the beach and back. The girl, who said her name was Hoa, was 13, but I had thought her eight, perhaps nine. I was still struggling to get used to the age:size ratio thing. For me it was merely a question of adjusting the sights, but for others, malnourished and under-sized children are perfect targets for pae-dophiliac fantasy – and sadly reality, too. To the paedophile pimp, young Vietnamese teenagers are not children but can easily pass for them. Venturing only rarely and briefly to the beach in Vietnam, I did not see the things other Westerners told me of: fat, hairy European men playing 'uncles' with gangs of young Vietnamese boys in the surf at Nha Trang; small girls 'massaging' foreign men on the sand, before disappearing who knows where for that few extra dong. I knew what I had seen in Hoi An was merely the discreet tip of a large and ugly iceberg.

Despite the pylons, Lang Co was beautiful, the atmosphere relaxed and undemanding. Had I been alone I might have stayed and not gone on to Hué until later. But it was out of season, the water was cold and the waves and breeze too high for all but the bravest. The summer months of May and June are when it all happens at Lang Co and in some ways I was glad to have been there almost alone, with only the gentle hum of the pylons to break the silence between each crash of the surf.

After Lang Co, the coast slipped away and we were once more inland, passing paddy fields and palms dotted with conical hats that seemed always to be lower than the wearers' buttocks, as the women planting or pruning or weeding bent from the hip until their faces were almost touching their knees. Water, food, rice seedlings, all and more were carried in the *don-ganh*, a yoke-like pole with containers hanging from each end, the Vietnamese equivalent of a shopping trolley or a wheelbarrow. I had already noticed that only women seemed to carry the *ganh*, using the shuffle peculiar to carriers every-where in Asia. There were no men among those weaving delicately along the levees that separated the wet rice fields.

As we drove, I looked at maps of Hué, trying to orientate myself prior to arrival. Hué, former imperial capital of Vietnam, city of the Forbidden Purple City and the Perfume River, last resting-place of Vietnamese emperors. Reading about Hué as I sped towards it, it seemed to be a place of tremendous cultural and historical significance, though much of the physical evidence of this had been destroyed during the 1968 Tet Offensive. I was eager to walk where princes and mandarins had strolled under parasols, discussing Rousseau and Pasteur, eager to see the Perfume River – the *Huong Giang* – and its dragon boats. My city map showed the centre of Hué as a place of arrow-straight streets and precise canals; at its heart a vegetable plot that had once been the Forbidden Purple City, the private quarters of the emperors and their families. It sounded like a bizarre soap opera and I would soon be in it.

chapter nine

THE IMPERIAL CITY

From the south, Hué is entered by crossing the An Cuu bridge, which spans a small tributary of the Perfume River. As with all the towns and cities I had seen in Vietnam, there had been no 'approach' to Hué, no distant view, the land being flat for many miles around. Only when I walked up from the Embankment to Charing Cross on my return to London did it strike me that, with one exception, I had always walked on flat ground in Vietnam.

Once over the bridge we were in the New City, still called by some 'the European quarter'. Our driver had no idea where he was once we were off the main road and road maps being apparently deemed an unnecessary luxury – maybe they simply didn't exist? – we drove round and round for some time looking for the hotel Annalena had selected. As the driver got increasingly annoyed and frustrated, the scenario began to remind me of my arrival at Nha Trang with the Danes. Perhaps there was something about a Celt travelling with Norsepersons that brought bad luck to all concerned?

As we drove I looked at a few places to stay myself, none particularly interesting. I didn't really want to be in this colonial part of the city with its quiet wide streets and empty feeling. But Annalena argued strongly for the saving of money by sharing, which I don't think was necessary for either of us – perhaps that was an excuse we both gave for not being alone.

We eventually found the imaginatively named Tourist Villa, which was as well since the driver was beginning to take sexual interest in Annalena, brushing past her each time we stopped to check the names of the hotels we saw. As he hadn't made any such gestures towards her earlier in the day, Annalena decided it was merely an unusual ploy to get rid of unwanted passengers. We paid him at the hotel gates, but as with the Saigon–Nha Trang Driver from Hell, he hung around a long while, talking to the small pregnant hotel manager, probably answering her questions about where we'd come from and what we were like.

I decided to stay at the Tourist Villa, it being now late afternoon, and asked for a single room, only to learn that there was only one room left and that Annalena and I would have to share it. I had no objection to sharing again with Annalena, who was an ideal roommate, quiet, thoughtful and clean, but at the time I badly needed to be alone and didn't feel like sharing anything with anyone. Fortunately Annalena understood my state of mind, having, she told me, experienced 'women's problems' herself. I settled down to stay one night and decided I would move nearer to the heart of the city the following day.

From the road the Tourist Villa looked like a European house, but behind it was a row of motel-style rooms fronting onto a patch of sad brown grass with plastic tables and chairs and it was here that we were put. As I stepped from our room to hang underwear, still wet from washing in Hoi An, on the line stretching across the hotel garden, I saw two familiar figures reclining in the plastic chairs. The Genet–Beau Gestes from the Vinh Hung who had told Tuan fibs about their nightly escapades recognized me and nodded coolly and in tandem. They were chatting with two other men and looking quite as large as I remembered.

While driving around the New City looking for the hotel, I'd realized we were pretty much in the suburbs. There were no cafés, shops or any places of interest within walking distance, so a few hours after arriving we called two cyclos and set off for the Phu Xuan bridge and our first glimpse of the Perfume River.

It was the rush hour, but the population of Hué is small compared with Saigon; fewer than quarter of a million people live within its boundaries. As we approached Hué's main bridge, however, the traffic bottle-necked and we were caught in the usual crush of bicycles, cyclos, trucks and a rare car or two. Taking advantage of the momentary lull, I stood up on the footboard of my cyclo in order to peer over the high-sided bridge and glimpse the river below. I'd seen it only briefly as we approached the bridge and now I wanted a decent look. In the seconds before we started jolting along again I saw a wide expanse of water gradually turning colour as the sun lowered in the sky. It was beautiful, but we were already moving towards the Citadel.

We rode only to the far side of the bridge and then walked from there along the wall which bordered the river. On the far bank we'd just left, I saw large and once elegant buildings standing among palms and other trees: the houses used by former colonial officials and their families. Behind me were rows of gaily lit and gaudily signboarded shops selling everything from electrical plugs to incense and beyond them rose the walls of the Citadel, outer layer of an onion skin at the heart of which lay what had been the Forbidden Purple City, inner sanctum of the emperors of Vietnam since 1804. Despite having checked the city map in the car, it was impossible to tell, looking at the wall and a small narrow bridge between the shops, that the Citadel was built within a series of moats. In Anthony Grey's novel *Saigon*, the protagonist spends time in Hué during his childhood and Grey's description of the Imperial Palace and the canals surrounding it were vivid. I wanted to see how much of what Grey had described, though fictionally, of the Hué of the 1920s was still visible in the mid 1990s.

My first view was disappointing. The small bridge before us – no more than 10 yards long – crossed nothing more than a ditch full of stagnant water that I could smell rather than see in the fading light. Not realizing that this was merely the smallest and least significant of an intricate series of waterways, my heart sank a little. As it was almost dark we decided against venturing into the blackness on the other side of the bridge and planned our visit for the following day.

We walked slowly north along Tran Hung Dao Street, the river always on our right, just looking and taking in the sounds and smells of another place, another set of images. The shops lining the street were various and their fronts were architecturally more Western than others I'd seen in Vietnam, though the goods and produce weren't Western at all. There was something slightly run down about everything I'd seen so far, reminiscent of the trading-post atmosphere of the Hai Van pass. My first impression of Hué was of a large but strangely empty place, as though it had once held far more people than it did now, like an old shoe that has stretched with use and flops around on the wearer's foot.

I don't know quite what I'd expected, but I think I was suddenly struck by the reality of Vietnam's poverty when I reached Hué. Saigon is Westernized and vast, the new Bangkok some say, though it would be a great pity if that prediction proved true. I had merely passed across the face of Nha Trang and Hoi An was an anomaly not to be found elsewhere in Vietnam or indeed Indo-China, but Hué confronted me with the real Vietnam very quickly, despite its being an important tourist centre. In 1994, the French magazine *VSD* referred to Hué as 'the most beautiful city in Vietnam' and 'a place of tourist interest that shouldn't be missed'. Many travellers and businesspeople I spoke to, both at the time and since, agree with *VSD*, but I could not. There was activity and there were people, but Hué had none of the bustle of Saigon, none of the peace and tranquillity of Hoi An and, somehow, on first acquaintance, was not a comfortable place to be. On reflection I felt as though I were locked in an amalgam of museum and graveyard, that the *raison d'être* of Hué was the preservation of what was gone.

This is acknowledged even by the *Vietnam Investment Review* which, in attempting to make Hué sound appealing to foreigners, actually outlined my own feelings about the place:

> During the day, Hué looks and feels like a city with a full and vibrant past, now partially buried beneath the bustle and detritus of a modern daily life. But at night, with the glare of reality dimmed to a timeless light, the ancient city takes on a lyrical quality that lets visitors drift back to the days of courtly style. Many people say one can best capture the sense of an illusory world, of a time gone by, in the boats that rock gently on the Huong River…

Hué seemed to me a rather unsuccessful kind of Disney project. Perhaps when the intended renovation and rebuilding take place, the city will truly return to life. But I saw none of that; beautiful buildings were falling down and rotting almost in front of my eyes and little else, either spiritual or corporal, seemed ready to take their place, though doubtless much was and is happening beneath the surface that a visitor on a first or even a dozenth impression might not see.

We walked to the Tran Tien bridge, sister to the Phu Xuan, intending to walk across the river and back to the New City to eat. But the bridge was closed; dark and silent with heaps of what looked like rusted machinery blocking the way. It was clearly marked on the map and the guidebook had said nothing about it being closed or collapsed – it was impossible to see what the problem was in the darkness. So we asked in various shops if this were indeed the bridge marked in the guidebook or some other, undisclosed bridge. After several attempts and much assistance by kindly people, including a maker of spectacles who stood on the pavement trying to translate and answer our questions while holding several pairs of spectacles in one hand and wearing two more on his head, we discovered that it was indeed the Tran Tien bridge and that our plan to walk would have to be shelved as it was closed for rebuilding. I wanted to ask how long the rebuilding had taken and when it would reopen, but such questions were not appropriate to the moment. Hailing the nearest cyclos, we retraced our steps and soon after were on the other side of the river, paralleling Tran Hung Dao Street and heading directly towards the Floating Restaurant.

As we walked along the narrow gangplank that led to the circular restaurant floating at the river's edge I immediately recognized the Genet–Beau Gestes and their friends from the Tourist Villa arriving immediately ahead of us. I was hopeful that the food would be as good as the *Lonely Planet* claimed because nothing I had seen in any of the street cafés had looked very enticing, particularly with my gut disturbance still ongoing. But after an hour we were still waiting to be served. The all-male party had eaten and left, served unctuously by every female member of staff, none of whom seemed to have any time for women customers. When the food came it was ghastly. I picked at bread and attempted the raw beef which had to be cooked in boiling water over a charcoal fire, but the fire went out and I lost interest. I was also cold. For the first time since leaving London I was actually feeling chilly – not the unpleasant damp chill of Hong Kong, but a real English chill, like September evenings when no one wants to believe the summer is over and the leaves haven't yet started to fall.

We walked back across the gangplank and the thick tropical grass to where our drivers were waiting, though we'd told them not to. Annalena wanted to look at the shops and I quickly saw that there was a lot more by way of material goods on this side of the river than on the other, which made sense as most of the larger tourist hotels are situated along the New City riverside and it was for their well-heeled guests that the very many antique and silk shops catered. We saw beautiful things of incredible quality and skill: carvings, paintings, weapons, perfume bottles made from bone and old ivory. Masks and crucifixes hung on the walls alongside cabinets containing the ubiquitous dogtags. Here in Hué I noticed the saleable paraphernalia of war was rather underplayed in favour of older and less potentially offensive items from the city's history.

After a long walk beside the river, during which our drivers followed us, trying to tempt us into their vehicles with many smiles and hand movements, we tired of antiques and allowed ourselves to be driven back to the hotel. Turning off the very long Le Loi Street, we passed a large building which occupied an entire street corner. A rather forlorn sign read 'Morin Hotel'. This was the place Pia and Kosh de Silva had told me about in Saigon.

Turning to Annalena, who was slightly behind me at this point, I shouted, 'Let's go there for breakfast, shall we? They have toast.'

'All right,' she yelled back and asked me how I knew about the toast. I was just telling her about the de Silvas when I saw an enormous rat cross the street in front of my vehicle and run up a set of dark side steps to disappear into the bowels of the vast Morin. Looking up at the ceilings of the illuminated first-floor rooms, I saw strip after strip of bare lath; what plaster remained hung precariously by, I assumed, the animal hair originally mixed into it as a strengthener a century and more before. Naked light bulbs showed lines hung with washing suspended inside the bedrooms; the whole place had an almost tangible air of decrepitude and decay, even from a passing cyclo.

The following morning we were woken at 5.30 a.m. by the thoroughly disgusting sound of someone doing a naso-pharyngeal spring clean. The night porter was pacing noisily up and down the wooden walkway outside the guest rooms and practising his spit shots. Anna-lena lay with the pillow over her head, I put in my earplugs and tried unsuccessfully to fall asleep again.

Having decided I wouldn't be staying in Hué long enough to warrant a change of hotel, I partially unpacked my bag the following morning. The bulb in the bathroom was broken and although we'd asked for a replacement several times the previous evening, we'd ended up having to use candles. We were in the same ablutive dark-ness the following night and only got what we needed by suggesting in appalling French that we might not feel it right to pay the bill in full as we'd not had full service.

Normally when travelling in developing countries I expect prob-lems with service and communication. I am, after all, in a country quite different from my own by my own choice. The difficulty that I, and many other Westerners I spoke to, found in Vietnam was one I had not encountered before and can only be described as 'di-chotomy'. Superficially, Vietnam offers a semi-Western style tourist and accommodation service, with travel agents and tours and starred hotels. Beneath that lies an mass of confusion around expectation and standards of service of which the General Director of Tourism, Do Quang Trung, is aware. In late 1994 he commented publicly that:

> Despite all the improvements and progress, I must admit myself that the tourism industry is still far behind. Successes are very lim-ited. The industry in general is now facing a critical and obvious lag behind both international and regional scales...
> *Vietnam Investment Review*

The Director went on to admit that poor service and high prices have turned many foreigners off making a return visit. Hopefully the tourist authorities will realize in time that development does not only mean 'more' but 'better' – a few courses in hotel management for existing staff would be more useful than several high-rise hotels.

Such things are easily seen in hindsight; at the time I felt con-flicting emotions when faced with certain cultural differences in Vietnam. It seemed trivial and petty to complain about a light bulb and be irritated by someone spitting outside my bedroom when only

26 years earlier 10,000 people had died in this city in the space of a few weeks. The briefly successful VC apparently shot, battered, strangled and buried alive over 3,000 South Vietnamese government officials, Buddhist monks, foreigners, priests and liberals during the Tet Offensive of 1968, before they were overcome in their turn. It was in attempting to dislodge the VC that the Americans and South Viet-namese forces shelled and partly destroyed the city, including the Forbidden Purple City. Many more civilians were killed, along-side thousands of NVA soldiers, hundreds of South Vietnamese soldiers and 150 US Marines. The 3,000 civilians 'removed' by the Communists and NVA on the taking of Hué were buried in mass graves around the city which were located only years later. I had imagined death under my feet in Saigon and the delta, but there I had also seen restoration and invigoration; here the museum-grave-yard feeling persisted. It wasn't easy for me, or I believe for many Western visitors, to establish a balance and feel that I had a right to certain standards and conditions of comfort in what purported to be a Western- style hotel, charging close to Western prices, and not feel trivial in my demands. Perhaps the manager had lost all her family in 1968, maybe the Spitting Man had received some terrible throat wound which meant he couldn't swallow properly. Yet I knew if I carried on thinking along such lines that I would become paralysed. Perhaps all the difficulties had a purpose. I was learning something in Vietnam: how to get what I needed without being swamped by guilt. Maybe watching the French, who appeared to have no qualms or doubts and a rock-solid belief in the absolute necessity of comfort and elegance, had helped?

We breakfasted at the Morin Hotel on pancakes and jam in preference to toast. Annalena had set her heart on chocolate syrup; everywhere we ate she asked for it, always without success. From time to time she'd get vague reports of sightings and hear ghostly syrup stories which I never believed myself, but in true Scorpio fashion, she never relinquished the quest.

The inside of the Morin was not quite so awesomely bad as it had seemed in passing the previous night. Wandering within its vast perimeter I discovered that the building, which I was convinced had once been a French barracks, was comprised of two large courtyards.

One courtyard, the back wall of which I'd seen from the street the previous evening, was a hostel/hotel for Vietnamese. The other, which had flowers, fountains and much topiary as well as small white stork-like birds roaming freely, was for Westerners. I was struck by the difference between the two courtyards, though by most Western standards even the upgraded side would probably have been shut down on health and safety grounds. But the atmosphere was great, or rather it had an atmosphere. Eating and drinking under the trees was very pleasant and afterwards, when we walked over to the small travel bureau which occupied a tiny section of the vast and echoing lobby, I could almost see French officers clanking around in spurs and swords, smoking *fin de siècle* Gauloises and eyeing-up each others' creases. Now there was only a small woman in a beige parka pointing to maps of the DMZ and telling us about the daily tours the hotel organized.

I considered a trip to the DMZ. It would mean seeing Khe Sahn and Hamburger Hill, places so vividly described by Michael Herr in *Dispatches*. But on consideration, I decided that it would look nothing like the picture in my mind and that the DMZ was for US veterans, not for people like me. I still had gut problems despite Lomotil tablets and decided that a visit to the local hospital was probably more sensible than a tour of the DMZ anyway. Annalena had decided on a tour of Hué's main tourist attraction, the tombs of the Nguyen dynasty emperors, who 'ruled' from 1802 until the deposition of the last emperor, Bao Dai, in October 1955. Quite apart from the gut issue, I felt that I had no great desire to spend a day wandering round more death, though some of the tombs are reputedly very attractive indeed, having gardens, lotus ponds and temples within walled courtyards, though most of the valuable tomb decorations disappeared during the war. I simply wanted to meet local people and talk to them, as far as that was possible. At the tombs I guessed it would be the usual 'You want guide' racket and I couldn't face that again. At least at the hospital I might learn something – and not just about the state of my guts.

I had an excellent time at the Hué Central Hospital, though less than productive as far as the bowel business was concerned. I got to talk to people who actually wanted to talk to me for no reason other than interest, which was most refreshing after the tourist rounds I'd been doing with Annalena. As I sat in the large lobby/reception area waiting to be seen by a doctor, a small crowd of people gathered to stare. Most of them looked quite unlike any Vietnamese I'd yet seen, and recalling Norman Lewis' black and white photos of tribal people, I realized with great excitement that I was looking at and being looked at by people I had not thought I'd see on this journey. I was glad to have decided against the tombs of Minh Mang, which sounded like some unfortunate social disease, and that of Tu Duc, which sounded like a cartoon character, or an Ozzie with scotophobia. The staring people wore quite ordinary clothes, but their faces were very different from the typical Hué citizen. Broader, flatter and more defined, their features reminded me strongly of tribal peoples I'd encountered in central India, semi-naked people whose men still carried bows and arrows, fermented their own tree sap and frequently killed each other, to escape, I'd been told in serious jest, the tyranny of their much older wives.

Outside the front of the hospital, dozens of people squatted, preparing or cooking food over small portable stoves. I thought perhaps this was the equivalent of a hospital canteen, then I remembered that in most developing countries, a patient's food is brought in by family or friends. What if the person has no family or friends? Well, I pondered, there'd hardly be any point treating someone who was starving to death.

After a short wait, I saw a slender young woman in a white frilly blouse and emerald-green crimplene bell-bottom trousers sashay towards me. She told me to follow her and in a small clean room she took my details and I showed her the international sos Tourist Assistance card I'd been given by the Vietnam Embassy in London which should have entitled me to free treatment. She stared at the card and shook her head. She had never seen one before and would not accept it. I wasn't particularly surprised.

The woman asked about symptoms in rather difficult English which was still better than my French. I only realized that she was the doctor when it became clear that no one else was going to see me. I wanted a white coat – the '70s disco outfit gave me no confidence at all. She might have been anyone. She said that I would have to give a 'sample' and I tried unsuccessfully to explain that that might not be too easy as I'd taken drying up-pills. She didn't recognize the words 'Lomotil' or 'anti-diarrhoeal', but when she handed me the sample pot I went to the extremely clean lavatory and did my best. Sadly, my best wasn't good enough; I struggled to produce a sample the size of my little fingernail bearing no resemblance at all to the exploding bowel syndrome I had just so vividly described in a mixture of English, French and expansive gesture.

Having produced the pathetic specimen, I sat once more in the reception area, clutching my pot and waiting for the lab assistant to come and get it for testing. The small crowd formed again and I pulled faces at a small tribal girl who pulled them right back at me then laughed. One of the women sat down next to me, a child in her arms. The child instantly seized a handful of my hair and began stroking it and rubbing it between her rather grubby fingers. Seeing that I didn't pull away or complain, the laughing girl came and sat on my other side and began to do the same thing. I stroked her long rather tangled hair in return, which made her giggle. She looked at me very closely, her dark eyes shining like lacquer, touching my skin and my clothing and staring at the colour of my eyes, so different from her own.

I wished I could ask where these people lived. Perhaps they lived along the Laotian border, only 40 miles away; perhaps further. There would be no hospital of this size any closer than Da Nang. The French name *Montagnards*, 'mountain people', seemed polite compared with the word *moi*, 'savages', used by Vietnamese, embarrassed perhaps, as many developing nations seem to be, by this too tangible evidence of 'backwardness'. The Vietnamese government, like others in Indo-China, is currently trying to tempt tribal peoples away from the slash and burn agriculture they've practised since time immemorial and resettle them in 'Vietnamese' areas and ways. Eventually, of course, the minorities would then disappear into the majority and the 'problem' would resolve itself. These people in the hospital were far more interesting and memorable than some old tomb which, after all, the world is pretty well full of, the living being a minority too. Perhaps the Vietnamese tourist authorities will realize that before it's too late.

While the stool test was going on, I was allowed to sit in the lab and watch as the very pleasant female lab technician donned gloves and mask and did the business. I looked at the oddly familiar colours, the pale institutional green of the walls, the elderly woodwork and chipped paint of the lab's surfaces, and wondered why that particular shade of green should be so internationally popular in hospitals, prisons and schools? A young male doctor came and sat with me while I watched and we attempted to chat in French, except his was even worse than mine and we eventually gave up and merely smiled at each other.

Nothing was found in the sample, and I felt relieved until the assistant to the woman in emerald green appeared and tried to sell me all sorts of antibiotics and stomach medicines. The test had cost 20,000 dong, about $10, which was way over the odds, but I was happy to give money to this hospital and only hoped it didn't get side-tracked along the way. I couldn't ask why I was being given medication if there was nothing wrong with me, so I paid for the charcoal tablets and refused the antibiotics. It was the right decision; within a day the problem had disappeared entirely.

Outside, the hospital grounds were busier than ever as the time of the evening meal approached. The driver who'd brought me was long gone and I called another, rather shifty-looking man, who drove with difficulty between the makeshift cafés and take-aways which had been set up along the dirt road leading to the hospital. Under dark canvas awnings, families sat to eat on upturned boxes or filled metal containers and small baskets with rice and vegetables for their sick relatives languishing within. It reminded me of pictures of monastic hospices, a soup-kitchen without the desperation or maybe a meals-on-wheels service.

I had arranged to meet Annalena at the Morin Hotel for dinner but as that was an hour or so away, I decided to see the inside of the Citadel. The sun was beginning to drop in the sky but I felt sure there was time to see what I wanted. We crossed the river and I explained to the driver that I wanted to see *inside* the Citadel.

He nodded and said, 'One dollar, one hour.'

Thinking that was pretty fair and having little idea of what I was agreeing to, I nodded and in the bliss of ignorance set off.

We crossed the small teeming bridge over the stagnant canalette that I'd seen with dismay the previous evening and drove under the large stone gateway into a different world. The second layer of the onion skin resembled a large park filled with enormous stately trees and space; so much space and so few people. And quiet, so quiet after the noise and traffic outside.

The driver gestured vaguely towards the wall of the Imperial Enclosure which rose up in front of us and began moving around it. Confused, I made pointing, diving gestures, to which he merely nodded and smiled. After 15 minutes and no gate, I realized we were riding around the outside perimeter of the enclosure and that the driver had no intention of taking me to the entrance, which we had in fact already passed, because he wanted money for as long a time as possible – hence 'one dollar, one hour'. I was furious, knowing full well that he'd understood my wish to go inside. The *Lonely Planet* guide informed me the Ngo Mon gate, the entrance to the Imperial Enclosure, closed at 5.30 p.m. I looked at my watch. It was 5.20 p.m., we were 10 minutes' hard cycling from the gate and it was getting darker all the time. Reaching the Ngo Mon, I told the driver to wait and fled for the still open gate, at which moment a previously invisible official stepped out and told me they were closed while another told me I must pay to go in. If it had been still light I would have paid up, but it was almost dark now and rushing past the officials, I said, 'I only want to look,' and they let me go.

Inside I felt even sorrier that I was too late to see it all. It was perfect. In front of me stretched a wide paved pathway edged by water. It led to a tall Chinese-style gateway and beyond it a beautiful building with red tiled roof and pillared portico. I was looking at the Thai Hoa palace, one of the earliest buildings in the Citadel which the Emperor had used for official interaction with his mandarins. On all sides were trees, black now in the rapidly fading light. In the distance, I could see a small group of foreigners slowly strolling and wondered how much they'd paid to be allowed in after hours.

I realized quite suddenly that I was alone, completely alone, and that everywhere around me was silence and peace. Hué was two set of walls and a canal or three away. There were no 'guides', no postcard sellers and I *was* standing, albeit briefly, where mandarins and princesses had walked under their parasols, though I made no attempt to visualize such a scene, being utterly content in the present. I felt the most wonderful sense of freedom and was contemplating running, or rather trotting, at full tilt up the pathway leading to the palace, simply from excitement, when I heard the voice of an official.

'You must leave now. Closed now. You come back tomorrow, OK?'

I didn't want to come back tomorrow, when there would be dozens of foreigners and 'guides'. I wanted to remember even the small part I saw, just as it was: pink and pale grey clouds leading the eye to a point just behind the roof of the palace, tempering the ochre-red of its tiles; the walls already beginning to merge into the blackness of the surrounding trees; the tranquillity which the combination of architecture and landscape was surely intended to create. As I reluctantly followed the official, I knew that behind me lay the heart of the onion, the Forbidden Purple City, preserve of emperors, concubines and eunuchs. Knowing that it was now a large allotment made leaving a little easier.

Passing through the Ngo Mon gate, I turned and looked up at what I hadn't had time to notice in my dash to see what lay behind it. The gate, a spectacular nineteenth-century Vietnamese building, rose above me, its open two-tiered structure incredible in the pink light now warming everything it touched. The fine columns and delicate tracery of dragons and serpents fighting their way along the cornicing were black on pink against the evening sky and turned the building into an enormous piece of surreal lace.

Passing the Flag Tower from where the North Vietnamese had flown the flag of the National Liberation Front for those three and a half weeks in 1968, I felt my passion for Vietnam rekindling. Five minutes alone and in peace was all it had required.

That evening, Annalena and I ate at the Morin Hotel. We sat and chatted with two young Englishmen we'd met briefly at the railway station earlier that morning. Like us, they'd been trying to understand the ticketing system and to find a timetable for trains to Ha Noi. I had wanted to travel by train in Vietnam. For the first time in my life, I could afford first class and was keen to see the north coast. But once again it was not to be. All four of us had given up and left the station no wiser, despite vigorous attempts to engage railway staff in conversation. During my solitary meanderings around Hué, I'd been to various tourist agencies trying to discover whether it was possible to reach Ha Noi from Hué by boat, even non-tourist boat. Again I met nothing but shaking heads and blank looks that asked, 'Why would anyone want to do such a thing?'

After dinner, the four of us were joined by two very strange people. The first, a young American who said he was 19 but looked a combination of Castro in the '70s and Jim Morrison shortly before he did his impersonation of Marat, was someone you have nightmares about, a less entertaining and madder version of the Flying Dutchman of Hoi An. He had been to the DMZ that day and insisted on pulling out a series of photos he said his father had taken when he'd been stationed at Khe Sahn during the worst of the fighting there. He handed them round, then started complaining, 'Careful, careful how you handle it, man. That's precious, you know.'

My countrymen were looking at the many rather bland photos of planes and hills out of pure English politeness rather than any genuine interest. My initial interest had been genuine, but faded fast, to be replaced by a silent question about the mental stability of the man in front of me, as he continued harassing his audience: 'Hey, man, hey, don't get your fingers all over it. Those marks, they don't come off. I don't wanna take them back to my dad looking like a pig's ass.'

After 20 minutes of aggressive and bigoted ear-bashing about the war, US involvement and his father, I'd had enough. So too had my three companions and as though on an invisible nod, we changed the topic entirely and talked about London. His limelight turned off, the Appalling One slunk away. I felt rather sorry for him and wondered whether it was his upbringing by 'Khe Sahn Sam' that had endowed the unfortunate youth with the social assets of a defunct pole-cat.

The second person to join our table was equally eccentric, but with the added social advantage of being vastly entertaining and extremely informative. She was a Canadian woman in her late fifties or early sixties who seemed to have travelled almost continuously throughout her life and had lived on and off in China for many years. I asked what she did and was told something rather vague about teaching. She said she had been born in Sweden, which made

Annalena curious, but now held Canadian citizenship. Her accent was a mixture of too many things to unravel and when told that three of us were British, she proceeded to remind us that most northern Europeans are of Viking descent. It seemed very strange to be sitting in a dark courtyard in central Vietnam, listening to splashing fountains, toad sounds and a discussion on Dark Age genealogy.

'The French,' the woman said, 'or the Normans, anyway, are all Vikings. That's what "Norman" means, of course, "Northman". And of course the British, all Vikings!'

She ended rather triumphantly but I begged to differ, making it quite clear that the Welsh are just about the only real British and that Celts and Vikings were quite different from each other.

'Ah,' she said, seeing her opportunity and going for the jugular, 'but what about the Irish, they're Celts, aren't they, but Dublin was a Viking city. That's why Dubliners have pale blue eyes and many of them are blond!'

I was about to come back with some pert response, when she continued, 'And the Scottish, of course, and the people of Yorkshire – York was a Viking city and...'

One of the Yorkshiremen with us laughed. His name was Eric.

The next morning, we were woken at 6 a.m. by the same hacking and gobbing. I considered leaping up and making a scene with the porter, but guessed that the ensuing racket would wake even more people than his disgusting habit and I would probably be the one generally vilified. However, I planned my revenge with care and as soon as the manager arrived, I shot from my room before the porter could leave and, with Annalena bringing up the rear, accosted her.

'*Madame*,' I began, certain that my French wouldn't stand up to such a test, '*ce matin et le matin* yesterday,' pointing backwards over my shoulder, '*c'est terrible. Dormir, c'est impossible.*'

I noticed the Spitting Man, drawn perhaps by guilt and a phlegm-laden conscience, standing on the grass not far away, ears tuned like a bat in broad daylight. My voice rose as I became increasingly impassioned under the influence of the Gallic language: '*C'est impossible ici. Sommes-nous dans un hôtel ou une toilette? Chaque matin...*'

I made hawking noises because I don't know the French for 'nasopharyngeal spring-clean' and suspected the manager didn't know it either. Behind me Annalena was making similar noises and repeating, '*C'est grotesque, grotesque. C'est très mal.*'

The porter, who had never been directly referred to, turned a strange dark red colour and I suspected that if he had not previously harboured a dislike of women, particularly Western women, he certainly would in future. Caught between her guests and her staff, the manager was also red, but looked as though she was trying hard not to laugh out loud. She said something to the man in Vietnamese, who attempted the pillar of salt trick on me and Annalena before stomping off in high dudgeon and rather lop-sided heels. There was no apology from anyone, but I was fairly certain it wouldn't happen again. Satisfied, I returned to our room. The scene was over. Annalena at least would benefit from it.

I left for Ha Noi that afternoon, having chased an air ticket round and round Hué after being advised, wrongly, that there were no flights out of Hué until after the New Year – which almost made me panic. What the ticket sales staff omitted to tell me was that they were not Vietnam Airlines at all, as almost every tourist going to that bureau assumed, but merely a ticketing outlet. The real Vietnam Airlines was in a posh hotel at the upper end of Le Loi Street and of course there were plenty of tickets to Ha Noi.

Annalena walked with me to the hotel gates, carrying one of my bags to the cyclo. We kissed goodbye and promised to meet up in Ha Noi and as I sat with my bags piled in front of me, she waved me into the distance. I felt quite sad for about 300 yards. I seemed to have said a lot of farewells in a short space of time and had enjoyed Annalena's cool Scandinavian assurance. Then the same exhilaration I'd felt on leaving Nha Trang began to sweep over me. I was alone and moving north once more.

chapter ten

HA NOI – CITY OF LAKES

From the air, the landscape of the Red River delta looked almost empty; a flat grey emptiness seemingly devoid of life until the scarlet roads with their occasional cyclists stood out like veins on an unhealthy skin. As the aircraft swung round for the final stage of its descent into Noi Ba airport I looked more closely at the roads of bright red dirt leading off the single metalled one we seemed to be following. This simple factor of human geography told a great deal about the state of Vietnam's economy, the distance it still has to go before the word 'developing' is no longer associated with it. Strange, I thought, as the wheels touched down and the non-Westerners clapped, that an application of asphalt, or the lack of one, can so affect the way an entire nation state is viewed.

Noi Ba was small and quiet compared to Tan Son Nhut but unsurprisingly, the taxi touts were out in force. I shared a car with a nice British couple and a handsome yellow-eyed French youth who was spending *le weekend* in Vietnam, '*A voir comment il semble.*' The British couple had been advised on a chain of hotels which was quite pleasant – rather like English guest houses – and reasonable. My immediate feeling about Ha Noi, as the manager of one of the hotels took me on his scooter to another hotel, my bags in tow on yet another scooter, was that people made more effort and were even politer than those in the south.

The small hotel in Ha Noi's old quarter, which the French knew as *la cité indigène*, was clean and cheap, and the room reminded me of my retreat in Pham Ngu Lao. The old stone balcony overlooked a small but busy street, a street of wood-turners where almost every shop doorway had a craftsman sitting cross-legged making a door handle, a toy, a bowl or a box. Door handles seemed the most frequently produced article, the craftsmen handling the rounded wood as they might a familiar but well-loved woman. The finished objects lay in neatly heaped baskets on the pavement, a powerful resin smell rising from them and mingling with the garlic and herbs from the cook shops on the opposite side of the narrow street.

The balcony gave me what I have always loved, no matter which country I'm visiting, be it Scotland, Italy or Burma: a spot from which to look at the life of a place, undisturbed and largely unnoticed.

On the opposite side of the street, a shop and the property above it was being gutted and renovated. The workmen, like workmen everywhere, spent their break time sitting on the pavement, watching the world pass by while smoking and drinking tea bought from the next-door café. From time to time, a man on a shiny scooter would appear and give instructions from a squatting position in the gutter. Unlike workmen in most places I've seen, when these builders worked, it was with a will. From behind the long off-white net covering the French windows of the balcony, I watched, with a certain voyeuristic frisson, as the men, stripped to the waist, heaved and sweated and drilled before returning to sit and drink tea and smoke once more.

From the balcony I also saw the *xich lo* drivers in their green jungle hats, so different from the baseball caps of Saigon's cyclo drivers. Many, both young and old, are former soldiers, unable to find work in a country where, according to the Vietnamese Veteran's Association, only 20 per cent of ex-servicemen receive pensions – most of those being officers. I later noticed, as I used cyclos to get around in Ha Noi, that the drivers were often more aggressive than those in the south, expecting higher fares though fewer spoke English and distances were often shorter. Had I been more accommodating, every journey would have cost $1 minimum. Evidently the minds under the green jungle helmets still thought attack better than defence.

Some of the buildings in the old quarter had been renovated and were not all in keeping with the spirit of architectural harmony. A few of the newer shop-fronts were of concrete, stained by the chemical reaction of rainwater seeping over metal balconies, windows and railings. Each street seemed a single unbroken block of shop-fronts, presumably with flats or offices above. Corrugated metal roofs covered concrete balconies which alternated with much older red tiles and original plaster. Washing lines and awnings mixed with the trailing green of potted plants. I loved it all, even the fact that it was cold on the balcony, that the people in the streets below wore woollens and jackets under their conical hats or topis. It was dry and it never occurred to me, having seen rain only once in Vietnam, on my arrival in Nha Trang, that it wouldn't stay that way.

The hotel was only a short walk from Hoan Kiem lake, the heart of Ha Noi and a place where Vietnamese legend and history intertwine to produce a powerful national symbolism. On the afternoon of my arrival I walked through the streets of the old quarter to the north end of the lake, crossing the The Huc bridge, a footbridge leading to the Ngoc Son temple. This pagoda sits picturesquely on a small tree-covered islet in the lake and commemorates the legend of the Restored Sword. This story, which is perhaps one of the most famous in Vietnamese culture, tells of the fifteenth-century emperor Le Loi who was given a divine sword with which to drive the Chinese out of Vietnam. His success exceeded all expectations and under his rule and that of his immediate successors, Vietnamese culture regained much of what it had lost to the dominant Chinese culture and language. Laos came under Vietnamese overlordship during this period and the Later Le Dynasty rulers, as Le Loi and his descendants are referred to, began moving south, edging into the Cham territories of what is now south Vietnam.

The legend didn't end with Le Loi's successes, however. Some time after his victory, the new ruler was relaxing on the lake when a huge golden tortoise rose up out of the water to seize the transcendent weapon and, taking it down into the depths, restored it to its divine originators. I never discovered how Le Loi felt about having his good luck charm taken from him in so abrupt a manner, but he seems to have survived it well. His dynasty ruled directly for 100 years and nominally until the Tay Son Rebellion of the late eighteenth century.

Looking at the calm water of the tree-lined Lake of the Restored

Sword, I thought how, had this legend occurred in certain Western countries, the lake would probably have been dredged, sifted and thoroughly ruined in an effort to turn the metaphorical into the literal. In Ha Noi, city not only of lakes but of artists and writers, I was to learn a little about the juxtaposition of art and life in Vietnamese society.

On the second day after my arrival in Ha Noi, mindful of the time I felt I'd spent unprofitably in Saigon, I set off round the corner to Hang Quat Street, home of the disputed Darling Cafés. The Darling Café dispute is a factor of Ha Noi tourist life I never entirely understood, but is revealing of aspects of Vietnamese business life nonetheless. What I did realize was that there was fierce competition, or apparent competition, between two cafés almost diagonally opposite each other on Hang Quat Street, each with 'Darling' above its door and catering to foreigners much as the Sinh Cafés had done in Saigon. Both establishments asserted that they, and no other, were the *real* Darling Café. The significance of the word 'real' in this instance lay in its implication of 'original' and the competition was related to the fact that the *Lonely Planet* guide had recommended the *original* Darling Café to its readers. Large numbers of tourist dollars lay at the heart of the Darling dispute which, shortly before my visit, had become so fierce and long-running that the *Vietnam Investment Review* felt impelled to step in to muddy the water still further with an article declaring, 'The Real "Darling" Found at "The Green Bamboo".' Now, the Green Bamboo is a restaurant some distance from Hang Quat with no Darling pretensions at all except in the metaphorical sense applied by the journalist and the fact that the owner of the Green Bamboo, according to the article, set up the original Hang Quat Darling praised with such Euripidean consequences in *Lonely Planet*. In true tragical style, the creator of the *original* Darling claims he was turned out after the greedy landlord raised the rent in order to take over and run the place himself. Reading the article while sitting in one of the 'unreal' Darlings on Hang Quat, I enjoyed the wit of the *VIR*'s Machiavellian collaboration which, in one simple gesture, side-stepped the apparent protagonists, introduced another with an apparently 'real' claim and began the process of revenge.

In one of the unreal cafés, I ate a decidedly unpleasant banana pancake, which tasted as though it had been fried in suet, while reviewing the tour possibilities pinned to the walls. As with the Phu Quoc island tour from the Sinh Café, the one I was most interested in was the longest and furthest away. Unlike the Mekong jaunt to Phu Quoc island, this north-west tour visiting Sapa, a former French hill-station, Dien Bien Phu, site of the French defeat, and the hill-tribe peoples of this mountainous and inaccessible region, would be hell. It was a four-wheeled drive for six days over some of the worst territory in the world. I didn't have six days. I was bound for Lao Cai and China and argued to myself that I would see the north-west of Vietnam through the window of the Lao Cai train. So instead I chose a two-day tour of Halong Bay in the north-east and, having added my name to the list on the wall and paid my deposit, left to walk around the old quarter and take cyclos to various parts of Ha Noi in a search for some of the contacts Dwayne had left for me on his kitchen noticeboard in Hong Kong.

One man Dwayne had urged me to meet was a returned refugee now working as a translator. His home, in a market area in the west of Ha Noi, was pleasantly medieval. In a large downstairs room about a dozen men and women sat on mattresses around coffee and tea urns. This was the first time I had seen apparently able-bodied people not working in the middle of the day. All were wearing outdoor clothing, though the weather seemed almost warm to me. No one spoke English, though many tried. The cyclo driver, an attractive young man in a green topi, made it clear to the assemblage that I was looking for someone who lived at this address. Recognizing the name, they all smiled and nodded with one accord, which left me no wiser as to whether the man was in, out or even about. Eventually, I grasped that he was at work and would be back by 5 p.m. I thanked all the people in the room, who seemed politely curious as to what I wanted with their brother/son/neighbour/friend and left, indicating that I'd be back. I did return later that day, but I never got to meet the mysterious translator.

Driving away from the market, where women in long plastic capes laid three or four fish on upturned boxes or carefully arranged and re-arranged oranges in a basket on the pavement's edge, I saw something that has remained clear in my mind ever since. I had seen similar things in India and Burma – beggars playing music, beggars who were blind singing to those they couldn't see. But in the short time it took for me to pass this particular group of beggars I knew I was seeing something quite uniquely Vietnamese. Three young men were roped together, one behind the other. The first man had no legs from the mid-thigh down and walked on artificial limbs with the aid of crutches. The man behind him, the singer, had no eyes and carried a small amplifier in both hands as though it were a object of reverence. The last youth had eyes but no sight and was playing a very large electric guitar. The music was not like anything I'd ever heard before, neither traditional Vietnamese nor Western but somehow and effortlessly both. The man's voice, strong through the amplifier, seemed to me both defiant and tearful, and the poignancy of the sound and the greater poignancy of the spectacle made me want to weep. The sound followed the cyclo out of the market street and for several blocks beyond as the driver picked up speed on the clear roads.

Before leaving England, I had arranged to meet up with an acquaintance, a former UN worker in Ha Noi who was spending Christmas with friends in the city. The day after my arrival, I telephoned the number she had given me, only to discover from her host that she was leaving Vietnam in a few hours. So far, I'd had no luck with any of my Ha Noi contacts and knew, from my experiences in Saigon, that it would be a loss if my stay proved barren in that respect. My fondest memories of Vietnam were already those times I had spent with Vietnamese people in a one-to-one situation, a privilege not easily come by in developing countries. Still hopeful, I telephoned a woman whose number Tim Page had given me with vague indications that she was a journalist. Madame Khiem was at home and cordially invited me to her house at whatever time was convenient.

The cape-wearing women in the market near the translator's house had evidently known something I did not. The wide plastic tubes fitted over bodies and the see-through plastic 'shower caps' fitted neatly over conical hats should have told me more about the weather than about the sartorial tastes of Ha Noi women. But evidently I had been too long around London's Soho. The day after my arrival in the City of Lakes it began to rain and, with the exception of brief interludes when the sun came up for air, rarely stopped. Also, when the sun went down behind houses and trees on the wide boulevards and narrow streets, the air became cold. Ha Noi is 1,062 miles north of Saigon and it felt like it. However, I had a heavy thermal top with me which I'd bought with the Chinese part of my journey in mind and a lightweight waterproof, so I felt I could deal with anything the skies over Ha Noi threw at me.

It was dry when I set off on the 20-minute cyclo journey to Madame Khiem's home on the south side of Hoan Kiem district. But it shortly began to rain and to my enormous surprise, the driver jumped off his saddle and began erecting a clear plastic contraption over the passenger seat which looked like a cross between an oxygen tent and a baby-carriage cover. I immediately felt most uncomfortable as the plastic, though it may have once warranted the epithet 'clear', did so no longer. This meant that I could see absolutely nothing, but could still hear the screeching and braking of the surrounding traffic. I had always imagined, foolishly no doubt, that by staying alert while riding in a cyclo, I could avert being squashed in a head-on collision by throwing myself from the seat. That fond illusion was now denied me, being effectively locked by rain under the plastic, which grew increasingly opaque the more I breathed.

I was extremely relieved when we stopped in a quiet street west of Hoan Kiem lake. From the outside, Madame Khiem's house looked quite ordinary, a door fronting onto the street like all the rest. Inside, however, was quite different; it was the house of a person of means. Madame Khiem shook my hand as she opened the door and smiled. I was empty handed, probably not the politest state in which to arrive at a stranger's home in Ha Noi, but Madame Khiem, who was dressed in jeans and a multi-patterned jumper, welcomed me courteously and offered me a seat in the stone-tiled reception room.

For the next four hours we talked about many things and I learnt about my host's family, her mother and aunt in particular. I was introduced to her daughter-in-law and as I watched her spare, silent husband preparing food in the kitchen area, I felt I had stepped into a distinctly matriarchal domain. Madame Khiem told me that she worked for an educational organization and had been a journalist, writer and translator for many years; her husband, now either retired or unemployed (I never quite learnt which), had been a cabinet-maker. Madame's son had been at college in New Zealand, which surprised me as he spoke almost no English, or perhaps he simply didn't want to speak to me.

Madame and I talked a great deal about writing while her young daughter-in-law, also a woman with literary leanings, looked on, listening to our conversation. As I drank cup after cup of black tea and ate cream horns, I learnt that Madame Khiem had translated novels and poetry from Vietnamese to English and wrote poetry herself, often under a pseudonym, as her mother and aunt had done before her. I found the idea of a literary dynasty fascinating and was particularly surprised to learn that Madame's mother had no idea her daughter was anything other than a journalist. I quickly perceived that a very specific distinction was being made between journalist and 'literary' writer. In Britain, people as diverse as novelists, copywriters and management consultants can refer to themselves as 'writers'; in Vietnam there is no such semantic slackness. According to what I learnt at Madame Khiem's, a 'writer' is a person who writes from the heart about the serious issues of life, particularly love and loss.

I recognized in our discussion many of the same sentiments that had first forced themselves to my attention on reading *The Sorrow of War* and again I was struck by the juxtaposition of reserve and sentimentality in Vietnamese culture. I was shown poems and short stories by a number of different women writers and given copies of some to keep, which I greatly appreciated. All were unashamedly sentimental, yet with an edge that was hard to define. Despite my early academic background in literature and critical theory, and time spent as a publisher's reader, I found it difficult to pin down the 'Vietnamese style', if there is such a thing.

I realized after about an hour's conversation that Madame Khiem was someone who enjoyed answering questions about herself, so I asked why her mother didn't know she was a writer.

'Because writers have sad lives,' she said, 'and my mother would worry about me and be upset if she thought I was a writer.'

'But why does she think writers have sad lives?' I asked. 'Does she think that *all* writers are sad or unhappy, just because they are writers?'

'All Vietnamese think this about writers,' replied Madame

Khiem, 'that they are unhappy and have unfortunate marriages and sad love lives. My mother has not had a happy life, neither has her sister, my aunt, so she thinks about herself also in thinking of me.'

We went on to discuss Madame Khiem's mother and her practice of leaving her elderly husband at home each day and travelling across the city to write in a small flat near the Hoan Kiem lake.

'It's very important to her that she has her own life and work, although she's in her seventies now. She and my father have lived together for many years but not always happily, they are too different.

'When Vietnamese people think of writers, they think of a person having many lovers, of never being happy with their husband or wife. Some people think that of me…' there was a pause, 'but it's not true of course, though I have many friends who are men, all over the world.'

She named particular British journalists that I'd heard of and I wondered whether I was meant to believe Madame Khiem's delicate protestations; perhaps the subtleties of upper-class Vietnamese inexactitude were simply too sophisticated for me to appreciate. I wondered whether Madame's mother and aunt had been especially unhappy women in respect of their private lives, but decided against asking something quite that delicate. So it was a surprise to be told, as part of general discussion, that a friend's daughter who had recently married had only done so because she was several months pregnant. I was rather glad to discover that the cool, reserved young women I had observed from Saigon to Ha Noi had the same desires, weaknesses and humanity as the rest of the female world.

Following on the 'young love' train of thought, I mentioned my discussion with Phuong whose glass slipper key-ring I'd been given in Saigon.

'She was 22,' I said, 'but told me she'd never had a boyfriend.'

Madame smiled. 'Of course,' she said, 'the young woman would tell you that, and for two reasons. At that age she almost certainly would have a boyfriend, but it would not be proper for her to tell you, a stranger and a foreigner, that, because it might seem like boasting.'

I thought of Phuong, the ease with which she blushed and her apparent lack of comprehension of the stone genitalia in the Saigon museum and secretly thought it unlikely she had lied to me. But, used to the brazen ways of Western women, perhaps I was simply unable to judge such things.

Madame Khiem told me a great deal about sad love stories and their place in Vietnamese literature, all of which I found enthralling. I was glad to have read *The Sorrow of War* as it gave me a reference point for much that we discussed. One particular theme that remained with me long after Madame's telling of it was the fate of Northern women during the anti-US war whose lovers were fighting in the South. Some of these women longed for their partners so strongly that they left everything – parents, children, farms – to walk the length of the country just to find their man. The tragedy of these women – and I never quite grasped how much of the story was fact and how much literary fantasy – was that the journey itself, its privation, malnutrition and disease, destroyed whatever looks and youth they might have had, reducing them to shadows. Their teeth and hair fell out, their skin turned grey and when they eventually found their husbands or sweethearts – if these were not already dead – the men would either not recognize their former loves or would run screaming from creatures they imagined to be vengeful ghosts. My sceptical Western imagination found the ironic relation between the search and its results rather too contrived for the stories woven from this theme to seem entirely believable. But one of the beauties of Vietnamese writing is precisely that, a non-linear approach to time and structure where 'truth' and 'non-truth' blur and merge into a fluid landscape somewhere between dreaming and reading, vision and nightmare.

To my surprise and pleasure I was invited to join the family for their evening meal in the large dining-room. I now had the opportunity of looking at the many paintings and photographs which hung on the walls around me. I immediately saw one which, coming directly after the sad stories of love and war, produced a bizarre reaction. It was as though all the feelings accumulated during my journey thus far were focused on this one object as it hung in a plain grey frame on the wall at the foot of Madame's polished stone staircase. The image was of a young man in green fatigues running into the foreground of the painting, a radio pack on his back.

As I stared, transfixed, Madame was saying, 'The artist sold his wedding ring to buy the materials for this. It's painted in lacquer, which is very expensive. He wanted to paint it very much because it was something he'd seen during the war and he wished it to be remembered. In the background you see a Vietnamese radio unit. The Americans have just picked up the unit's signal and are already on their way to bomb it. But this man here, running towards us, is carrying the radio and also the signal and he will lead the bombers away from his friends and the real radio, so that they will be saved and only he will die.'

I had struggled not to cry from the moment I set eyes on the picture, before any words were said about it. Now my stiff upper-lip collapsed and with my hands over my face I wept silently, quite unable to think about face or loss of it. I couldn't even attribute my reaction to PMS, which had thankfully fled.

Madame paused politely for me to recover, then continued, through my mumbled apologies, 'The artist is a friend of mine. All the paintings here are by friends of mine. They know I have many foreign visitors and so they leave their work with me and sometimes people buy them.'

The thought that I might possess this painting had never occurred to me; suddenly it seemed a possibility. I very rarely see specific material objects and think 'I must have this' and it seemed odd that I might buy something that had caused such a response in me – almost like buying love or pity. I said nothing for a while, not wanting to ask business questions when I was at an emotional disadvantage. So we looked at other works, of flowers and houses.

In the dining-room, I noticed several photographs of Madame Khiem with important people, including the military genius of Dien Bien Phu, Vo Nguyen Giap. Despite his advanced age, General Giap looked tall beside the diminutive Madame Khiem, his round face pleasantly benign under snow-white hair.

A few days later, in one of the many contemporary art galleries near the Hoan Kiem lake, I saw two portraits of the General. One, a large watercolour, showed a young Giap in remote countryside, perhaps Pac Bo, standing very slightly behind and looking, with an expression difficult to fathom, at a youthful and dark-bearded Ho Chi Minh. In his khaki shirt and shorts, the future victor looked like a boy scout about to rub two sticks together. I took a photograph of this painting, intrigued by such a simple image of two men who had, together, overcome empires. The flash of my camera reflected in the picture glass and many months later I noticed that it had formed a yellow five-pointed star on the forehead of General Giap. The other portrait, an official-looking work of an elderly man in uniform, showed the same round benignity as the 'scout' picture and when I thought of the deeds done in the intervening years of this man's life – 'utterly ruthless' were the words I most often heard associated with his name – I wondered how it was possible for so little to show. Perhaps here was the antithesis of Dorian Gray.

After dinner, I explained my visa dilemma to Madame, who told me not to worry about it. There was an official charge for having the wrong exit stamp and I would simply to have to pay that at Lao Cai. I would have to pay some Ha Noi fat cat to change the exit stamp anyway and then the Lao Cai border guards might decide to charge me just for the hell of it, so I might as well save myself the bother of hanging around offices and just pay at the border. If all else failed, I'd have to slip the Lao Cai guards a few dollars and it would all be OK. I felt greatly reassured by Madame's casual approach to officialdom, but I still harboured visions of being stuck forever in a freezing, if beautiful, hell-hole miles from an embassy, surrounded by heroin traffickers and the smoky-quartz smell of opium.

I thanked Madame Khiem for her warm hospitality and fascinating discourse. Before leaving, I stood in front of the 'heroic' painting and looked at the tiny pieces of eggshell representing smashed stones set into the lacquer, the copper and bronze sheen of paint indicating fire, and the old-gold horizon, filled with peace and menace both, broken by the single branch of a palm. My heart in my mouth, I took the step and asked Madame how much the picture might be. She told me what she had paid the artist for it and that she would like to sell it on for a little more to give him an extra 'present'. I thought the sum very reasonable, though I was concerned about carrying a large rigid item on my back through China to Hong Kong and London. I asked her if I might think about the logistics of such a purchase and telephone her in a few days, to which she replied that being very fond of the piece herself she was in no hurry to sell it.

It had stopped raining when I left Madame Khiem's house. She had hailed a cyclo in the street and asked the driver to take me to *Ga Ha Noi*, Ha Noi railway station. I was on my way to book the only berth available, a 'hard sleeper', i.e. a plank, to Lao Cai, and quite suddenly, as I sat in the damp and shifting seat of the pedicab, China and its vastness assumed a reality I hadn't truly considered before. I felt that buying the ticket, which proved remarkably easy, was a psychological step north; that I was on my way once more.

But before thinking seriously of China, I was headed for Halong Bay, the north-east of Vietnam and, of course, the city of Ha Noi itself.

chapter eleven
THE FLAT LANDS

The day after my visit to Madame Khiem's, I was up at 6 a.m. There might have been a sense of flashback to Saigon and the morning of my delta tour, but the 18°F difference between Saigon and Ha Noi made it less easy to spring out of bed and a cold shower was out of the question. At least it wasn't raining as I peered through the dusty glass of the French windows into the already busy street and removed my earplugs.

Wearing a waterproof jacket and with my exceedingly large thermal top stored in my bag, I strolled round the corner and into Hang Quat Street. Outside one of the pseudo-Darling Cafés, the white minibuses, which seemed a prerequisite for Vietnamese tourist operators, were lined up like hearses at a Filipino funeral.

There were only three other people besides myself on the bus when it left from outside the café. Our guide, a tall, fleshy young man in baseball cap and shades who told us his name was Pete, spoke fast and furiously in a language that bore less resemblance to American than he imagined and less still to English. None of the local cafés were yet open for food or drink but Pete told us that we would stop for breakfast before leaving Ha Noi, which seemed a little odd; however, undismayed by the lack of sustenance and wider companionship, we set off with light hearts and stomachs on what was to be a far longer journey than any of us could have imagined as *la cité indigène* slipped away behind us and we drove on through the busying streets and boulevards of Ha Noi.

The next two hours were spent driving around the inner city suburbs looking for the hotels where the rest of the tour passengers awaited us. As each person had been told the same time of departure, we became accumulatively later and later until, by the time we stopped for coffee and a bread roll, my stomach thought it was lunch-time and the sun was rising rapidly above the mist and grey-ness of the city morning.

I was glad, however, to have been able to look at the streets of Ha Noi when they were still relatively empty. The wide boulevards had a distinctly behind-the-Iron-Curtain feel to them in the harsh northern light and the people who were up and about wore mainly dark colours or the ubiquitous jungle green. Looking around, I could understand a little of what the north and south each disliked or distrusted about their neighbour. There seemed a seriousness, a rigour about what I had seen of northern life so far and a quietness which contrasted sharply with the colour and noise of the south. But in many ways it seemed not so different from north/south animosity found in many countries of the world, from the United States to Wales.

When we left Hang Quat, the bus passengers had consisted of a friendly middle-aged German couple, a large bearded Austrian and myself. Before breakfast we'd taken on board two Italians, four Isra-elis, a Japanese, an Australian and two quite spectacular Frenchmen who started complaining before we'd even finished breakfast. It was obvious that we were in for an interesting two days.

Outside Ha Noi the Red River is truly spectacular and truly red. It had a quite different quality from any of the other large rivers I'd seen in Vietnam, possibly because my view of it was almost exclu-sively through the metal struts and spars of the Chuong Duong bridge. But what it might lack in bucolic charm as it flowed out of Ha Noi, whose name means 'City on a Bend of the River', it made up for in grandeur. Only the Mississippi where it marks the Tennessee state line had seemed more splendid and solemn as I crossed it and that had lacked the rich, mulligatawny colour of the Red River.

Leaving Ha Noi, the Red River is crossed by two bridges. As we drove over the new-looking Chuong Duong bridge, avoiding a broken-down lorry and its load of paper, now fluttering like giant snowflakes into the path of oncoming vehicles, I saw, a few hundred yards to our north, the much bombed and much repaired Long Bien bridge which appeared to be for the use of cyclists and pedestrians only. According to the *Lonely Planet* guide, at one time during the Vietnam war, the Long Bien, which was a favourite target of US bombers, was guarded by 300 anti-aircraft guns and 84 SAM missiles. This array of weaponry didn't stop the bridge being repeatedly hit and repeatedly rebuilt, often overnight. But it was only when some particularly ingenious Vietnamese hit on the idea of putting American POWs who, ironically, were mostly airmen, to work on the bridge that the US stopped the bombing raids. I wondered whether it was still considered not quite safe even after 20 years and if that was the reason for no motor vehicles using it.

Once away from the city, we passed through a brief industrial hinterland, with small factories and chimneys whose smoke contributed to a general greyness in the atmosphere. Then we were in the countryside and, unhampered by buildings, the flat landscape stretched into the remote distance broken only by the levees bordering the biggest rice paddies I'd ever seen. Rice is one of the most important of all Vietnam's exports and since collectivization was abolished in the mid-'80s, production has increased by 50 per cent. Since the early 1990s, Vietnam has leapt from being a net importer of rice to the world's third largest exporter. Such expansion is happening everywhere in Vietnam and as we drove across its earth, I felt the energy again and saw it in the faces of the women who irrigated the fields we passed by hand; bucket after bucket of muddy water fed into the vast channels and ditches.

The sky cleared and it was under a surprisingly bright cyan sky dotted with soft speeding cumuli that we drove east through the Red River delta, along a reasonably good road, towards our destination of Bay Chai on the coast of Halong Bay in the Gulf of Tonkin.

As we travelled further into the delta, the road rose to a level about 5 feet above the waterlogged earth until we were on a narrow causeway cutting across what resembled green marsh but was actually newly transplanted rice crop. Irrigation lines were etched deeply into the earth's surface. The grass-covered levees formed low walls between fields and beyond them occasional hamlets showed pretty white walls and red tiled roofs. The wind blew strongly; through the moving window I watched its invisible fingers whipping up the shallow water round the spindly legs of china-white wading birds and redirecting the fronds of coconut palms due south. Being raised, even slightly, above ground level meant our bus was buffeted as the wind whistled through the half-open windows. I watched the driver struggling with the steering-wheel from time to time and wondered vaguely what would happen were we to land upside down in an water-filled irrigation ditch. My confidence in Vietnamese emergency services being of the limited variety, I decided accidents were best not contemplated.

For a few hours, the landscape remained unchanging; the villages we passed through had a pleasant but bland uniformity of dun-coloured dogs, variegated pigs and strutting cockerels. At the entrance or exit, depending on one's perspective, of each village was a grey-white lime pit. As in most developing countries, rural Vietnamese build their own homes and the communal lime pit provides material for both mortar and whitewashing. For some reason I found these pits fascinating, perhaps because my only previous acquaintance with them had been at the peak of the UK AIDS hysteria in 1985, when one dear old lady of 80 reputedly advised the *Sun* newspaper that all gay men and people with AIDS should be shot and thrown into lime pits. Looking at the seemingly innocuous lime pits of north Vietnam, surrounded as they were by playing children and their pets, all of that seemed very far away.

We had been given a packed lunch along similar lines to that of the Sinh Café and around lunch-time we arrived at a ferry crossing. Despite attention to my map, I really had no idea where we were or what route we'd followed from Ha Noi. I asked what water we were crossing, but Pete wasn't too good on local orientation himself and dealt with that by smiling and refusing to understand questions. I later discovered, as I stood on a second ferry, that both crossings were of tributaries of the Red River and both were part of the massive delta system.

As we waited for the first ferry, our tour party was joined by another busload of tourists, among whom I recognized the young Japanese woman with the voice like Henry Kissinger. Although inevitable, it always seems strange to see an even vaguely familiar face in a foreign place and we were pleased to meet each other again. She had a young Japanese man in tow and both seemed to know the

Japanese member of our party. There was much smiling, bowing and exclamation beginning, 'Ah!'

It was during the enforced idleness on the south side of the ferry that I first got the measure of the Israeli members of our group. So far, they had spoken to no one, but it was evident from their manner that they were not enjoying themselves. The roadway leading to the water's edge was lined with stalls selling fruit, soft drinks and the inevitable out-of-date biscuits. I bought a fruit that I had never seen before and subsequently learnt was a custard-apple and, by watching a local, discovered how to open and eat the thing. As I spat the large black seeds into the water an Israeli girl joined me and asked in good English what it was I was eating.

I replied, 'I don't really know. I just wanted to try it.'

She looked sceptical. 'I'm afraid to eat things here. You don't know what's in them or who's touched them.'

I looked at her in astonishment. 'It's actually rather nice,' I said, feeling suddenly defensive of Vietnamese fruit. 'And anyway, what could possibly be wrong with the inside of fruit?'

I could see her beginning to weaken. 'Can I try a little bit of yours?' she asked. This seemed odd to me – after all, she didn't know what ghastly hidden diseases I might have. But in the cause of international relations I said that yes, of course she could have some.

She tasted it and broke into a relieved smile. 'I know what it is now, we have this at home in Israel.'

I smiled back, imagining a blow had been struck for fruit all over the world.

'Only ours are better,' she concluded, before thanking me and turning away to inform her friends in rapid Hebrew that it was safe to eat this, because they'd eaten it before, in Israel.

Suddenly the affectations, protestations and general tactlessness of the French I had met during my journey paled into insignificance and even seemed amusing beside the sullen ungraciousness of these particular tourists. During a subsequent conversation over dinner that evening, I was asked – I was virtually the only non-Israeli that the four deigned to address – if I'd been to Israel. When I replied that I had, my standing rose still further. Luckily no one thought to ask me what I'd thought of the place – that was taken for granted –

and I was in too polite a mood to shatter their illusions.

The two Frenchmen were proving a source of general entertainment. Their complaints, which they were polite enough to make in English so that they could be generally enjoyed, had not ceased since they boarded the minibus outside their suburban hotel, but it was all done in a deliberate spirit of hopelessness which the rest of the passengers found funny. Because of the way the men were dressed and because they were together, I thought it likely they were gay, but in later conversation discovered my error. They were merely very camp and seemed quite consciously to behave like a long-faced comedy duo. The tall man, Frank, said he was a teacher in some rural region of central France, but his snakeskin cowboy boots, sprayed-on Calvin Klein jeans and orange and pink paisley denim jacket did not in the least accord with my idea of rural French pedagogues – though admittedly whatever ideas I might have had on the matter were drawn solely from reading *Le Grand Meaulnes*. The other man, Pierre, was the small silent sidekick who giggled a lot behind his hand while Frank moaned loudly, waving his long paisley arms in all directions. During a particularly vociferous scenario when Frank's upper body was more mobile than usual, I caught the flash of a gold medallion as it swung free, probably trying to escape the frantic orange and pink jacket.

Both of the two roll-on roll-off ferries were quite ancient and seemed entirely covered in a thick black-brown tar. It was necessary to approach with caution, as the motion of the water caused them to move as one tried to step on, threatening to trap feet between the weight of the drop-gate and the blackened concrete ramp. Getting off usually meant jumping into several inches of water. Each journey took about five minutes and on the second crossing, as we nosed slowly closer to the far shore, I watched a high-chimneyed power-station grow larger and more dominating on the approaching bank. I never discovered what the station supplied, or to whom, but already signs of a small but growing industry were forming around its base. Looking at the rural scene from mid-water, the grazing water buffaloes, sampans driven by nothing other than muscle and bamboo poles, the village of white-washed buildings and trees on its low promontory, I tried to imagine a vast industrial complex here, but imagination failed me.

We arrived at our destination of Bay Chai shortly after midday. It had taken us more than six hours to travel 100 miles. The bus dropped us at our hotels. For some reason we were divided between two or three hotels on a road that looked like, and actually was, a building site. My room was basic but serviceable. The extra blankets piled on a chair suggested that the coming night might be a cold one, which made the blue mosquito net seem rather incongruous. We were allowed 15 minutes to dump our belongings in our rooms before being rushed off to lunch at a tourist-filled restaurant on the tree-lined seafront. I too was a tourist here, just as I had been a tourist at the coconut toffee factory in the Mekong. It was a strange, unfamiliar feeling being shepherded and directed, but behind that feeling lay a small sense of relief at not having to think and plan for oneself, for a day or two.

There was something peculiarly southern European about the atmosphere of Bay Chai. That may have been the result of its being constructed literally and metaphorically around the burgeoning tourist industry drawn to the region by the spectacular limestone islets of Halong Bay. But the location itself had a decidedly Impressionist charm; looking through the pines from the dust-yellow road bordering the sea and across the water to Hong Gai, the *ville indigène* of Halong Bay, the vista was pure Pissarro. Sadly, the view I saw with such pleasure is unlikely to last long. The entire Halong area is currently under development by Singaporeans and Taiwanese eager for more than a nice view and a few noodles; one Malaysian company plans a $100 million resort to include a several hundred room hotel, tourist houses and sports centre at Bay Chai.

After my visit to Halong I chanced on an article in a Far East newspaper in which the reporter suggested that the return journey from Halong to Ha Noi:

> ...would be much more interesting with a stopover for an afternoon, or even a night, at the Macau-owned Do Son Casino, near the port town of Haiphong, about halfway back... The few existing two-star hotels and karaoke lounges [of Bay Chai] might have enough old-world charm to satisfy the French tourists visiting a

former colony, or Taiwanese or Koreans seeking cheap entertainment, but not most of the choosy and luxury-loving Singaporeans.
The Straits Times

The entire article made me cringe as I envisaged the delightful views I had been fortunate enough to see disappearing into the abyss of Singaporean requirement. The juxtaposition of the words 'karaoke' and 'old-world charm' caused me to doubt the mental stability of the reporter and the reference to the casino made me wonder about inducements. Some months later I heard that the Vietnamese government had prohibited the opening of any more casinos and was glad.

After a plain but pleasant lunch, we walked across the road and along the beach to where the tour boats were anchored. One's role was very firmly defined on the sides of the boats in large painted letters which read 'Halong Tourist'. The space between the high-sided boat and the pebble beach was bridged by a single, narrow, wooden plank. The drop from the top of the plank was about 15 feet and I quailed at the thought of running up the thing with an unsteady left foot. I was relieved to see others around me quailing too and cheered up considerably, if meanly, at the thought of French Frank and his smooth, leather-soled cowboy boots. Seeing the general disquiet among the less than athletic, Pete the Tour – as I privately called him in traditional Welsh style – seized one end of a long bamboo pole and, sending one of the boat men up the plank to its other end, created a very useful handrail. All of us were struck by the simplicity and inventiveness of the thing and I thought how dulled our initiative must be.

The open-sided boat deck was a very odd mixture of styles. Cascades of plastic hibiscus tangled with pointless muslin curtains. The roof of the deck was supported by pale yellow columns and under it were two glass-topped tables. Padded benches ran along each side of the deck on which we sat in relative comfort and looked out at the incredible view stretching before us as the boat moved towards open water and the phenomenon of Halong Bay and its many thousand islets. Vietnam's tourist officials had begun to refer to Halong Bay as the 'eighth wonder of the world' by December 1994 and though that's perhaps an overstatement, the sight was truly stunning, an amalgam of Thai island paradise and China's Guilin panorama.

The words *Ha Long* mean 'the place where the dragon comes down to the sea'. Like many such places in Vietnam, there is a legend attached to Halong Bay which tells of the dragon who once lived in the mountains above the bay. One day it decided to go for a swim, but on its way down to the sea its flailing tail gouged out the land it passed over; as it dived into the sea, displaced water flowed backwards, filling the gorges and hollows and leaving only a few scattered peaks of land standing above the water. Although no one now believes that there's a dragon living in the bay, there have long been sailors' tales of an enormous marine creature called the 'Tarasque' which reputedly haunts the depths. Apparently, some of the more intrepid of Bay Chai and Hong Gai's boat owners have organized Tarasque-hunting parties aimed at Western tourists, much as Scottish tour operators have Loch Ness monster outings.

I saw nothing of Tarasques or even ordinary monsters as we moved through the pale blue water of the bay. On our left, the village of Hong Gai lay under its towering cliff and I wondered how a place could survive in such a position, imagining the small fragile-looking houses crushed between the sea nudging their doorsteps and the overweening limestone tower rising vertically at the rear. Looking later at maps of the bay, I realized that the scattered islets and islands acted as a breakwater against storm waves and the limestone cliffs sheltered rather than menaced the inhabitants of Hong Gai.

Within sight of Hong Gai, we passed what appeared to be a floating petrol station. Diesel pumps, shaded by rusted metal awnings, stood sentry on the deck of a elderly barge. Drums and cylinders leant precariously against each other in the sunlight as though whispering greasy secrets. There was even a small building of yellow corrugated iron perched on one end of the barge and outside it a lone youth clad only in underpants crouched, fiddling with the base of a TV aerial mast.

After 20 minutes the water around us had turned a dark turquoise-green. The sky, never entirely clear, was a hazy blue and the temperature cool and pleasant as we neared the limestone stacks which often rose directly from the water without the preliminaries of shore or beach to interfere with the perfect 90° angle created by their upward thrust. The tree-clad peaks were fabulous and the chiaro-scuro effect of layer on layer of islets rising one behind the other was both beautiful and awe-inspiring. It seemed at times as though the gigantic chalk cliffs hung mysteriously, supported by nothing more than sea vapours.

One of the most obvious natural distinctions between parts of the globe is the quality and colour of light and the way it affects what and how the observer sees. Looking at the chalk peaks of Halong Bay, I appreciated for the first time the extraordinary quality of medieval Chinese landscape paintings, which had captured just such views in Guilin and the Lijiang valleys. In Britain, with its cold northern light, such paintings, seen only on the pages of a book or hanging on a wall, had always seemed to me beautiful, but obscure and unconvincing. Now, I would go home and view with new eyes.

After moving south and east for about an hour, we were completely surrounded by the high green-covered rocks and out of sight of the mainland. When the boat's engine was turned off, the silence was intense. We anchored near a group of islands which had a small beach and were told that we could get off and walk up to see the caves and grottoes hidden high up within the limestone. I decided to take the opportunity to relax and as the majority of the party clambered down the plank and up the steep and invisible path to the caves, I sat and had a cup of tea provided by the boat driver and listened to the sounds of the water hitting the hull. The few of us who'd chosen to stay on the boat looked about and the Australian member of our group, a nurse from Canberra, pointed out, with some surprise, that there were birds in the trees covering the cliffs. I wondered why she made this observation until she added that they were the only birds she'd seen in the north of Vietnam. When I thought about it, this seemed true; I remembered the sounds of a million sparrows twittering outside my window in Pham Ngu Lao, but couldn't recall seeing or hearing a single bird since leaving Hué. We wondered why that might be and someone suggested they'd all died of fright as a result of the heavy bombing of the Ha Noi–Haiphong region during the Vietnam war, though if that were true there'd not be a bird almost anywhere in Vietnam. Someone else thought they might simply have flown away as a result of their habitat being destroyed. In fact the observation wasn't accurate – though not exactly teeming with bird-life, the north of Vietnam does have feathered creatures.

As we rocked gently under the chalky overhang, awaiting the return of our companions, a boat, rowed by two women, came along-side. Looking rather like a larger, longer version of the coracles I'd seen at Lang Co, the boat was made from rattan and tarred to keep out the water. Thinking of garden furniture, I looked at it, foolishly expecting to see it fill up with water and sink, but rattan is both durable and extremely versatile and the Vietnamese, who know how to exploit such things, are currently producing a rattan bicycle for export.

While one woman dandled her baby and waved bottles of Coca-Cola at us, the other let go of her oars and began attending to her make-up in a small hand mirror. I watched, intrigued, as this woman, who wore a close-fitting knitted yellow cap buttoned under her chin, blue tartan socks and no shoes, turned her head this way and that, catching her reflection in the glass. She seemed to be applying pow-der – or perhaps she was keeping an eye out for the Tarasque over her shoulder. These women lived in the sampans moored around the bay. Their lives were spent on the water in what most Westerners would consider intolerable conditions, yet everything about them was clean and fresh: their appearance, their baby, their boat.

My attention was drawn away from observations on cleanliness by the arrival of a similar rattan boat containing an unusually tall and broad woman. I instantly thought of the pirate warnings I'd read, of the frequency of attacks in Halong Bay in just such situations. Perhaps the rower was not a woman at all but a pirate in a bizarre form of drag; s/he did have permed hair strangely reminiscent of some 1930s schoolgirl. Whilst thoughts of Angela Brazil and Daisy pulling it off muddled with Captains Blood and Hook, the woman – as she proved to be – produced armfuls of out-of-date coconut bis-cuits and tried to sell them to us as we drank our tea. Wise to the 'ancient biscuit' trick, I made the mistake of pointing to the date on the packet and shaking my head. The woman seemed to find this very funny and descended into her boat to reappear a few minutes later with the dates changed in pencil by an unsteady hand. She pointed at the new date and, laughing, made a thumbs-up. While I could admire the boldness of her plan, I still had no intention of buying her wares. Seeing that I would not be swayed, the woman began to abuse me in Vietnamese whilst looking me straight in the eye. Though I didn't understand the words, I had a fairly clear idea of what she was saying and guessed that my parents were unmarried and my pocket tighter than my anus.

Realizing she'd lost the day financially, she decided she could still win it morally and, seizing the baby from the next boat, held it out to me and made eating gestures. I naturally declined, saying it looked inedible in its raw state. I could see that she was beginning to enjoy herself when the boat driver intervened, looking quite shocked at the extent of her obscenities, and told her to leave. Still cursing and giggling alternately, she clambered down from the side of our boat, where she'd been hanging on a rope-ladder, and struck up a conversation with the women in the boat whose baby she'd borrowed.

Soon afterwards, our party returned, Frank muttering and flapping as his boots skidded on the pebbles and slipped on the wood of the gangplank. The biscuit-woman seized her opportunity and managed to make a sale to the unsuspecting Germans.

As we set off back towards Bay Chai, the driver and his assistant began to play music tapes. The two which seemed to be his favourites, or perhaps he imagined they were our favourites, were Simon and Garfunkel's 'I Am A Rock', which seemed bizarrely appropriate, and the Eagles with that old chestnut, 'Hotel California'. Is there no escape, I thought, as memories of the Christmas cupboard flooded back. The entire situation became truly surreal, however, when, in the silence following the last bars of 'I Am A Rock', the friendly German man who had boarded the minibus in Hang Quat began to whistle 'Hitler Has Only Got One Ball' very loudly. I struggled unsuccessfully to recall whether it was also the tune to something else and wanted very much to ask him if he knew what it was he was singing, but decided eventually simply to enjoy the weirdness of it all.

That evening we ate well at the restaurant near the beach. Someone asked for chicken, which meant a death sentence for the bird happily pecking away in a bamboo cage on the pavement. One minute it was alive, then there was much squawking followed by a thud and it was merely another ingredient for *ga chien sa ot*, fried chicken with chilli and lemongrass. To several of our party, including myself, this summary execution seemed rather shocking, yet it was a salutary experience for us, in the era of unrecognizable cuts of pre-packaged flesh, to be reminded that death and dinner are as intimately related now as they ever were.

The following day was cold and grey. The sun struggled to show itself but, unconvinced, I put on my waterproof jacket and took my thermals. The entire morning was spent doing exactly what we had done the previous afternoon, but what had then seemed charming and exotic seemed madness in the grey rain-slashed light of 9 a.m. as the open-sided boat headed out across increasingly rough water. Within half an hour all four Israelis were lying down in a closed section at the back of the boat, retching and mumbling among themselves and refusing to speak to Pete the Tour. It actually became quite dangerous to walk hand over hand along the foot-wide deck space that led to the hole-in-the-floor toilet at the rear of the boat. But it was a curious experience watching everything fall into the water as it flashed only feet away from one's vital organs.

As it grew ever colder, the whistling German pulled out a large bottle of some local fire-water he'd bought in Ha Noi and kindly shared it with whoever could stomach it. It certainly raised cold damp spirits and, in the single photograph of myself taken onboard the boat, I am sitting wrapped in a wool shawl wearing gold-rimmed glasses and an inane grin. Despite doing an unwitting impression of Red Riding Hood's grandmother on acid I look relatively normal compared to the bearded Austrian sitting next to me. In his pink cagoul, its pointy lime-green hood half covering his face, he needed only a large toadstool to be crowned as the only Teutonic King of the Leprechauns.

I enjoyed Halong Bay, though the second boat trip had been an unnecessary experience. The weather was beginning to close in right across the delta region as we set off on our return journey to Ha Noi. The clouds were low and grey and without the blue of the sky and yellow of the sun, the landscape seemed drained of colour. Everything took on the brown of wet dust – chickens, ducks, sparrows, dogs, earth, houses, water, water-buffaloes, all were a uniformly neutral shade. But when colour intruded into this dun world it did so with panache; dark red lotus flowers seemed particularly vivid rising from their brown-black watery bed and pink hibiscus cascaded over metal-stained walls. In occasional fields of rice, a saffron blouse stood out like a sunflower and when the green of grass was torn it once again revealed the vermilion soil beneath in flashes of bloody colour. When the rain and mist intensified, I started making notes for a short story and looked up only rarely, but on one occasion I saw a flat grey landscape of dykes and paddies, broken in the middle distance by a young girl in a scarlet coat riding her bicycle into the wind.

Passing through a village about halfway to Ha Noi, I saw an elderly woman sitting in the shelter of her doorstep combing her hair which, though yellow with age, swept round her shoulders and reached almost to her knees. Moving at high speed through the streets, the unexpected intimacy of this image was quickly succeeded by four women, all wearing scarves over their lower faces, welding the underside of a truck beside a chrysanthemum allotment. Worn and weather-beaten houses proudly sported the date 1990 or 1991 over their door frames. Even the pale greens and yellows of new buildings had turned to dust colour.

It was early evening but already dark and raining again when the minibus dropped the last of its passengers on the corner of Hang Quat. The whistling German and his wife, the Austrian in the pointy hood and I stood around for a few minutes in the rain shuffling our feet and saying goodbye before we drifted off to our respective hotels.

I was alone again, but this time I had reached my destination and my thought was no longer 'Onwards and upwards' but 'What now?' There was no going further in Vietnam and in the cold dark wetness of Hang Quat, I felt the difference between 'alone' and 'lonely'. It was New Year's Eve. I didn't feel quite as enthusiastic or jolly at the thought of the Lao Cai train and 16 hours on a plank as I'd hoped I'd feel when purchasing the ticket. The prospect of one of the most awkward border crossings in the world followed by days on a Chinese bus filled me with gloom.

I felt tired, cold and utterly unintrepid as I walked into one of the fake Darlings and asked for noodle soup. The windows were steamed up and all around me depressed-looking travellers huddled in the miasma caused by their own damp clothing. As I peered miserably into my greasy soup, I thought of Saigon, of prawns and squid pancakes, warmth and sunlight, and wondered why I was going in the opposite direction.

chapter twelve

WINTER FLAMES

Before leaving England for Hong Kong, I visited a well known astrology shop in Covent Garden to have a personal 'astro-cartography' map made. This particular aspect of astrology, which looks at the world map in relation to one's place and date of birth, has been around for a long time, occasionally being used to predict world events. President Kennedy was seemingly warned, by whoever had studied his astro-cartography, to avoid Dallas, Texas, on the last day of Scorpio 1963 – his equivalent of the 'Ides of March'. The warning passed him by and Kennedy ended his days in similar style to Julius Caesar. Of course, Kennedy might equally well have lived to a ripe old age and fallen under a truck in Topeka, hindsight always being better and all that. But I had a curiosity to see what, if any, aspects my own birth details had in relation to Vietnam. Ten minutes after paying my money, the computer churned out my map, and I went and sat in a café in Neal Street, Covent Garden, and stared in nervous disbelief at the black line of Pluto Descending cutting through Ha Noi. In the interpretation booklet that came with my map, the following apparently applied to any sojourn I might make in Ha Noi:

> There is great danger under this line, and the battle of selfhood is with a hostile world that seems intent on extinguishing you. The world withdraws from you and leaves you to do battle with the very things that are closest to you. If you win this battle you will be free from dependency for the rest of your life. There is alienation and destruction here, but these are the keys to a new life. There may

also be a desperation born of fear of always being alone and all in all there is too much danger here for prolonged residence.

On first reading this, I did what many people do with astrology: accepted the good bits and cast aside the bad as being nonsense. I did wonder vaguely what sort of difficulties might present themselves, but persuaded myself that as I wouldn't be taking up a 'prolonged residence' the warning didn't apply to me. Then I more or less forgot the whole thing. On arriving in the cool sunshine of Ha Noi, Pluto's black line had seemed no more than a distant smudge on the horizon. It didn't occur to me to relate the warning to my lifelong aim to visit Vietnam or think that this might be the place where Vietnam would test me rather thoroughly.

The evening of my return from Halong Bay, things started, little by little, to go wrong. The rain became relentless and without heating my room was damp and dreary. In all my life I had never been alone on New Year's Eve, and whilst that prospect in itself was not a problem, my general situation was unconducive to solitary pleasure. Eating the eternal noodles in another fake Darling Café, I considered the opening lines of one of Keats' less stimulating poems:

O Solitude! if I must with thee dwell,
Let it not be among the jumbled heap
Of murky buildings...

As I tried to remember the next line – something about 'Nature's observatory' or possibly 'lavatory' – an American guy started talking to me and, both being alone and far from home, we chatted for a while and arranged to meet later to go to a bar or café and see the New Year in. I began to cheer up a little and wandered around the various shops in the old quarter, beginning to buy gifts for friends back home – T-shirts, more incense, paintings.

I sat for a time in a small friendly pagoda observing the people at prayer, the intensity with which they prayed on their knees, incense sticks held between the palms of joined hands. I didn't understand the significance or function of most of the images and decoration that I saw, but it was warm in the temple, warmer than in the cafés and certainly warmer than in my room, and I suddenly had a faint glimpse of how pleasant the inside of a church must be to any Western urban itinerant.

In the streets around Hang Quat, boys were lighting strips of firecrackers; the noise was deafening and could be quite nerve-racking when the crackers exploded unexpectedly only metres away. I watched the smoke and fumes rise from the burning strips to hang almost unmoving in the cold moisture-laden air. After walking aim-lessly for an hour or so, I returned to my hotel and had a hot bath in an attempt to raise the spirits.

I waited in the reception of my hotel at the agreed time for the American, but after 15 minutes he hadn't appeared and in a fit of pique I left and, climbing under the plastic covering of the nearest cyclo, set off for the International Telephone Exchange. I decided to try and cheer myself up by calling members of my friends and family. After five or six phone calls, I had only succeeded in speaking to the friend of a friend's friend. It was about 9.15 p.m. in Ha Noi and mid-afternoon in Britain. Everyone – even my parents – was out and about. Feeling worse than ever, I returned to my hotel to find a dis-appointed and apologetic message from the American, who'd turned up three minutes after I'd left. The dark finger of Pluto was begin-ning to poke me more firmly in the ribs; I was clearly meant to be on my own and not have a good time.

The ease with which I'd made friends and acquaintances further south appeared to have utterly deserted me. It seemed that the weather had affected everyone and almost all the foreigners who sat in the cafés and restaurants of the old quarter looked morose and ill-tempered, as though a silent mildew were invading their perspec-tive on life. Hoping against hope to come across someone I'd met in the balmy south, I'd left little bits of forlorn paper fluttering on the message-boards of the Darlings. Each time I went for a coffee or a pancake they were still there, looking more and more soggy; sad messages sent into a void.

Inspecting the notices on one occasion, I saw an advert for an AIDS Benefit at the Ha Noi Opera House. Because of my own past history in AIDS work I took particular notice of this and felt rather cheered up at the thought that things were happening in Vietnam on that front. The terribly British name of the event's organizer also brought a smile to my face, though I was sorry to see that I'd missed the occasion, which had taken place the previous evening.

By 11 p.m. I'd accepted that this particular New Year's Eve was not going to get any jollier; there'd be no 'Auld Lang Syne' for me this year. Walking and riding around in the fume-laden rain had made my throat sore and my eyes water and I thought of one of the last of Dr Lo's blue pills much as that same short-lived poet who longed for 'Nature's lavatory' must have felt on considering draining a cup of hemlock. I decided to go to bed and sleep and when I woke up it would be a new day, a new year, and I would be on my way to a new country; everything would seem quite different. I swallowed the pill, put in earplugs against the noise of the firecrackers still popping fiercely in the distance and snivelled myself to sleep.

The next morning, I awoke believing I had sunk Lethe-wards almost as far as the defunct Keats. What had been a minor sore throat the previous night was now raw flesh. More seriously still, the breathing problems I'd had in Hong Kong seemed to be hanging around again. By the time I spoke to Madame Khiem and arranged to pay her a farewell visit later that afternoon, I felt extremely unwell. I checked out of my room, sad that my feelings on leaving it were not as happy as on my arrival. It was too wet to stand on the balcony and the semi-naked workmen were nowhere in sight – probably recovering from a grand old time the previous night.

Leaving my bags behind the reception desk, I wandered off for a final glimpse of Ha Noi. I had put this time aside to view Ho Chi Minh in his mausoleum but I'd heard that it was closed, or rather his mummified remains were not on view due to their restoration. Being New Year's Day, *Tet Duong Lich*, public buildings and cultural centres such as museums were closed. Vietnamese New Year, *Tet Nguyen Dan*, which corresponds to the Chinese lunar New Year, is usually four to six weeks after the 1 January festival and is far more significant in Vietnamese culture. I couldn't imagine how many firecrackers would be let off at the 'real' Tet celebrations.

On my way to Madame Khiem's, mindful of my manners, I bought several bunches of the beautiful flowers I'd seen being sold all over central Ha Noi. I had often looked at the flowers and thought how lovely they were and was glad to have the opportunity to buy them. Then I went to a 'French' pâtisserie in Hang Bong Street, reputedly the best in Ha Noi, and while the cakes and pastries I'd chosen were boxed and wrapped, I ate a quick Danish pastry and downed a *café au lait*.

Sitting inside my oxygen-tented cyclo, the box of cakes perched precariously on my knees, I began to feel increasingly ill. As the rain-drops ran down the plastic and dripped onto my unprotected ankles, I started to snivel, partly from gloom but mostly, I soon began to sus-pect, from depression as the result of a viral infection. There was a certain Hardyesque satisfaction about water flowing inside and out my little tent. The driver of course was completely soaked, the cov-ering of his plastic jungle hat darkened by the rainwater and his clothes a sponge. He didn't seem in the least bit moved by his own plight, which made me feel not a whit better about my own. I was quite glad it was pouring so that tears could pass as rain.

Madame Khiem was pleased to see me and most appreciative of the flowers and cakes. I looked at my favourite painting again and told her what I had decided: that it would be foolish to carry such a large heavy item overland to Hong Kong and back to Britain. Even if it wasn't stolen, damaged or confiscated, I would be squashed under too much luggage. Madame listened with perfect equilibrium and said she was quite glad as it was a special picture and she was very fond of it.

We ate cakes and drank tea and I began to feel faint. My ticket to Lao Cai was burning a hole in my money pouch and my mind, unsettled by illness, was feverish and unable to make logical deci-sions with regard to what I should or shouldn't do in the next 12 hours. The thought of the hard sleeper in my condition was desper-ate, but I had the ticket and had told myself that I would go, regard-less of comfort or consequences. I was trapped in a situation entirely of my own making. The truth, when I faced it, was that I didn't want to go to China. I had imagined I wanted to go, but I didn't. In good weather and rude health, I would have been excited. Now I was merely afraid, afraid of being seriously ill in the middle of nowhere, with no help and no immediate means of returning home, afraid of mental and physical discomfort and, most importantly, afraid under the circumstances, of the unknown. For several hours these entirely reasonable fears fought a solid battle with a much stronger though less rational fear: of failure, of failing myself. As I sat under my plastic in the rain, in the pâtisserie, at Madame Khiem's, the fight raged inside my enfeebled brain until I knew I was becoming paralysed by it. It was so very difficult for me to admit to myself that I'd had enough, that I was tired and unwell and that I wanted to go home. I thought of the English youth in Hong Kong and his fear of public failure. At 19 I would have felt the same; now the tribunal was more severe. The prospect of standing before my own tribunal as a traitor to the cause of onward and upward was dreadful.

When I voiced some of the more superficial fears I was contending with, Madame Khiem was kind, but I got the distinct impression that she thought all my difficulties were mere fantasies – which, of course, relatively speaking, they were, but fantasies as real as nightmares from which one wakes up screaming. On a practical level she assured me that I could probably get a refund for my ticket if I went back to the train station. Although the money involved was negligible, her words offered me the beginning of a way out. I looked again at the painting on the wall behind me. If I didn't go to China, who knows, maybe I could have the painting after all. Still undecided, I thanked Madame for her kindness and advice and, climbing under yet another mobile cucumber-frame, set off for a part of the railway station I hadn't been to before, in a part of Ha Noi I'd not yet seen.

As I rattled and bumped along the pot-holed road to the main station I decided that if I got a refund on the Lao Cai ticket then I wouldn't go to China at all, but would make my way back by air to Hong Kong and my homeward flight. If I were refused a refund, then that would be a sign that I should go on overland. Despite the mental game-playing, however, I knew by the time I reached the station that I was too ill to go anywhere and then, having been helped by a very kind elderly woman to recover most of my money, realized that in fact I had nowhere to go. I'd checked out of my hotel and still had to pick up my bags. It was 6 p.m. on New Year's Day. I'd made one of the hardest decisions of my life, was increasingly unable to breathe and had nowhere to stay. It was still onward and upward, just in a different direction.

The receptionist at my hotel was most apologetic as he explained that my room was no longer free, but he kindly offered to find me another hotel within the chain and rang several places. Within 15 minutes the manager of another hotel arrived and I found myself on the back of his scooter heading who knew where.

The Cuu Long Hotel in Hang Bong Street was considerably more upmarket than any I'd yet stayed in, having heating, air-conditioning and a TV. It had the added advantage of being almost next door to the pâtisserie, so whatever happened, I knew I wouldn't die of malnutrition. When told it was 30 dollars a night, I negotiated it down to 20. I had cause over the next few days, as I lay with what I suspected might be pneumonia, to be grateful that my room near Hang Quat had been taken and that I was at least ill in suitable surroundings.

Lying in the large and very comfortable double bed, watching endless music video shows on the English language stations broadcast from Hong Kong, I wondered what to do next. I still needed to get back to Hong Kong for my return flight to London, but that was not for several days and I tried hard in my fevered state to think and plan logically. I needed to book a flight from Ha Noi to Hong Kong to ensure I didn't miss my London connection. I made several phonecalls to Vietnam Airlines from my bed and also confirmed my Hong Kong–Moscow flight.

I was concerned at being too ill to fly, and as things seemed to be getting worse rather than better and experience had taught me that such illnesses could last for weeks, I decided some treatment was in order. Having scoured the *Lonely Planet* guide, I set off hopefully towards the traditional medicine pharmacy on the south-east side of Hoan Kiem lake. Staggering from cyclo to counter, I found there were indeed medicines in the pharmacy, but none that I would have called 'traditional'. Few of the French-made pharmaceuticals seemed to be regulated and I was offered all kinds of drugs that, under other circumstances, I might have been interested in trying.

Feeling very rough indeed and with sweat running races down my face and under my thermal top despite the cold, I pottered round the Hoan Kiem art galleries while I thought about what to do next. I saw the General Giap portraits among many other wonderful pieces and looked carefully at the price of everything. I was thinking increasingly about Madame Khiem's 'heroic' painting and judged from what I saw in the galleries that the price she'd quoted me was very fair. In the galleries I was astounded at the quality of the work and the great range of topics covered. I saw many paintings that I would dearly have loved to buy, but none grasped my imagination as the heroic one had.

In one gallery I saw the dark bronze bust of an old woman, her face deeply lined with wrinkles and sadness. On a small brass plate below the bust I read the woman's name and her contribution to the Vietnamese fight for independence: five sons, four sons-in-law and a grandson. I ran my finger along the lines of the woman's face and tried to imagine what it must feel like to be so old yet so alive amid such death.

Despite feeling increasingly unwell, I loved looking at the works of art. In the private galleries I talked to the artists, as they sat huddled over small gas stoves wearing old coats, hats and fingerless gloves. They looked like vagrants but their work was marvellous. Huge sweeps of pale colour lit up stretched silk, and jungles and deserts hung before me. Most of the younger artists had moved away from images of war; it was only in the public galleries that I saw paintings of women soldiers carrying arms to their male colleagues deep in the jungles, stretcher-bearers silhouetted against skylines and children darting into underground bunkers – images to take away in my mind's eye and remember.

It was raining heavily again as I left the galleries, having decided on my next move. Plan B involved taking another cyclo to the Traditional Medicine Hospital; encouraged by my experiences with Dr Lo in Hong Kong, I thought I'd see if the Vietnamese equivalent was as successful. It was a long damp journey and I huddled inside my waterproof jacket under the plastic, trying not to cough because it hurt. I could actually feel my bronchioles closing in, restricting air to my lungs, and was glad I'd remembered to bring my inhaler.

The Traditional Medicine Hospital in Ha Noi is situated behind a high wall and for a brief moment I thought I was looking at some kind of compound. But I found the entrance and, asking my driver to wait, pushed open the creaking gate. Inside, the building seemed utterly deserted; dark corridor after dark corridor stretched before me, silent and empty. Cubicle-type rooms led off the corridors, but each one was vacant, its door padlocked. I was considering leaving and going back to my hotel when I caught the faint whiff of moxa, a herb burnt on acupuncture points in Chinese medicine. I sniffed my way to the bottom of a wide stone staircase and as I walked up it, the moxa smell grew stronger.

I emerged from the dark stairway into a dimly lit corridor in which I could see distant figures flitting from room to room. At least there was life here and therefore hope and, still following my nose, I ended up outside a large treatment room with a number of tables on one of which lay a woman almost completely covered in acupuncture needles. The only other people in the room wore white coats; one was placing glowing moxa on the end of the needles stuck in the patient's back, while the other waved what looked like an enormous spliff over various un-needled parts of the woman's anatomy. 'Now's your chance to run away,' I thought to myself, but I'd already been spotted by the spliff-waving woman, who ushered me into the room and, having sat me down, tried to work out my symptoms by gesture alone. I had assumed that speech would not be necessary as most acupuncturists can judge the extent and nature of a patient's problems by feeling the 'pulses'. No such diagnostic technique was used, so I pointed to my upper chest and made wheezing noises.

The treatment was nothing if not vigorous. About halfway through, I realized that the medics, whose status I never ascertained, thought I had a sore throat and were treating me accordingly. By means of rather desperate gestures I indicated that my throat wasn't too bad but that my lungs were very bad indeed. I didn't have my phrase book with me but even had I known the words *benh suyen*, 'asthma', and *chung sung*, 'inflammation', I doubt whether I could have made myself understood, so complex is the tonal phrasing of Vietnamese. Even names like Hang Quat had to be pointed to or written down for cyclo drivers because my accent rendered the sound meaningless. I was more than ever grateful for the level of literacy in Vietnam.

My gestures were rewarded by having a long needle slipped delicately behind my sternum between the collar bones. Oddly enough, none of the treatment was painful and while one woman wired me up to the electrics, the other lit a moxa-spliff and began warming the needles. I lay wondering what expletives to yell in case of extreme pain, but luckily none were needed.

Just when I thought it was all over and I could get up, I was treated to a rather violent head massage, complete with finger cracking and palm slapping. Utterly dazed, I staggered up and, thanking both women very cordially, paid $10 – I didn't even bother with the embassy's SOS card – and wobbled out into the corridor. The spliff-woman followed, quietly handed me her private card and offered to visit me in my hotel room if I needed further treatment. Pocketing the card, I walked out into the rain and set off with my shivering driver, back to the Cuu Long and my warm room.

The following day I had an idea of blinding brilliance and despite the fact that the lungs had worsened and I was now having to use my inhaler frequently to prevent choking, I dressed and set off for the Aeroflot offices two streets away. Seeing me gasping and sweating my way down the stairs, the hotel manager packed me onto his scooter and drove me round to the airline office. It was raining and as one of my hands clutched his ribcage, which surprised me by its delicacy and smallness, the other struggled to hold a large umbrella over both of us despite the hostile blusterings of the wind.

Thanking the manager for his kindness, I darted into Aeroflot and asked to be rerouted from Ha Noi to Moscow rather than Hong Kong to Moscow, on medical grounds. My appearance and the noises my lungs were making convinced the cautious but efficient counter staff that my request was genuine. They were more than happy to oblige me, but would have to check the validity of my ticket with their London office first and find out whether there was any room on the Ha Noi–Moscow flight in two days' time. All this was complicated by the fact that London was a working day behind Ha Noi and it was still the New Year holiday in Britain. My fingers and every other part of my anatomy crossed, I left the office saying I would telephone the following day. I knew that, whether I was suffering from pneumonia, asthma or an unknown virus, my lungs really wouldn't stand the flight back to Hong Kong followed by a very long westbound flight to Moscow, then London. I was beginning to fear something I'd never had the misfortune to experience: a full-blown asthma attack – on board a Russian aircraft.

Returning to the hotel, I stopped off at the pâtisserie, which was also a restaurant, and discovered a particularly delicious pie filled with an apricot-type custard. After that I ate a large bowl of rather excellent 'beef' noodle soup which, I was quite certain from the colour and texture of the meat, was dog. The soup was followed by a piece of something that looked, but didn't taste, quite like quiche. I tried to remember the old saying about starving one illness and feeding another. I couldn't remember whether it was the cold that should be starved or the fever, but I was hungry and between mouthfuls of food took mouthfuls of air.

The front of the shop was completely open to the world and the counter and till staff stood around muffled in thick coats and scarves. The customers too wore all their heavy outdoor clothing, because we were in a sense outside and it wasn't easy to perch on the foot-high stools that served as seating around the equally low tables. I watched other foreigners talking, gesturing, coughing and sneezing while putting away large quantities of cake and *pho*. It could have been anywhere in the world, except that we were rather closer to the ground than in most restaurants and the wind was blowing rather keenly.

Back in my warm but humid room, I found everything had been cleaned and tidied and that several aspirin and four antibiotics had been put on my bedside table. I felt very touched, but also concerned too for the way in which many people in developing countries view antibiotics as something that can be taken for infection in the same way as an aspirin is swallowed for a headache. Shortly afterwards, the young woman who seemed to be the housekeeper cum receptionist knocked on my door. She was carrying a tray with a thermos flask of hot water, a plate full of sliced limes and a small pot of honey. I'd asked for these things earlier in the day, but hadn't really thought I'd get them. It was very encouraging to feel that the people of the hotel were so kind and thoughtful.

I thanked the young woman and told her that she was kind and that I appreciated this, to which she replied, 'Not kindness, it my duty help you. When young, I away from home in strange house. I very ill, but a woman she look after me like she my mother. So you see, I know how is be ill and no at home. You take these,' she pointed to the red and black capsules, 'you feel better.'

I smiled and nodded.

Later I pondered the distinction between kindness and duty and the very different approach of the Vietnamese to these things. The concept 'duty' has so many negative overtones in Anglo-Saxon culture that if someone said they were helping another from 'duty' it would almost be considered an insult. Somehow the word 'duty' impersonalized the help given in the Cuu Long Hotel, perhaps making both the giving and the taking easier, but it in no way detracted from the quality or quantity of help and kindness which I received with everything from my laundry to my food, which, as I got progressively more unwell, was brought to my room.

By early evening I was bored and fed up and my ribs hurt from coughing. Vietnam TV was showing video after video of insipid singers, male and female, wailing depressive songs at the camera whilst walking in artificial gardens. English language TV was little better; I learnt that Britain's main cultural export in the late twentieth century is the music video, seemingly the tackier the better. For want of anything better to do I began to take an interest in international sports and was grateful when the news appeared every hour or so. I had three of Dr Lo's blue pills left. One would be vital for the flight. I hoped the other two would be sufficient until my departure – whenever that was.

The following morning I woke up unable to hear and hardly able to speak. Having rallied myself a bit with a blast of the inhaler and a glass of hot water, lime and honey, I decided that traditional medicine had had its chance and that I must go for the big guns. With my choice of Western doctors limited to the French and Swedes, I chose the latter and on telephoning the Swedish Embassy clinic was told Dr Svensson would see me if I got to the embassy compound before midday.

I had a hot bath, pulled on my still damp clothes and asked the manager to call a taxi for me. As we pulled up outside the rather ugly compound, the driver tried to cheat me by saying he had no change for my dong and wanted dollars. In no mood to wrangle, I gave him what I thought the ride was worth and, despite his protestations, walked into the clinic.

It was a strange place, the Swedish Embassy clinic, like a small and rather depressing piece of northern Europe slotted uncomfortably into an equally depressing piece of Asia. The tall, blonde and very buxom clinical assistant was the largest person I'd seen in weeks and reminded me of the 'Doctor' films of the late 1950s or a Mel Brooks creation.

The doctor, a thin man with grey-white skin and grey-blonde hair who looked as though he had been away from Europe too long, shook my hand and in perfect English asked my symptoms. He looked only marginally healthier than myself; Vietnam, or perhaps some other damp, developing place, had sucked all the moisture from him. He listened to my lungs and told me that my upper respiratory tract sounded a complete mess and that it was probably a viral infection aggravated by asthma. I explained about having to fly and the effects of aircraft air-conditioning on my lungs, even when healthy. Going to a cabinet, which he unlocked with a key hung round his neck, the doctor poured eight small white pills into an envelope.

'These are cortisone tablets,' he said. 'Take them all before you get on the plane and the problem with the lungs will not be so bad. I think the problem is a viral one and not pneumonia, so there may not be much point in antibiotics, but I'll give you penicillin anyway. You never know.'

And that was that. The only other thing needful was to pay, and that required undoing my left boot and removing from under the insole the $100 bill that had been secreted there in a plastic cash bag since leaving London. The bill for a 10-minute consultation with medication was $99, the single largest expenditure of my entire journey. I'd grown quite fond of that $100 bill over the weeks – we'd been close after all – and I felt quite sad as I handed the note to the nurse who took it as though it were the most normal thing in the world to accept warm dollar bills out of people's boots.

When I got back to the hotel, I immediately called Aeroflot to see if they had any news of my flights. To my enormous relief they said that London had confirmed my original booking and that I had been authorized to fly from Ha Noi. The 'but' part came at the end of the conversation: only the part of the journey from Ha Noi to Moscow was confirmed and there would be no seats free from Moscow to London on the day of my arrival. Was I willing to fly anyway? I said, 'Yes, of course.' The prospect of being stuck in Moscow was infinitely less problematic than the thought of going back to Hong Kong and I was confident that if I could still breathe I could talk my way onto a Moscow–London flight if I had to.

Initially the counter staff had advised me that there might be handling charges for the reticketing, which I was more than happy to pay. When I arranged to pick up my tickets later that day, I asked what the charge would be and was told nothing, because I was sick. As I put the telephone down I felt a load fall away from me. I was going home. If I could have shouted with relief I would have, instead I merely squeaked and staggered down the three flights of stairs to the pâtisserie for a few more apricot pies. I wasn't yet out of the flames, but I felt now that things would be all right. The tribunal was silent as I sat on my 'milking-stool' and ate my pie. I had learnt that there are kinds of fear I'd not imagined – like fear of fear.

chapter thirteen

DEPARTURE

I had a single day left in Vietnam and the problem of the exit visa raised its head once more. The thought of there being some hold-up at the airport after the efforts of myself and Aeroflot and in my current state of health made me concerned. So I spent much of my last morning wandering the streets in a cold sweat searching for the appropriate government department. By dint of much walking, I discovered the correct building, but of course because it was still the New Year holiday, everything was closed. My attempt had failed and deciding there was no point in worrying about what couldn't be changed, I began instead to think once more about the heroic painting.

That afternoon I telephoned Madame Khiem at her office and explained what was happening with regard to China and my return to England. I said that I was now in a position to buy the painting and asked if I might do so, to which she replied that I might. We agreed that I would pick it up the following morning on my way to the airport and that I would leave the money with her son or husband who would receive instructions for removing it from its present frame. Putting the phone down, I knew I'd committed myself to the largest non-utilitarian purchase of my life and felt quite elated. Clearly there was something in all that stuff about 'retail therapy'.

Continuing the 'therapy', I tottered off to make a few remaining purchases. I had promised a herbalist friend some old-fashioned hand-held scales for weighing small quantities of herbs. I explained to the cyclo driver what I was looking for and to my surprise, we had only gone round and round for about an hour before actually finding a herbalist which sold scales. There is always a particular joy about getting precisely what one wants and even when the owners of the strange-smelling shop told me they wanted $20 for two small scales, I maintained my good humour and simply laughed, or rather wheezed and spluttered, though quite a crowd had gathered. The shop, which was hung about with fascinating bundles of dried things that didn't bear close inspection, was in a narrow back street and I realized as the crowd pressed closer round me that I hadn't seen another foreigner for some time. Still, I moved to get back into the cyclo, muttering, 'Twenty dollars, ha, ha, ha!' which did the trick, as the price immediately fell to $10. Entertained passers-by pressed round eagerly and one man from the crowd took it on himself to argue the price with me, though as far as I could see he was nothing to do with the shop at all. The 'herbal' smell was beginning to make me feel rather sick, so from $10 I offered $5, still way over the odds, but I just wanted to go back to my clammy room or anywhere away from the sickly sweet smell and bits of animal parts hanging inches from my face. I stuck at $7 and the scales were wrapped in pieces of the 'Ha Noi Gazette' or whatever the newspaper was called and as we rattled over the pot-holes and ancient cobbles, I found I'd quite enjoyed the experience after all.

That evening, having dosed myself with large quantities of whatever I could lay my hands on, I called a taxi and set off for a newly opened restaurant belonging to one of Vietnam's most famous writers, Nguyen Huy Thiep. I'd learnt about the place in conversation with a Dutchwoman some weeks earlier. She'd visited the restaurant, which was on stilts, shortly after it opened in November '94 and had found it full of artists, musicians and the most tremendous atmosphere. So I set off to cross the Red River once more, for the Hoa Ban restaurant was on Nguyen Van Cu Street, the other side of the Chuong Duong bridge.

I don't know quite what I expected to find at the Hoa Ban but it certainly outstripped any of my expectations. On my last night I found myself in the sort of company I'd longed for in Vietnam. Shortness of breath virtually forgotten, I listened while students and artists argued together and although I couldn't understand a word, I picked up the intensity with little trouble. Two young men who spoke some English drew me into conversation. They told me that the others had been talking about the difficulties of publishing in Vietnam despite the relaxation of political restrictions. Now the problem was not one of content, but the very narrow field of interests that publishers seemed to have.

I asked about the owner of the restaurant, who unfortunately wasn't present. I should have liked to have seen the famous writer whose publisher, I have since read, once described him as being like the mythological Chinese character Monkey – having many aspects and many lives. My two new acquaintances, whose names I was never able to pronounce, told me all they knew about Thiep as I dug through a plateful of surprisingly delicate-tasting pangolin. I noted that the young men seemed extremely proud of Thiep and his achievements, though he wasn't known to either of them personally.

'He is very important Vietnamese person,' said the older of my companions. 'His writing was in the beginning of *Doi Moi*. You understand *Doi Moi*?' I nodded, having grasped the basics of the cultural openness programme called *Doi Moi* which began in the late 1980s in Vietnam and which has allowed a flowering of intellectual and artistic progress as painters, writers and film-makers take their places on the world stage. I asked Thiep's age and background and after some discussion in Vietnamese was told he was 44 and came from the highlands. One reason the Hoa Ban restaurant was on stilts was because it represented the homes of Thiep's youth; the jungle animals, the pangolin, venison and skunk on the menu were from the forests Thiep had grown up in and written about in his stories. *Hoa Ban*, so my young friends told me, is the name of a white jungle flower which blooms only in the northern highlands.

I said I wished I had read Thiep's work but that as I couldn't read Vietnamese that would not be possible.

'Oh no!' I was quickly corrected. 'Nguyen Huy Thiep has books translated! They are in French and also English. So you can read!'

I felt my ignorance acutely.

They continued, 'He has made films also. Do you know *The General Retires*?'

I admitted that I did not. I asked if Thiep still wrote now that he had a restaurant to run.

There was some hesitation and a brief discussion in Vietnamese.

'He has not written much, no,' the younger man said. They seemed to want to say only positive things about their hero but at the same time did not want to tell untruths. 'He has done other businesses and he had drama company. My friend was in this company. It was very good to make Nguyen Huy Thiep's work for people to see. But without money what can you do?' He looked crestfallen for a few moments, perhaps at the thought of his friend's lost opportunity, perhaps at the failure of Thiep's plays to see the light of day.

His friend said, 'I heard Thiep talking the other day, to people at that table there.' He pointed to a table in the middle of the room, now full of what looked like policemen. 'He said, "To survive is important for everyone and that it is hardest of all for writers to survive." I don't know all that he meant,' the young man smiled, 'but he also said that when you fall in love then unhappiness starts and for writers this too is hardest.'

I thought of what Madame Khiem had said to me about the Vietnamese love/hate affair with writing and found it confirmed in the words of these two young men. It seemed to me that Thiep had decided there were more sociable and less stressful ways to make a living than writing and had sensibly decided in their favour.

I couldn't manage all the pangolin, particularly after seeing a fat snake about to be digested by the 'policemen' at the centre table. Although there was none on the menu, I harboured a dread of seeing monkey served up and luckily was spared that – which was doubtless even luckier for any unfortunate simian in the vicinity. My two young friends tried to persuade me into trying all kinds of Vietnamese wines and beers, but I resisted, knowing that combined with vast qualities of medication, alcohol would leave me in a heap.

Finally, I thanked them for their company and their conversation and we all shook hands. I felt sorry to be parting yet again as I walked back onto solid ground and set off for the Cuu Long Hotel one last time. Although I had not met the famous writer, symbol of *Doi Moi* and one time flag-bearer of Vietnamese writing, I felt I knew him as I knew few other people that I'd actually met in Vietnam.

It had been perfectly acceptable for the young men in his restaurant to discuss the fame and exploits of Nguyen Huy Thiep, but no doubt if I'd asked about their girlfriends or career prospects they would have dried up entirely. Though Confucianism is officially long dead in Vietnam, its precepts and courtesies live on.

The following day my single task, having packed (which was simple as I'd never unpacked at the Cuu Long), was to find something suitable to protect the heroic painting. I remembered a row of shops selling bedding and mattresses at the end of Hang Quat Street and set off the short distance from Hang Bong Street by cyclo. I quickly found exactly what I was looking for: a length of two inch thick heavy duty foam rubber. The elderly man who served me was Vietnamese–French and spoke to me in French. We came to an immediate understanding about the foam, but I was left struggling to recall the French word for 'string' then realized I'd never known it in the first place. Under his beret the old man was perfectly composed as, flushed and sweating with fever, I did a dreadful version of a Balinese temple dance indicating winding string. He gave me several metres free and threw in the plastic covering for the foam rubber. He doubtless thought I wasn't the full dong.

Packed and ready to leave, I paid my bill and gave all my dong and loose dollars to the young woman who had done her duty so thoughtfully. She accepted them graciously as the reward of that duty. I shook hands with the manager who'd driven me around on his scooter in the rain and told him, truthfully, that I would tell people that his was a very good hotel. He seemed pleased and as the taxi drove off in the still pouring rain towards the Vietcom Bank and Madame Khiem's house, he and the young woman stood and waved to me.

At the central Vietcom Bank of Ha Noi I withdrew a sizeable sum of money on my credit card. Waiting for the transferral to be approved and the money counted, I watched as several bank clerks weighed large bricks of notes on antiquated scales before tying them up with what I thought at first was odd-looking string (clearly my Balinese dance had affected my brain), but which, on closer inspection, proved to be lengths of a dried tropical grass. The grass lay in semi-opened bundles all over the floor behind the service counter. I watched in fascination as each bundle of notes was counted by one clerk, passed to another and recounted, passed to a third who weighed it and finally to a fourth who tied it firmly with grass. In one corner of the office, a pile of such bundled notes stood about 4 feet by 5 feet. There lay millions and millions of dong in a country where such sums would never be seen by the average person in a lifetime. Yet it was all incredibly casual; the chatting during the counting, the stacking, the grass. Then my cash was being counted out and I was off in the taxi once more.

I expected the picture would be out of the frame when I arrived but it was not. Perhaps, even after my last call, Madame had not truly believed that I wanted it, that I would actually come for it and take it away. Perhaps it had become part of her home and she really didn't want to part with it. Her silent husband and taciturn son removed it from the wall, where it left a large mark, as pictures invariably do, so they hung the empty frame back up, which somehow looked worse. I felt rather sorry to be taking it away, but when I touched it for the first time and ran my fingers over the eggshell stones and walls and touched the face of the radio operator as he ran out of the picture towards me, I knew that it was mine and that even though the board was much heavier than I'd expected, I would have carried it anywhere. The foam rubber fitted exactly, the string was just the right length and the whole thing slipped perfectly into the plastic covering which was tied in a large knot that I could use as a handle. I counted out the notes and laid them on the table where I had drunk so many cups of strong black tea and listened with such pleasure to Madame's conversation. Her son signed a note I had already written out stating that I had bought the picture in good faith and what I had paid for it; this was to cover me should I be stopped and asked for details at Noi Ba airport, as I knew departing foreigners often were.

There were now two pieces of luggage and a large painting to carry and I was still pretty feeble. I'd taken half Dr Svensson's cortisone tablets, deciding to keep the other four for emergencies, so my breathing was easier, but I was rather uncertain on my legs and not particularly lucid in the brain department. Despite all that, I felt in good spirits as I set off on the last stage of my last journey in Vietnam.

Fortunately I didn't know quite how long the remainder of my homeward journey was to be – ignorance undoubtedly was bliss in this particular instance. As I checked in at Noi Ba and saw how very few other passengers there were on my flight, my heart rose even higher at the prospect of quantities of empty seats and lots of space to lie down with the last of Dr Lo's blue pills.

No one questioned any of my belongings as I checked in; my note from Madame's son remained in my pocket. Approaching the passport control desks, however, my pulse began to dance to a tune even faster than that of the virus. Nonchalantly I handed over the small maroon booklet which, in this circumstance, was me. Opening my passport, the officer paused when he came to the words 'Lang Son' and looked at me suspiciously.

'This wrong exit,' he said and I suddenly noticed that he had one eye considerably larger than the other.

Not wanting to irritate him by staring at his problem, I looked down and said apologetically, 'Yes, I know. I tried to change it in Ho Chi Minh and here in Ha Noi and now I am sick and must go home early.'

I wheezed in what I hoped was a convincing manner and smiled pathetically.

The officer looked utterly unmoved. 'I must show to superior,' he said, 'there will be charge,' and marched off, leaving me standing alone as the dozen or so other passengers drifted through the control without problem. I assumed hopefully that he meant financial charge and not any other sort and prayed that whatever was going to happen would happen fast. The next Aeroflot flight out of Noi Ba was in three days' time.

After about five minutes, the officer returned with his superior and about three other men in uniform. All five had a good look at me and mumbled together. I tried to look innocent and helpful at once and coughed and blinked a great deal, which wasn't difficult.

The superior, who spoke good English, came over to me and reiterated the fact that my exit stamp was incorrect.

'Yes I know,' I said, my smile starting to wear a bit thin as I explained all over again about my attempts to change it and the office being closed and my being ill and having to leave early...

The superior picked up the stamp that lay on the desk and, inking it carefully, pressed the word 'Used' over my visa. He closed the passport and, handing it to me, smiled and said, 'Have a good journey.'

I hesitated. 'Do I have to pay?' I asked him, thinking it was probably better not to mention it, but wanting to know the worst.

He shook his head. 'No charge,' he said, 'because you are ill and have to leave early.'

It was the strangest feeling. I thought of all the occasions between Saigon and Ha Noi when people had tried to catch me out, overcharge me and basically rip me off. I expected that in any poor country and though sometimes irritated by it, it had never surprised me. Now I was truly surprised. Here was an official with a perfect right to obtain money and he didn't want it. I looked at him, wondering for a moment if I had understood him correctly, but he waved me through the control area and, picking up my painting, I slung it over my shoulder and walked.

The circular departure lounge at Noi Ba airport is surprisingly comfortable. In the duty-free area, young women in high heels and thick coats chattered over the scant selection of alcohol and chocolates. One, more daring than the rest, smoked a cigarette quickly and secretively, her lipstick clinging to the filter.

There were several Russians waiting for the plane and they were all pretty jolly. Perhaps even Russia seemed attractive and comfortable after Vietnam. One of them, who'd overheard my conversation with the passport official, asked how much I'd had to pay for my stamp. When I shook my head and said, 'Nothing,' he looked surprised and told me I was very lucky indeed. I didn't ask for details – I preferred not to know quite how lucky my escape had been – but when I thought about it later I realized that it was not so much an escape as simply another example of the unexpected.

I wondered whether the Russians were part of the dwindling number of advisers and officials from the former Soviet Union still remaining in Vietnam, leftovers of Communist co-operation. From thousands in the late '70s and early '80s the number of *Lien Xo*, literally translated as 'Soviet Union' but meaning anyone from there, had dropped to just over 200 by early 1995, their skills and technical abilities now considered inferior to those of the West.

I had thought, as did most of my fellow travellers, that our flight was originating from Ha Noi and flying directly to Moscow. Of course, the reality was entirely different. We watched a plane land

and a few people get off, then we were shepherded onto an extremely full flight which had just flown 'backwards' from the Laotian capital Vientiane to refuel and pluck the few passengers from Noi Ba.

I was relieved to discover that all the Ha Noi passengers were put into business class, which differed from economy class only in as much as the seats were fractionally larger and there were slightly fewer passengers. I had two seats to myself, but across the aisle was an elderly Vietnamese professor on his way to Moscow for a conference on malaria. While waiting for take-off, we had a most interesting talk about tropical diseases. He asked me the symptoms of my lung problem and nodded sagely when I told him about the rattles and wheezes. He agreed with the Swedish doctor's diagnosis and went on to explain that such respiratory difficulties were increasing in Vietnam, particularly around the time of winter festivals.

'You see,' he said, 'the reason for your problem is that firecrackers contain lead and when the cracker explodes, the lead goes into the air. If the air is dry or there is a wind, then the lead blows away quickly and does no damage. But in Ha Noi, for example, at this time of year, there is much heavy dampness and little wind. The lead hangs in the air for a long time and people breathe this for many hours, sometimes for days. If a person already has a weakness of the lungs or a virus, as you do, then the problem becomes worse.'

I remembered walking round and round Hang Quat on New Year's Eve in the rain as the firecrackers went off all round me and the great palls of grey smoke hung across the streets like muslin curtains. I had felt perfectly well at Halong Bay and fine physically until the day after New Year. Everything the professor said made sense.

He continued, 'I heard the government is thinking maybe firecrackers should not be allowed any more. Not only because of the big increase in problems with lungs, but because so many young children get injured, mostly at Tet when the crackers go on and on for days. The noise can be bad for old people too, bad for their nerves. But I don't think the government will stop it. It's part of Vietnam, firecrackers.'

He shook his head and smiled at me. Several months later, my 'Ha Noi lung' firmly behind me, I read that the lead in firecrackers had been distinguished as the cause of the increase in lung complaints in Vietnam and that the government had banned firecrackers at Tet and other festivals.

As we prepared to take off I asked one of the stewardesses whether we were flying directly to Moscow. She looked at me oddly and said, 'This plane goes to Bangkok from here, then we change planes and there is a new crew. You will go to Delhi and from there to Tashkent and then Moscow.'

I must have looked rather greeny-white at this news because she asked me if I were unwell. I said I was and asked for some oxygen, at which point I was supplied with a rather antiquated personal oxygen supply in a square leather carrying box. I'd never experienced pure oxygen before and the professor cautioned me against excessive inhalation. I'd recently read, however, that jet lag is not a product of exhaustion or time change but of oxygen deprivation and that 15 to 20 minutes of pure oxygen during a flight can prevent it. I was about to put this theory to the test.

When the wheels left the ground at Noi Ba airport I looked out of the window in the hope of having one last glimpse of Vietnam, but it was dark and the rain was falling heavily onto the tarmac as the Ilyushin rose into the air with its burden of several hundred passengers. Between Vietnam and Thailand I just sat and let the 'going home' feeling flow over me. For a few moments I allowed the tribunal to have its say, as I thought about the place I was leaving, the suddenness of it all at the end, the fact that I'd not done, seen or been all the things I'd intended when I left Britain. Then as the plane climbed south-west over Laos and towards northern Thailand, I closed my eyes and with the oxygen mask firmly grasped, thought of all the things I *had* seen and done, the people I'd met, the experiences I'd had, the friends I'd made and the memories I'd always have.

At Bangkok I wandered off the plane and pottered around the airport for about an hour. There were few transit facilities and I couldn't even find a seat, so I walked up and down pulling my expandable Nha Trang bag behind me on its noisy castors until some witty person passed me and, saying, 'Woof woof,' bent to pat the bag. Leaving Bangkok with a new crew, I had to go through a rigmarole in order to get the oxygen supply back again and have a seat where I could lie down. But the professor explained to the crew how unwell

I was, which worked, as I found myself upgraded yet again, this time to first class. The seats were quite a lot bigger even than business class, but once more that was really the only difference and it was still all chicken and no film.

As we soared into the air above Bangkok, I looked down at the enormous road junctions and multi-laned highways which I knew had been dirt road when I'd first landed in Thailand 13 years earlier. I hoped that the predictions about Vietnam being the next Thailand would not be true, that somehow Vietnam would continue to avoid as much of the West as was possible, even if that did make travel uncomfortable for people like me. But I knew that wouldn't happen, that high-rise hotels were already starting to soar over Saigon and it was only a matter of time before they'd be disfiguring the skies along the coast, alongside Japanese and Singaporean golf courses, Taiwanese nightclubs and American banks.

It took 18 hours to reach Moscow from Ha Noi. Thanks to Dr Lo I slept at least eight of those hours very soundly. My sole memory of Delhi was of a few Indian people getting on the plane and walking up and down the empty aisles; everyone had got off but me. Taking off from Delhi, I vaguely remember a stewardess locking my safety belt as I lay across two seats. Due to Dr Lo's Midazolam, I was entirely unable to do it up myself. Of Tashkent I remember nothing at all.

At Moscow there were, of course, seats on the next flight to London, though it meant a four-hour wait. Wandering round and round the oddly designed building that had seemed so vast and shiny on my first transit in 1982, I thought how small and provincial it all seemed now. I had a ham sandwich and half a pint of Guinness in the Irish pub, which was staffed entirely by Irishmen, then went and looked out through the vast glass walls at the grey skies and greyer snow of Russia.

During the final leg of the journey on an aircraft full of extremely Russian-looking Russians I felt quite jolly and by the time we landed at Heathrow I was almost refreshed. My fellow passengers who'd travelled from Ha Noi had been relegated to economy class after Bangkok and, by the time we reached Heathrow, were looking utterly wiped out. Apart from shortness of breath, I felt rather good given my state of health during the previous days; the complete lack of tiredness seemed to me complete and satisfactory evidence of the anti-jet-lag oxygen theory. Of course I'd had several hours of oxygen, not just 15 minutes, which may have had something to do with my liveliness. That and the fact that I'd slept very soundly indeed on comfortable seats in quiet surroundings. I was truly grateful to the cabin crews who'd make rest possible.

Driving through the ugly suburbs of west London in the back of a black cab, I experienced as I always do, the sense of displacement that follows a journey. When in a place like Vietnam, I find it almost impossible to imagine that somewhere like London exists, despite having lived there for many years. As I approached my home in the biting cold of a British January, the dull houses and pavements still seemed less real to me than the bright red earth and emerald crops of Vietnam. I thought that feeling would pass, that Vietnam would fade in my mind as faraway places inevitably do, but it has not happened. The blues of Lang Co and the browns and yellows of the road to Halong are as real in my mind as when I first saw them, perhaps more so, as my mind's eye sees and assimilates far more than my physical eyes could ever do.

When I next visit Vietnam, it may have changed little or changed a great deal, or both. I hope and partly believe that its harsh experiences with the West will make it wary of accepting too unquestioningly the 'materialist philosophy and the all-eclipsing ideal of the raised standard of living' that Norman Lewis presumed would take hold after the demise of French colonialism. Perhaps my fellow Welshman was right, just a few decades early in his predictions. Indecision hangs over the destiny of most nations and few more so than Vietnam as it is poised to leap into what we call the modern world; having beaten us, Vietnam has no need to join us in any but the most superficial material sense. How much of its own essence it will maintain in the face of this inevitable change is as unanswerable a question in the 1990s as it was for Lewis in 1950 when he wrote:

These were questions, since there is no yardstick for felicity, to which no final answer could ever be given. And even a partial answer would have to be left to an observer of the next generation.

Perhaps one of the most optimistic indicators of Vietnam's future comes from its own past and the writing of fifteenth-century soldier-poet Nguyen Trai, who wrote what amounted to a declaration of independence hundreds of years before many present-day Western nations existed:

> Our people long ago established Vietnam as an independent nation with its own civilisation. We have our own mountains and our own rivers, our own customs and traditions and these are different to those of the foreign countr[ies]... We have sometimes been weak and sometimes powerful, but at no time have we suffered from a lack of heroes.

E.J.C.